Unsolved Historical Mysteries

Unsolved Historical Mysteries

Answers to Outstanding Historical Puzzles

W.D. Rubinstein
Adjunct Professor of History,
Monash University, Melbourne.

EER
Edward Everett Root Publishers. Brighton. 2017.

EER
Edward Everett Root, Publishers, Co. Ltd.,
30 New Road, Brighton, Sussex, BN1 1BN, England.
www.eerpublishing.com

edwardeverettroot@yahoo.co.uk

Unsolved Historical Mysteries
Answers to Outstanding Historical Puzzles

W.D. Rubinstein

First published in Great Britain as *Shadows Past. History's Mysteries* in 2008.
This edition, with new Introduction, first published in 2017.

ISBN 9781911454441 Paperback.
ISBN 9781911454458 Hardback.

Cover designed by Pageset Limited, High Wycombe, Buckinghamshire.
Printed in Great Britain by Lightning Source UK, Milton Keynes.

Contents

'Little man whips a big man every time,
if he's in the right and keeps a-coming.'

Motto of the Texas Rangers (nineteenth century)

Introduction to the New Edition

Since this work, then titled *Shadow Pasts: History's Mysteries,* was first published in 2008, new works have continued to appear about all of the topics examined in this book. It is worth highlighting some of the more important of these, as well as outlining recent trends among writers on these topics.

The fiftieth anniversary of the assassination of President Kennedy occurred in 2013. As one might expect, this gave rise to a spate of new books on the events of 22 November 1963, although they certainly never stopped appearing, and there was no work which provided any new evidence to support the view that JFK was killed as the result of a conspiracy. Lance Moore, *Killing JFK: 50 Years, 50 Lies* (2013), which, as its title indicates, examines what its author claims are "fifty lies" about the assassination (e.g., "Lie Number 25: Oswald and the FBI- 'There was nothing to support the speculation that Oswald was an agent, employee or informant of the FBI'- Warren Report"), with discussions of why each "lie" is wrong, is typical of the more cogent works by Warren Critics which have appeared recently; the work usefully summarizes the current views of those who believe in a conspiracy. It would also seem that more fingers have been pointed than in the past on the role of Vice-President Lyndon Johnson in the assassination, as in Roger Stone and Mike Colapietro, *The Man Who Killed Kennedy: The Case Against LBJ* (New York, 2013). That the dark forces of the "new world order" were involved in the assassination is the thesis of Jerome R. Corsi, *Who Really Killed Kennedy?* (Washington D.C., 2013). That the Warren Commission and its Report were flawed is argued by Philip Shenton in *A Cruel and Shocking Act: The Secret History of the Kennedy Assassination* (New York, 2013); Shenton nevertheless believes that its conclusions, that Oswald and Ruby acted alone, are accurate. As before, on the other side, defenders of the Warren Report have been greatly outnumbered by its critics. The most important recent pro- Warren work (which appeared as the first edition of my book was in press) is certainly Vincent Bugliosi's *Reclaiming History: The Assassination of President John F. Kennedy* (New York, 2007), a massive (1632 pages!) account which concurs in the conclusions in Gerald Posner's *Case Closed* at four times its length. Bugliosi (1934–2015) was a famous Los Angeles lawyer who is best known for successfully prosecuting Charles Manson and his followers; his account of this, written with Curt Gentry, *Helter Skelter* (1974) was a best-seller. Bugliosi apparently obtained guilty verdicts in 105 of the 106 murder cases which he prosecuted. Bugliosi's expert, professional account of the assassination stands in obvious contrast to most of the works produced by the Warren Critics. More than half a century has now passed since that day in Dallas, and no new information has come to light which would definitely prove that the Warren Report was inaccurate, or which identifies the real killers.

Speculation about Jack the Ripper has also continued unabated, although perhaps not at the same rate as previously. My chapter on the Ripper referred to Patricia Cornwell's *Portrait of a Killer- Case Closed* (2002), which claims that DNA evidence exists that the painter Walter Sickert was the East End killer. A similar claim has been made about the suspect Aaron Kosminski in Russell Edwards's *Naming Jack the Ripper: New Crime Scene Evidence, A Stunning Forensic Breakthrough, The Killer Revealed* (London, 2014), which also uses DNA evidence from a shawl owned by Catherine Eddowes, one of the Ripper victims to identify Kosminski. The book was published to considerable publicity, although it quickly became the subject of much hostile criticism when scientists stated that the DNA evidence was, in fact, certainly flawed in a fundamental way. Another new candidate also entered the fray in the person of Michael Maybrick (1841–1913), the brother of James. Michael was a professional singer and songwriter (under the pseudonym "Stephen Adams") who wrote songs well-known at the time such as *The Holy Boy.* Bruce Robinson's *They All Love Jack: Busting the Ripper* (London, 2015) devotes 864 pages to advancing the case that Michael was the Ripper, who also polished off his brother James (who died of arsenic poisoning soon after the Ripper crimes) and forged his *Diary.* According to Robinson, whose book attracted much media publicity, Michael, a prominent Freemason, was being protected by Freemasons and high officials, and was "a psychopath shielded by servants of the Victorian state." Michael Maybrick was, however, eminent enough to have a biographical entry in the *Oxford Dictionary of National Biography,* where he is described as a "singer and composer." After his alleged murder spree, he moved to Ryde, Isle of Wight, where he served five terms as the town's Mayor, was appointed a Justice of the Peace, and became Chairman of the Isle of Wight Hospital. Readers can draw their own conclusions. Facts about James Maybrick and the Maybrick family have been drawn together by Christopher Jones in *The Maybrick A to Z* (Birkenhead, 2008), which appeared well before Michael Maybrick was named as a possible Jack the Ripper. Two other useful books on the background of the Ripper crimes are Neil R. Bell, *Capturing Jack the Ripper: In the Boots of a Bobby in Victorian London* (Stroud, 2014), which is the first work devoted to examining how the Metropolitan Police Force actually functioned at the time, and Patrick J. Gallagher, *The Forgotten Ripper* (2016), concerning four women, not thought to be Ripper victims, who were found murdered in or near the Thames between May 1887 and September 1889. The search for the Ripper goes on, with no candidate named in recent years whose case, in my opinion, is stronger than that of James Maybrick.

The popularity of the view that William Shakespeare did not write the works attributed to him has, it is fair to say, only grown in the past decade, so much so that supporters of the orthodox view of William Shakespeare have launched a concerted campaign to root out the heresy. This has resulted in the appearance of such works as *Shakespeare Beyond Doubt* (Cambridge, 2013),edited by Paul Edmondson and Stanley Wells, a collection of nineteen essays attacking the alternate 'candidates" root and branch, and James Shapiro's best-selling *Contested Will: Who Wrote Shakespeare?* (New York, 2010). Anti-Stratfordians have responded with their own collection of essays arguing that the Stratford man did not write the works attributed to him, edited by John M. Shahan and Alexander Waugh, *Shakespeare Beyond Doubt? Exposing an Industry in Denial* (Tamarac, Florida, 2013). As well, in 2007 the anti-Stratfordian group the Shakespeare Authorship Coalition launched a "Declaration of Reasonable Doubt," an online listing of the reasons why so many now question the orthodox account, which can be signed by those in agreement. By 2016 it had attracted 3672 signatories, including those of 624 academics. Some new and important points, omitted from the original petition, "Beyond Reasonable Doubt: New Evidence and Arguments Since the Declaration of Reasonable Doubt," may be read on the Shakespeare Authorship Coalition's website, under "Clarifications." Recent works arguing for specific candidates include the pro-Oxfordian Charles Beauclerk, *Shakespeare's Lost Kingdom: The True History of Shakespeare and Elizabeth* (New York, 2010), and John Casson and William D. Rubinstein, *Sir Henry Neville Was Shakspeare: The Evidence* (Stroud, 2016). There is a website devoted specifically to refuting the thesis that the seventeenth Earl of Oxford was Shakespeare, Oxfraud. Recent anti-Stratfordian works include Steven Steinberg, *I Come to Bury Shakespeare* (2013),and Richard Paul Rose, *The Shakespearean Guide to Italy: Retracing the Bard's Unknown Travels* (New York, 2011). Useful general works on this subject have appeared, such as Warren Hope, *The Shakespeare Controversy: An Analysis of Authorship Theories* (second edition, Jefferson, N.C., 2009), William D. Rubinstein, *Who Wrote Shakespeare's Plays?* (Stroud, 2009), and David Ellis, *The Truth About William Shakespeare: Fact, Fiction, and Modern Biographies* (Edinburgh, 2013). The period since the appearance of the first edition of this work has only strengthened my belief that Sir Henry Neville wrote Shakespeare's works, with much new and important evidence supporting this view having come to light.

Unquestionably the most dramatic development among any of the topics in this work since the appearance of the first edition concerns Richard III, and specifically the discovery in 2012 of his skeleton under the singularly unroyal venue of a carpark in Leicester. (Prior to the Reformation this was the site of Greyfriar's Church, which was abolished with the change of religion.) After it was definitely identified by DNA evidence as the King, it was reburied in 2015 with full ceremonial honours in Leicester Cathedral. The funeral service was conducted by the Archbishop of Canterbury, no less, and newspaper reports stated that thousands attended or stood respectfully outside, most of whom were apparently highly sympathetic to the former King, despite his evil mainstream reputation. The discovery of Richard's skeleton triggered more works on his life, for instance Josephine Wilkinson, *The Princes in the Tower: Did Richard III Murder His Nephews Edward V and Richard of York?* (Stroud, 2013) and the resolutely anti- Richard *Richard III- England's Black Legend* (London, 2013) by Desmond Seward. No new evidence, however, has been found that would bear on the question of whether Richard murdered the princes in the Tower, the existing facts, as before, strongly favouring the view that he was guilty of their deaths.

Several new and important books about Rudolf Hess and his flight to Britain have appeared since the first edition of this book. They agree with the thesis that Hess's flight was a "sting" operation orchestrated by the British. These include Peter Padfield, *Hess, Churchill and Hitler* (London 2013), John Harris and M.J. Trow, *Hess: The British Conspiracy* (London, 2011), and John Harris and Richard Wilbourn, *Rudolf Hess: A New Technical Analysis of the Hess Flight, May 1941* (Stroud, 2014). Harris and his collaborators suggest that the key agent in contacting Hess was Tancred Borenius (1885–1948), a Finn who was close to the Finnish government but was also professor of art history at the University of London. He enticed Hess to go to England at a meeting in Geneva in January 1941. They then go on to argue that Borenius was acting on behalf of the Duke of Kent and other aristocrats and right-wingers, who hoped, had Hess's flight succeeded, to get King George VI to dismiss Winston Churchill and put a pro-Appeasement government in power that would arrange a separate peace with Hitler. Padfield argues that Hess brought with him a detailed proposal for a compromise peace (in which Hitler promised to leave Britain and its Empire alone in return for a free hand in Europe), and that, when Hitler received the news of Hess's flight, he reacted calmly. These points have been made before, but without the new evidence presented in these three works. Against their view must be set the fact that it is inconceivable that King George VI would have dismissed a Prime Minister who enjoyed the confidence of Parliament, that the Duke of Kent, who died in a plane crash in 1942, was a strong supporter of the war effort, and that there is good first-hand evidence that Hitler reacted with fury when he heard the news of Hess's flight. It is, however, certainly possible that Hess was spurred on by a "sting" operation organised by British Intelligence, although the British government almost certainly had no knowledge of the flight until Hess landed in Scotland.

Concerning the question of whether Jesus survived, two of the authors of *The Holy Blood and the Holy Grail,* Richard Leigh (1943–2007) and Michael Baigent (1948–2013) have since died (the third co-author, Henry Lincoln (b. 1930) is still alive as I write this). Baigent and Lincoln sued Random House, the publishers of Dan Brown's *The Da Vinci Code,* for copyright infringement. To much publicity, they lost the lawsuit in 2007. (To my unlegally trained eye, it seems that they should have won.) Lincoln has recently published *Key to the Sacred Pattern: The Untold Story of Rennes-Le-Chateau* (Nashville, 2015), and other books on this topic continue to appear, for instance Conrad Bauer's *The Priory of Sion Hoax, Conspiracy or*

Secret Society? (2016) and Cyndi Wallace-Murphy and Tim Wallace-Murphy, *Rex Deus: The Families of the Grail* (Nashville, 2016). But no evidence has been forthcoming during the past decade that would support the claims made in *The Holy Blood and the Holy Grail.*

Unorthodox works on the Giza Pyramid and other ancient structures of recent years include Scott Creighton and Laird Scranton, *The Great Pyramid Hoax: The Conspiracy to Conceal the True History of Ancient Egypt* (Rochester, Vermont, 2016), which claims that in 1837 Col. Howard Vyse faked the evidence which has been used to date the Giza Pyramid, and the collection of essays edited by J. Douglas Kenyon, *Unseen Forces: A Guide For the Truly Perplexed* (Livingston, Montana, 2016), which includes many article on advanced technology in ancient times. This theme is amplified in Graham Hancock's *Magicians of the Gods: The Forgotten Wisdom of Earth's Lost Civilization* (New York, 2015), claiming that an advanced civilization, known to many ancient cultures, existed between 12,800 and 11,600 years ago, when it was wiped out by a comet- apparently it was not sufficiently advanced to prevent being destroyed. Sceptics about this issue remain, as for instance in Jeb J. Card and David S. Anderson, eds., *Lost City, Found Pyramid: Understanding Alternative Archaeologies and Pseudoscientific Practices* (Tuscaloosa, Alabama, 2016).

Publisher's Acknowledgements

The publisher would like to thank the following for their kind permission to reproduce their images:

Bear & Company Inc: Figure 8.1; **Getty Images:** Hulton Archive Figure 3.2, Figure 4.2, Figure 5.1; Keystone Figure 7.1; Donald Uhrbrock/Time Life Pictures Figure 2.2; Roger Viollet Figure 6.2; **Mary Evans Picture Library:** Figure 4.1, Figure 4.3, Figure 6.1; Interfoto 2.1; Douglas McCarthy Figure 5.2; **Mirrorpix:** Figure 3.1

Every effort has been made to trace the copyright holders and we apologise in advance for any unintentional omissions. We would be pleased to insert the appropriate acknowledgement in any subsequent edition of this publication.

Chapter 1

Introduction: The 'Amateur Historian' and the Study of History

It might be best to begin by stating what this book is *not* about. It is *not* a book about 'unexplained events'. Readers will look in vain in this work for any discussion of the Loch Ness Monster, UFOs, Bigfoot, haunted houses, or the like – although in one chapter, on the mysteries of ancient Egypt, we will come close to (but not exceed) reaching the limits of the rational. Nor is it a book about 'conspiracy theories', although it might seem at first glance as if it is. Some of the accounts posited by 'amateur historians' about history's mysteries in this book indeed entail the propounding of a conspiracy theory – most notably, perhaps, the many works about President Kennedy's assassination which argue that Lee Harvey Oswald, Kennedy's assassin, did not kill Kennedy acting alone but as part of a wider conspiracy, whose other members have never been apprehended. But other topics examined here certainly do not revolve around a purported conspiracy, and it is inappropriate to view them in this light. There is by now a wide-ranging literature, much of it very recent, on conspiracy theories, to which this work is tangential, although not irrelevant.[1]

What, then, is this book about? It is about subjects which have been written about and examined chiefly by 'amateur historians' but which are ignored, or generally ignored, by academic historians. Some other points of importance should also be made at once. The term 'amateur historian' is emphatically not used by me in a derogatory or supercilious sense, despite the fact that I have been employed as a university academic teaching history for nearly thirty years. I have enormous respect for many aspects of the work of 'amateur historians', and do not regard them with a sneer. An 'amateur historian' is simply someone who researches or writes about history but who is not trained or employed as a university academic. Many are professionally well-qualified in another field requiring considerable education, intelligence, and judgment – as lawyers, engineers, teachers, doctors, media producers, journalists, and in a range of similar occupations. Probably most of the men and women whom we will encounter here are university graduates of obvious intelligence, and virtually all have written and published about their subject of interest, often very widely, or they would not be noted in this book at all.

To qualify for inclusion in this book, there must be a considerable body of writing by 'amateur historians' about topics or interpretations which are normally ignored or shunned by academics. To be sure, there are partial exceptions to this definition. For instance, the question of Richard III and the princes in the Tower, a stock-in-trade among 'amateur historians', whose best-known modern exposition is arguably a detective novel, Josephine Tey's *The Daughter of Time* (1951), is discussed in every scholarly and academic biography of Richard III, in large part because it is unavoidable to examine what became of Richard's predecessor as king. Virtually every account of Richard III and the princes by an academic, it should be noted, has concluded that it is very likely that he was responsible for killing them, and virtually all reject more fanciful accounts of their fate. In contrast, however, academics as a general rule pointedly avoid entering into any real discussion of most of the other well-rehearsed topics in this book. Strikingly, for example, only one or two of the 25,000 college and university historians in the United States have ever written an account of President Kennedy's assassination which examines whether he was killed by Lee Harvey Oswald acting alone or as part of a wider conspiracy, although Kennedy's assassination is arguably the most famous, and conceivably most important event to occur in the United States since the Second World War. So far as I am aware, no university academic in Britain (or elsewhere) has ever attempted to solve the mystery of the identity of Jack the Ripper, and virtually all academic historians of late Victorian England would regard such an endeavour as outside their remit as academic historians. In the case of the Shakespeare Authorship Question, the bias among academics is even more blatant: among English literature academics, any discussion of the identity of William Shakespeare is regarded as taboo and *a priori* impermissible. In such an atmosphere, it is *only* non-academic historians who have made the running, a vicious circle which has led to mutual hostility and alienation.

What, it might be asked, do academic historians write about? It might be useful to cite some recent monographs and articles, chosen almost at random from current scholarly catalogues and journals, which indicate something of what academic historians actually write about. Some recent scholarly articles, by well-qualified and expert academic historians in leading academic journals include 'Colet, Wolsey, and the Politics of Reform: St. Paul's Cathedral in 1518', 'Containing Division in Restoration Norwich', 'Shipping and Economic Development in Nineteenth-Century Ireland', and 'Brazil as a Debtor, 1824–1931'. Recent academic monographs (the term for a scholarly work on a narrow subject) include *Cambridge and its Economic Region, 1450–1960*; *Economists in Parliament in the Liberal Age (1848–1920)*; *Elite Women in English Political Life,c.1754–1790; The Holy Land in English Culture, 1799–1917: Palestine and the Question of Orientalism;* and *A History of the Royal College of Physicians of London, Volume IV: 1948–1983.* I have selected these at random from among recently-appearing works by impressive scholars which have been published in leading journals or by major publishers. Some of these might be of interest to non-specialist historians, but it is obvious that they are highly specific and even technical works, certainly with dozens and even hundreds of footnote references, which are unlikely to appeal to non-specialist historians. It will be noted that all these works are on narrow, even arcane topics, although they certainly have wider importance and are set in a wider context. They are primarily addressed to other specialist historians and advanced students, often as part of a continuing debate among scholars about particular historical issues which generally remain unknown to non-specialists. Academic historians often write works of more general interest – sometimes, indeed, best-sellers – but in general scholarly works of history are of the narrow type noted here.

There are also a number of other factors which clearly demarcate *most* academic books and articles in history from the subjects considered in this book. Despite their frequent narrowness, academic writings in history are normally written in a much wider context, and are aware of this wider context, although their subject-matter might be very narrow. Thus, for instance, if the 'Jack the Ripper' murders were discussed at all by an academic historian, this discussion would not be an attempt to identify who 'Jack' actually was, but almost certainly an examination of the Ripper crimes in some wider and seemingly more important context – for what they tell us about the nature of poverty in the East End, prostitution in late Victorian England, the organisation of the police, the reaction of the press, attitudes towards Fenians or Jewish immigrants, and similar topics. The question of who 'Jack the Ripper' actually was would certainly be regarded by most academic historians as of far less intrinsic importance – indeed, of no real importance at all – when compared with these wider and inherently more important topics. A university historian might well write a monograph about, say, *The Kennedy Administration and Latin America, 1960–63*, or even a well-researched biography of President Kennedy, but he or she is most unlikely to regard the guilt or otherwise of Lee Harvey Oswald as a suitable topic for academic research. In other words, academics deal with 'serious' topics such as national politics, international relations, economic development, legislation, social conditions, perceptions of minorities, and the like, and generally eschew the lurid and the highly specific which lack this context. In many respects the concerns of academics are quite different from those of most of the 'amateur historians' whom we will encounter in this book. For the amateurs, the highly specific and the highly controversial are the stuff of history, a mystery to be solved, of far greater continuing interest than the wider context in which it might be placed. Who now *cares* what the Kennedy Administration's policies towards Latin America might have been, compared with the central and continuing mystery of what actually happened in Dallas, Texas on 22–24 November 1963? To those who cannot accept the findings of the Warren Report that Oswald and Ruby acted alone, but that President Kennedy was killed by wider, powerful forces, the existence and success of these groups, such that the perpetrators of the 'crime of the century' (as it is often termed in anti-Warren Report circles) have managed to 'get away with it' and continue to flourish for over forty years is certainly far more important for our understanding of American society and its real rulers than any minute examination of an aspect of the Kennedy Administration's policies, however thoroughly researched by an obvious expert.

One might ask: is there anything which is common and central to all, or virtually all, 'amateur historians'? In my opinion, there is one central common driving force behind the great majority of 'amateur historians', the sense that they are cleverer than the so-called 'experts', and are able to interpret the evidence, rearrange already well-known evidence, or find new evidence in a manner which will solve the great mystery. For this reason, much of 'amateur historiography' revolves around secret knowledge, allegedly suppressed evidence or belief-systems, and, often but certainly not always, conspiracy theories of one kind or another: the 'authorities' are fools, or they themselves are engaged in the deliberate suppression of the truth. Only a small handful of very clever, independent-minded outsiders have the wit to see or understand this – sometimes only that particular 'amateur historian', since there are invariably other dissenting historians and researchers whose pet theories are themselves inaccurate and misleading. In some cases, the 'amateurs' surely have a point. There is not the slightest doubt that, for instance, the academic specialists in English literature of Shakespeare's time have declared any real investigation of the 'Shakespeare Authorship Question' as *a priori* taboo, and will ostracise anyone, academic or non-academic, who even raises doubts that the Stratford actor wrote the works attributed to him. In most other cases, however, any claims of deliberate suppression are plainly untrue. The American government, for example, has never made any attempt to suppress the 'truth' about President Kennedy's assassination: the Warren Commission was disbanded after it completed its work in October 1964, and no American government body had any responsibility of any kind for publicising or defending an official 'line' or interpretation of the events surrounding JFK's death. Indeed, the innumerable theories and works about the 'actual' events of 22 November 1963 flourished precisely because for many years no one examined them critically. Nor was the American government or any of its agencies or bodies concealing any 'smoking guns': when literally millions of government documents relating, directly or indirectly, to Kennedy's assassination were finally made public in the late 1990s, absolutely nothing was found which has undermined the accuracy of the Warren Commission's finding that Oswald and Ruby acted alone. (As always in such cases, the American government was its own worst enemy in suppressing or classifying any document which did not raise *bona fide* concerns of privacy or national security, leading millions to believe that it was deliberately hiding something.)

'Amateur historians' are thus, very often, egoists and are almost always auto-didacts in the fields they are writing about, constructing a view of the world and of 'true knowledge' from their own ingenuity and against the views of most acknowledged 'experts'. Within reason, there is absolutely nothing wrong with these characteristics, which are valuable and which – many 'amateur historians' would be surprised to learn – are very similar to the central driving force among academic historians. Academic historians are judged and assessed by their academic peers mainly upon the originality of their work: the more original the contribution made by an academic in his or her published work, the more significant the historian is regarded. Of course, any original theory or finding must be supported by good and convincing evidence: without such evidence any historical thesis, regardless of its originality, will be dismissed by other academic historians. Since high originality is regarded as central to academic reputation among university historians, many try, both as young and senior scholars, to produce deliberately original works. Certainly, there are other ways of earning a high reputation as an academic historian, especially by writing the definitive and lengthy work on a particular topic, which does not necessarily entail striking originality. Nevertheless, independent and creative originality is probably the most important factor in producing not merely an academic reputation, but academic promotion to the rank of professor, book contracts, and appearances at conferences. While John Milton might have exaggerated in claiming that 'fame is the spur', he was not altogether inaccurate in explaining the main driving force behind 'amateur' and academic historians alike.

With this, especially in the English-speaking world and particularly in Britain, there is the peculiar tradition of auto-didactism, that is, of persons outside the academy, often self-taught, who have developed an interest in learned and serious subjects – in the case of many 'amateur historians' discussed here, often unorthodox subjects. Frequently, this interest becomes obsessive and all-consuming. Although not necessarily historically-minded, the 'train spotter' is possibly the most familiar manifestation of this in contemporary Britain. One frequently sees railway enthusiasts standing at the ends of platforms at British railway stations, recording in a notebook the types and numbers of railway locomotives and carriages passing through the station. This activity seems daft, if not demented, to those who do not share the train spotter's enthusiasm, at best a very peculiar harmless eccentricity, at worst, however, more than slightly sinister.[2] There are American parallels to this, most familiarly the twelve year-old boy who knows every baseball Major League batting champion since 1901, or the lay expert on the minutiae of the Civil War battles. Nor is this kind of auto-didactism limited to those without university of professional education. In this work, as noted, we shall encounter scientists and lawyers who know every detail of President Kennedy's assassination and believed there was a conspiracy, engineers who believe that the Great Pyramid was not a tomb but a power plant, a physical education teacher who wrote detective stories and arguably the most famous book ever written about Richard III and the princes in the Tower, a schoolteacher whose unorthodox theory of the Shakespeare Authorship Question has hundreds of devoted followers nearly ninety years later, and many others of like ilk. For the academic historian, meeting such people is often a disconcerting experience, since they often know far more about their subject than he or she does. One of the most memorable of the experiences I have had in researching this book has been to attend several sessions of the 'Cloak and Dagger Club', a society which meets every few months in a pub in Whitechapel to hear a speaker, in a room upstairs, give a presentation about Jack the Ripper or a similar topic (I am member number 219). Before each presentation, however, members of the club generally drink for an hour or so and discuss Jack the Ripper and his crimes. Virtually everyone there assuredly and plainly knows far more about the Ripper crimes than I do, and it would be impossible for me to equal their erudition – if this is the right word – on the topic of the Ripper without consulting a lengthy reference book on the Ripper crimes. Many there appear to know by heart and can recite all known information about every incident, every moment, and every person involved in any way in the Ripper crimes or their investigation; they are literally walking encyclopaedias of Jack the Ripper and his deeds. I would no more dream of challenging these Ripperologists about the minutiae of the Ripper crimes than in disputing the Periodic Table with a professor of chemistry or the Theory of Relativity with a physicist. Almost all of these Ripper experts have their own distinctive views on who the Ripper actually was, and often disagree among themselves. Many of these theories strike me as naïve and wrong-headed, yet virtually all of these Ripperologists are unquestionably experts, many of whom would certainly do well on 'Mastermind' or a similar television quiz, as specialists on Jack the Ripper. My guess is that few of these Ripper experts have much formal education. Many are certainly self-taught and none, of course, is an academic. Yet, on the subject of Jack the Ripper, most are veritable Nobel Prize winners who would certainly put me to shame in the details of the Ripper crimes they know by heart. (Unless this is misunderstood, I should also note that not a single member of the Cloak and Dagger Club has struck me as ghoulish, or having an unhealthy or depraved interest in the Ripper crimes; to a remarkable extent, their interest is purely objective.) Their enthusiasm for this aspect of modern history certainly surpasses that of most of my students and even many of my colleagues.

One perhaps curious feature of the 'amateur historians' is that they seldom appear to be intensely interested in more than one subject, certainly very seldom among the well-known subjects discussed in this book. Someone with an intense interest in, say, Kennedy's assassination, will seldom have an equally strong interest in Jack the Ripper or the ancient Pyramids. This might perhaps reflect the national orientation of these subjects – Americans seldom develop an intense interest in a European topic – but this fact also reflects a genuine feature of the mind of 'amateur historians', that they are experts on only one area. An author like Colin Wilson, the novelist and writer on the occult, who has in his time written on most of the subjects discussed in this book, is a genuine rarity. Admittedly, this also reflects the way academic historians nearly always deal with history: almost invariably, the specialists and experts in only one narrow area of interest – an 'expert' famously being defined as one who 'knows more and more about less and less' – and would never dream of writing, or even researching, a subject far removed from their established area of expertise. An academic expert on the Second World War might, conceivably, become interested in the flight of Rudolf Hess to Britain in 1941, but it is difficult to imagine that he or she would attempt to write anything on Richard III and the princes in the Tower, events of 450 years earlier, and virtually inconceivable that any academic expert on the Second World War would write on the building of the Pyramids – indeed, such an academic is all but inconceivable. There have been well-known and senior academic historians who have written on unrelated areas, but they are few and far between. Hugh Trevor-Roper (Lord Dacre of Glanton), who was Regius Professor of Modern History at Oxford, wrote *The Last Days of Hitler*, still probably the most famous work ever written on the death of the Führer, and was also (and primarily) a well-known expert on the English Civil War period three hundred years earlier, but he stands out as a most unusual exception.

1: INTRODUCTION

All academic historians teach a range of courses and seminars at their colleges or universities. Although many of them, particularly in the United States, contribute to broadly-based introductory courses on world or American history or general courses on historical methodology, nearly all their teaching will be in their area of established speciality. No university would expect an expert on the Crusades to teach a course on the history of the American Civil War, unless, most unusually, that historian had also developed a separate, established interest in the area, or unless no one else was on hand to give such a course. No academic historian whose speciality is the Crusades would feel remotely qualified to deliver lectures on the American Civil War or to mark or assess essays or examinations by students in the field, and much less to supervise a post-graduate thesis in the field. The core area of speciality of all academic historians normally remains that of his or her doctoral dissertation, typically undertaken and researched when that scholar was in his or her twenties or early thirties, and which in most cases forms the basis of their earliest published work. Young academics are normally hired on the basis of their doctoral dissertations, and to teach in that field or a closely related one. Academics may well get tired of working in that field, and certainly on that topic, but only seldom have the time or resources to become an expert in a separate, unrelated area, or to have their expertise validated by undertaking a second dissertation, unrelated to their first, or by publishing in this separate field. This may be unfortunate, and almost certainly many academic historians would benefit intellectually by developing a second historical interest unrelated to their first one, but it is a fact of life that few ever do so. This is perhaps not so very different from what 'amateur historians' habitually do: expertise in, and even obsession about, one particular topic might be a general rule.

The impression which may be given in this work is that 'amateur historians' deal exclusively with topics and theories which most would regard as eccentric or worse. It might be worth making the point explicitly that this impression is misleading: *most* 'amateur historians', however defined, work in two other areas unrelated to anything in this book – family history and genealogy, and local history. Hundreds of thousands of people are engaged in researching the histories of their own families. British newsagents stock three or four monthly magazines devoted to family history and genealogy, and the advent of the internet, with its increasing on-line availability of census records and local directories, has been a godsend to the area. Local historical societies, dealing exclusively with the history of a county or city, have been a well-known feature of British society for nearly two centuries, as have societies devoted to the history of a religious or ethnic group, an occupation or particular field, or a special interest such as railway or sports history. Anyone familiar with them will know they are generally the domain of keenly-interested, often very talented amateur rather than (except in rare cases) academic historians, and are often hallmarked by narrow antiquarianism lacking a wider context, although this may now be changing. It is likely that the 'amateur historians' engaged in all fields exceeds the number of academic historians, at least in Britain, by many orders of magnitude.

In recent decades, some academic historians have been influenced by so-called 'post-modernism', a faddish mode of historical analysis – if that is the right term – heavily influenced by 'cultural studies', 'post-colonial studies', and feminism. Post-modernism claims that history lacks a 'grand narrative', but consists instead of innumerable personal and individual 'narratives', each of which has its own integrity. There is something to be said for this viewpoint, which is far older than its proponents might realise. Leo Tolstoy, in *War and Peace*, made the point that the French invasion of Russia in 1812 was not simply the story of the life of Napoleon Bonaparte, as it is so often depicted in accounts of the French invasion of Russia, but is the life story of each of the 50,000 French soldiers who invaded Russia. While this is certainly true, even important and valuable, the question might be asked: how, in 1812, did 50,000 armed French peasants come to be in Russia? The answer, of course, is Napoleon Bonaparte – without him and his leadership they would have stayed at home – which is why, in a nutshell, 'post-modernist' approaches to history are inadequate (and are rejected by most historians). 'History' *must* privilege the source of causality, although this source (or sources) may well be a matter of dispute.

The relevance of 'post-modernism' and its implications for this book stems from the fact that we are dealing here with 'amateur historians' whose conceptualisation of history in their own minds often differs radically from that of academic historians. Should we accept their conceptualisation at face value as equal to that of academics? My personal view is no: their lack of sophistication and inability to place events in a wider context must rule out such a course. Nevertheless, it would do no harm for many academic historians to understand something of *vox populi* and how many 'ordinary' men and women conceptualise history and what they regard as its important events. 'Post-modernists' should, however, draw little comfort from this conclusion, since, perhaps paradoxically, the way many 'amateur historians' conceptualise history does *not* revolve around the individual experience of suppressed groups or the downtrodden, but very often – as the ever-popular subjects considered here make clear – around kings, rulers, the lurid, and allegedly well-kept secrets.

In this book, seven different topics are covered. These are among the most common and frequently encountered of subjects widely discussed and written about by 'amateur historians', but there are other topics which might be included in a future volume, such as the life of King Arthur, the alleged mysteries surrounding the death of President Lincoln, the fate of the children of the last Russian Tsar, and the identity of the 'Man in the Iron Mask'. Much has been written on these topics, although probably not so much as on the topics surveyed in this book. There are, in addition, two other very recent events which are well on their way to becoming classical discussion pieces among 'amateur historians', as well as among journalists and conspiracy theorists generally: the death of Princess Diana in 1997 and, of course, the terrorist attacks of 11 September 2001. The death of Princess Diana in a car accident in Paris has become a happy hunting ground of conspiracy theorists in England and possibly elsewhere. One national daily newspaper in Britain is famous (or notorious) for having a front page story almost every Monday – Monday usually being a day with little real news to report – alleging some new revelation about Diana's death. Normally, these front page stories are not reported in other newspapers, or on radio or television in Britain, indicating they had no validity.[3] September 11th has already spawned a virtual industry, much of it on websites but some that has been published, of allegations that President Bush knew of the attacks in advance or that the American government actually masterminded them.[4] These conspiracy theories appear to be without foundation, and offer a close parallel to many of the conspiracy theories about President Kennedy's death in emanating from the political left and seemingly secretive American government organisations or leaders as behind the attacks.[5]

In each of the chapters in this book I have set out the main issues, theories, and works which have attempted to grapple with each of these subjects and suggested unorthodox historical views. They are not arranged in chronological order. Instead, I have begun with what are probably the three most widely-discussed of these subjects, Kennedy's assassination, Jack the Ripper, and Shakespeare, and then moved on to cover the other topics in the book, concluding with the mysteries of the ancient Pyramids chiefly because the unorthodox theories which have been propounded about their construction and purpose are certainly the most radical and *outré* of all. One of my central purposes in writing this book, it must be said frankly, was to see whether I, as an academic historian, could do any better than the 'amateur historians' who have addressed these topics, and I have always given my own views about these subjects while presenting both the topic and the theories they have attracted as fairly as possible. In two cases (Jack the Ripper and Shakespeare) I have come to my own unorthodox conclusions; becoming interested in the Shakespeare Authorship Question inspired me to co-author (with Brenda James) a separate book on the topic, *The Truth Will Out*. Among other topics surveyed here, I have often emphatically rejected the conclusions of the 'amateur historians'. This is particularly true in the case of the assassination of President Kennedy, where I am certain that Oswald and Ruby acted alone and that there was no conspiracy of any kind. With other topics, for instance the engineering feats of the ancient Egyptians, I have no professional expertise or training enabling me to judge the unorthodox theories and have said so, always hopefully presenting these theories as fairly as possible and being guided by common sense.

Should academic historians take these subjects and the theories they have attracted more seriously than in the past? Perhaps, although one can understand why they have preferred not to. Certainly many students become more interested in studying history through these topics than the more normal substance of academic history, and certainly any rational approach to them requires students to bring the same evidential, forensic, and historiographical skills to bear as do any other topics in history. In the case of the Shakespeare Authorship Question, the blanket taboo on even discussing the topic, rigorously enforced by English literature academics (*not* by academic historians) is in my opinion counter-productive to our understanding of Shakespeare and his works. There is a world of autodidactical 'amateur historians' out there waiting for academic historians to discover them. It is possible that any such discovery would be good for professionals and amateurs alike.

Chapter 2

The Assassination of President Kennedy

The assassination of President J. F. Kennedy in Dallas, Texas, on 22 November 1963 was one of the watershed events of the twentieth century, destroying at a stroke Kennedy's innovative and enlightened 'Camelot' administration and – as is often suggested – leading to America's disastrous involvement in Vietnam and the other chain of horrors which followed during the next decade. It is, famously, one of a handful of events in modern times, such as Pearl Harbor (for Americans), and the attacks of 9/11, in which everyone alive at the time vividly recalls where and when they first heard the news. Yet – perhaps rather surprisingly – it continues in the eyes of many to be one of modern history's most enduring mysteries. Although Kennedy's alleged assassin was arrested ninety minutes after his murder, the assassination has often been termed the greatest unsolved crime in American history. While an official committee of inquiry into the assassination, headed by America's Chief Justice, Earl Warren, unanimously concluded in 1964 that Lee Harvey Oswald, Kennedy's assassin, had acted alone, that Oswald's killer Jack Ruby had also acted alone, and that there was no conspiracy of any kind, negative and hostile reaction to the Warren Report (as to the committee's published inquiry and conclusions are known) has spanned many hundreds of alternative accounts of the assassination, by theorists known as the 'Warren Critics'. All or virtually all of those critics argue that Oswald (if involved at all) was part of a much wider and well-organised conspiracy, normally viewed as centrally involving powerful right-wing and anti-Castro bodies and individuals and, often, the Mafia.

Virtually none of the Warren Critics is an academic historian, and although Kennedy's assassination occurred barely half a century ago, their efforts might well constitute the largest single body of work by amateur historians on any subject; certainly the number of books, articles, internet sources and the like rivals, and probably exceeds, the other enormously popular historical subjects discussed in this book such as the Shakespeare Authorship Question and the Jack the Ripper murders.[1] As will be seen, in general these works espouse one or another variant of what might be termed a left-wing conspiracy theory, pointing to powerful conservative and right-wing forces as responsible for Kennedy's assassination. In this, they differ from other examples of the works of amateur historiography discussed in this work, which do not as a rule contain an ideological component or edge.

The main facts of President Kennedy's assassination and the much-disputed events surrounding it are so well-known as to require only a brief summary. President Kennedy was visiting Texas chiefly in order to broker a peace deal between the liberal and conservative wings of the Democratic Party in that state, and also to win support for his own reelection in November 1964, Texas being regarded as crucial to Kennedy's reelection. Although Texas in general and Dallas in particular was widely perceived as deeply hostile to Kennedy, his trip to Texas had gone successfully and smoothly until the moment of his assassination. Dallas was notorious for its right-wing extremist elements which detested Kennedy for his weakness during the ill-fated Bay of Pigs invasion of Cuba, his alleged weakness towards Communism, and the liberalism of his administration on civil rights and welfare issues. President Kennedy and his entourage, which included the First Lady, Jacqueline Kennedy, the Governor of Texas, John Connally, and (riding in another car) the Texan vice-president, Lyndon Johnson, had just driven through cheering, friendly lunchtime crowds in the unseasonably warm downtown streets of Dallas, and were apparently well on their way to a major luncheon reception a few miles away. Just before leaving the city, three shots (as the officially accepted account of the assassination has it) rang out within about eight seconds. The first missed the president, the second struck him in the shoulder, wounding him, and then struck and seriously injured Governor Connally, sitting in front of the President, the third and fatal bullet struck Kennedy in the head, blowing out part of his brain and being responsible for his death. Kennedy was officially declared dead at nearby Parkland Hospital, where he was taken, at 1.22 p.m., about fifty-two minutes after he was shot.

At 1.51 p.m., a twenty-four year old employee at the Texas School Book Depository building, from which the shots were allegedly fired, was arrested following a struggle at a movie theatre in another part of Dallas. He was arrested not for killing the President, but for shooting and killing a Dallas police officer, J. D. Tippit, at approximately 1.14 p.m., in an area of Dallas not far from the movie theatre. Later that afternoon, he was also charged with President Kennedy's assassination. This young man, Lee Harvey Oswald (1939–63), had already led a life so strange as to seem out of a novel. Oswald's father had died young, and his mother, an itinerant nurse, had lived in several American cities. As a teenager in New York, Oswald encountered left-wing political propaganda and became an avowed Marxist, although never joining any Marxist or radical party or group. Oswald was, in fact, both a loner and a classical autodidact, devising his own explanation of the world through his own wide reading and experience. Remarkably, and confusingly, however, he saw no contradiction between the views he held and his joining the U.S. Marines at the age of only sixteen, serving for several years and learning to handle guns. Even more bizarrely, while in the Marines Oswald learned Russian, with the aim of emigrating to the Soviet Union. This he did late in 1959, being given a dishonourable discharge from the Marines as a result. Oswald lived in the Soviet Union from 1959 until June 1962, and married a Russian girl, Marina Pruskova, in 1960. In 1962 he returned to America, moved to the Dallas Fort Worth area, and held a series of low-paying dead-end jobs. During the working week he lived apart from his pregnant wife and baby daughter, who roomed with a Quaker couple, Michael and Ruth Paine, in suburban Dallas while Oswald lived by himself in a cheap boarding house in Dallas itself. In 1963 Oswald did several other unusual things as well. In March, using the name A. J. Hidell, he purchased a cheap mail-order rifle and a revolver. (According to the Warren Report the rifle was used to kill President Kennedy and the pistol to shoot J. D. Tippit.) Shortly after purchasing the Italian-made Manlicher-Carcano rifle, Oswald used it in an unsuccessful attempt to kill Edwin Walker, an extreme right-wing former general who lived in Dallas. Oswald also posed for backyard photographs taken by his wife holding the rifle and Communist newspapers, proclaiming himself 'a hunter of fascists'.

In mid-1963 Oswald went to New Orleans, where he founded a pro-Castro organisation, the 'Fair Play for Cuba Committee', of which he was the only member, receiving a good deal of local media coverage. He also went by bus to Mexico City with the aim of obtaining a Cuban visa from the local Soviet embassy, but was rebuffed. Oswald returned to Dallas from Mexico in early October demoralised and depressed, and began a poorly-paid warehouse job at the Texas School Book Depository building in central Dallas, a job found for him by chance by neighbours of the Paines.[2]

According to the standard account of the assassination, Oswald was desperate, demoralised, and virtually broke. His political hopes had come to nothing; his wife had given birth to his second child in a welfare hospital and was living on virtual charity. President Kennedy, in contrast, represented everything Oswald could never be: famous, powerful, rich, cultured, glamorous, and surrounded by America's greatest and best. As a Marxist, Oswald – it is often forgotten – also detested Kennedy for deeply-held political reasons. According to the Warren Report, at 12.30 p.m. on 22 November 1963, Oswald fired three shots at President Kennedy from a hidden 'sniper's nest' he had prepared on the sixth floor of the Depository building, using the mail-order rifle which he had brought to work with him that morning concealed in a paper bag. As soon as he fired his last shot, Oswald fled from the Depository, returned to his boarding house, where he grabbed the mail-order revolver he had kept there. He was wandering, perhaps aimlessly, around the local streets when, at about 1.14 p.m., he was stopped by Police Officer J. D. Tippit, riding alone in a police car, who had been given a radio description of the alleged assassin which resembled Oswald. Oswald then fired four shots into Tippit, killing him. Oswald again fled aimlessly to a local shopping precinct, sneaking into a local movie theatre without paying. There, he was arrested for Tippit's killing. Oswald nearly shot and killed a second policeman while being arrested.

After two days in police custody, a time when he was charged with Kennedy's murder and repeatedly proclaimed his innocence on national television, Oswald was himself shot and killed. This occurred on the morning of Sunday, 24 November 1963, in the basement of the Dallas police headquarters when he was about to be transferred to the local gaol. Oswald was shot by Jack Ruby (1911–67), a local man whose life story was also a strange one. Ruby was born in Chicago to a dysfunctional Jewish immigrant family; his father was an alcoholic, his mother mentally ill. Unlike many others from eastern European Jewish immigrant backgrounds, Ruby had little formal education and was not successful at business or professional life. As a teenager, Ruby ran errands for members of Al Capone's Chicago gang, but was not directly involved in organised crime as an adult. Following service in the Second World War, he settled in Dallas in 1947 where he was a ne'er-do-well fringe businessman, engaged in a long string of unsuccessful business ventures. By 1963 he was involved in running two unsuccessful nightclubs, a rock-n-roll venue compèred by his sister, and a striptease nightclub, the Carousel Club, which he ran himself. Ruby was in considerable financial trouble, owing substantial amounts to the U.S. government in unpaid taxes, and had become addicted to anti-depressant pills. He was unmarried, living with a male roommate (and a dog) in a cheap rented apartment. He habitually carried a gun, seen by him as necessary in his all-night bar frequented by drunks and toughs, where all transactions were in cash. He was well-known as a violent man with a quickfire mercurial temper, and had been an amateur boxing champion as a youth. Unlike Oswald, who was intensely political, Ruby was almost apolitical and politically unsophisticated. He was an admirer of President Kennedy, in particular because Kennedy had made many high-profile Jewish appointments to his administration, something which Ruby, extremely touchy about his Jewish background, greatly admired.[3] Ruby later said that he shot Oswald to spare Jacqueline Kennedy the necessity of returning to Dallas to testify at Oswald's trial.[4] On Sunday morning Ruby managed to walk down to the basement of the Dallas police headquarters just as Oswald was about to be placed in a police van for his transfer to jail, and shot Oswald, who died an hour or two later in the same hospital as President Kennedy. Ruby's shooting of Oswald was unforgettably seen live on television and in renowned photographs by journalists then present. Ruby, immediately overcome by police, was eventually tried and sentenced to death for Oswald's murder. (Ruby expected to be proclaimed a hero and the death penalty conviction is seen by observers as the result of a bungled defence by his lawyer, the famous trial defender Melvin Belli.) Ruby died of cancer in prison three years later.

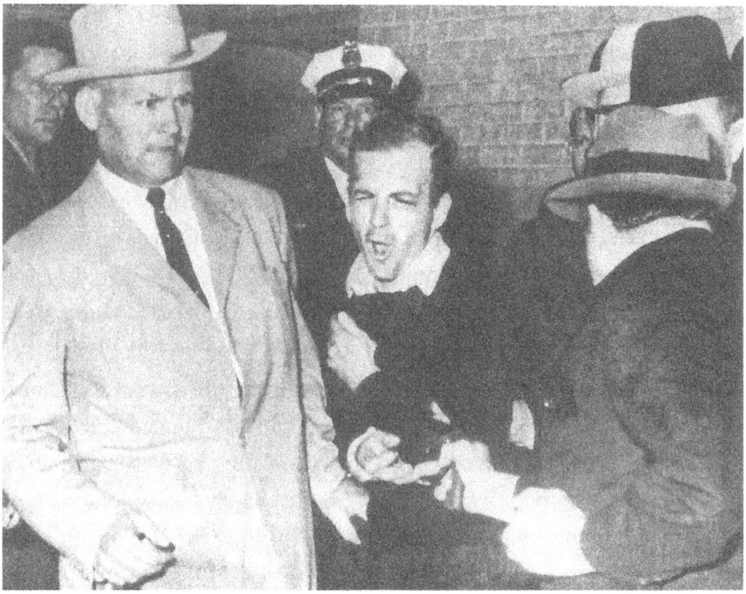

Figure 2.1 Jack Ruby shoots Lee Harvey Oswald: one of the most famous photographs of the twentieth century, a murder filmed live on national television. Mary Evans Picture Library/Interfoto

Since this sequence of events was so epochal, unexpected, and improbable, doubts about Oswald and Ruby emerged in the minds of many almost from the instant the killings occurred. The new president, Lyndon Johnson, also believed that an international conspiracy, headed by the Soviet Union, might have been behind Kennedy's assassination, and was very keen to lay all such concerns to rest. Within days of these events, Johnson appointed a high-level panel to investigate and report on the assassination. It was headed by Chief Justice Earl Warren (and hence known as the 'Warren Commission') and consisted of six members besides Warren, all of whom were well-known, heavyweight mainstream public figures: Allen Dulles, former head of the CIA; former World Bank head and High Commissioner of the American zone in occupied Germany, John J. McCloy; Republican Senator John Sherman Cooper; Democratic Senator Richard Russell; Republican congressman (and future president) Gerald Ford; and Democratic congressman Hale Boggs. It was given virtual *carte blanche* powers by the president, with the FBI and other federal agencies compelled to cooperate with its requests. Johnson also made it the only government body empowered to investigate the assassination, thus preempting an investigation by Dallas officials or by Congress.

The Warren Commission was also provided with a full-time staff of twenty-eight who actually carried out the investigation. Most were lawyers with Ivy League backgrounds, young and very bright. Most of the lawyers worked in private practice; only a few worked for the federal government.[5] In practice, since all the Warren Commission's members except Dulles had full-time jobs, the Commission's report – the Warren Report – was prepared by its staff, especially, it would seem, three of the young lawyers it employed, David Belin, Wesley J. Liebeler, and Arlen Specter. In particular, the Commission's key conclusions appear to have been those of Specter, then a thirty-three year old graduate of Yale Law School (and in recent years a prominent Republican senator from Pennsylvania).

Despite what its critics have claimed, the Commission did a genuinely remarkable job and produced a twenty-seven volume report, containing about ten million words, by 24 September 1964, only ten months after it had been appointed. Whatever might be said about the career of J. Edgar Hoover, the FBI which he headed appears to have carried out its role in the preparation of the Commission's report in an exemplary way. On the Commission's behalf the FBI conducted 25,000 interviews, while the Secret Service interviewed another 1550 persons.[6] The Commission itself heard testimony from 552 witnesses, of whom ninety-four appeared before it in Washington D.C. The conclusions reached by the Warren Commission, the officially accepted account of the assassination, are well-known: Oswald killed Kennedy acting alone, and was in turn killed by Ruby, acting alone. There was no conspiracy of any kind. Oswald and Ruby had never met, and were not acting on behalf of any other individual or group. During the assassination only three bullets were fired, all by Oswald, all from the Depository building. No one else was involved.

Having completed its Report the Warren Commission disbanded. It was never reactivated, and no government agency existed to defend its conclusions or respond to its critics. Even before its Report was issued, however, there were already many theories of conspiracies; indeed the Report itself responded to those which had already been aired in a thirty-one page section entitled 'Speculations and Rumors'.[7] Although the Commission did an outstanding job, there was much about its format which could well arouse legitimate suspicions. All of its members were Washington insiders, and all – with the striking exception of Earl Warren – could be described as politically right-of-centre. None, even those who were lawyers, had any real or recent expertise in ballistics or forensics. The membership of former CIA director Allen Dulles has appeared suspicious to many Warren Critics. Most importantly, however, the Warren Commission was not a trial: the dead Oswald had no defence lawyer and the Commission did not have to prove his guilt beyond a reasonable doubt to a randomly-selected jury. Nor was it possible to appeal the Commission's conclusions to a higher court. Its task was merely to arrive at a conclusion, using such evidence as it liked, to support its findings. In practice, the legal staff of the Commission presented its theories to the Commission's members, who acted as a kind of jury. In the end, all signed the Report, although several members reportedly had doubts about the view that the second bullet, the so-called 'magic bullet', hit both Kennedy and Connally.[8] Had Oswald not been shot and killed by Ruby, however, he would have been subject to a jury trial with very different procedures, above all with a proper (and probably very well-known) trial lawyer. The prosecution would have had to convince an independent jury that he was guilty, and, if convicted, Oswald would presumably have attempted to appeal to a higher court to have the verdict overturned. It is unlikely, moreover, that Oswald's trial could have proceeded before the second half of 1964, and would probably have been lengthy. (Although Ruby's shooting of Oswald was utterly beyond question, having been seen by millions on television, Ruby was found guilty in March 1964, four months after the assassination.[9] It seems very likely that Oswald's trial would have taken significantly longer.) The weight of evidence against Oswald was so great that it seems difficult to believe that he would not have been convicted (and quite possibly executed), but his lawyers would naturally have mounted a spirited and clever defence.

Even before the Warren Commission officially reported, however, the first salvos had been launched in print against the view that Oswald had killed Kennedy, acting along. Apparently the first anti-Warren book published in the English-speaking world was the now almost unknown *Who Killed Kennedy?* by Thomas G. Buchanan, which appeared in mid-1964. It was published by Secker and Warburg, the prestigious London house which had published Orwell's *Animal Farm* and *1984.* Buchanan was a Southern-born American who was educated at Yale and George Washington universities, and lived in Europe, especially Paris, after 1945.[10] According to

Gerald Posner, he was also a member of the Communist Party.[11] Buchanan's work first appeared in French in *L'Express* in early 1964. To a surprising extent, many of the familiar themes and theories encountered in anti-Warren writings ever since were to be found in Buchanan's book, although with original twists. Buchanan repeatedly likened Kennedy's killer(s) to John Wilkes Booth, Abraham Lincoln's assassin, who also turned out to be part of a much wider conspiracy. According to Buchanan, 'Lee H. Oswald could not possibly have been alone [in the assassination] and the assassin could not possibly have been a leftist'.[12] There was another assassin standing on the railway overpass in front of the motorcade.[13] There were certainly more than three shots, and it would have been virtually impossible for Oswald to have fired them all.[14] Oswald was seen downstairs in the Depository building immediately after the assassination.[15] Oswald had several accomplices, and the Dallas police appeared to know all about Oswald's life and lifestyle at once.[16] Ruby, a Chicago 'gangster', was of course a part of the conspiracy.[17] Oswald, Ruby, and Officer J. D. Tippit probably knew one another.[18] The assassination conspiracy was made possible by 'complicity between Dallas police and gangsters'.[19] Behind them were, in all likelihood, the FBI and, certainly, Texas oil millionaires and the 'Texas oligarchy' which had 'a deep hostility to measures undertaken by the Kennedy administration'.[20] Another factor in their motivation might have been the recently-signed agreement between Enrico Mattei of the Italian oil trust, and the Soviet Union, which threatened the power of the Texas lobby. Mattei died in October 1962 when his plane exploded in mid-air.[21] Many of these points – but not the last one about Enrico Mattei – became stocks-in-trade in dozens of anti-Warren books published over the next four decades. It is surprising that Buchanan's work is not better known than it is, especially as his avowed leftism set the stage for so many other Warren Critics.[22]

Two years later, after the Warren Report appeared, the earliest of the attacks on the Warren Report were published, Harold Weisberg's *Whitewash* and Mark Lane's *Rush to Judgment*. Weisberg, a former Senate investigator, returned to the theme many times over the years. Nearly thirty years later, he produced *Case Open: The Unanswered JFK Assassination Questions* (New York, 1994), a response to Gerald Posner's *Case Closed*, and in 1995, *Never Again! The Government Conspiracy in the JFK Assassination* (New York, 1995). Weisberg, it must be said, is a virtually incoherent writer whose books are poorly organised and have no indexes. Like many others, he believes that the 'government conspiracy' central to the assassination was 'virtually on the very highest possible [level],' and involved J. Edgar Hoover, Deputy Attorney-General Nicholas de B. Katzenbach, and possibly President Lyndon Johnson.[23] In 1966, Mark Lane, a left-wing lawyer and former member of the New York state legislature, published *Rush to Judgment*, probably the first anti-Warren book to become well-known; it sold over a million copies.[24] Lane argued that the Warren Commission was seriously flawed in its composition and proceedings, a perfectly arguable point with an important element of truth. But Lane also went much further, alleging assassination conspiracies. Many have been critical of Lane's methodology, which his critics claim involve taking remarks out of context and using sources without attribution.[25] More highly regarded was *Inquest: The Warren Commission and the Establishment of Truth* by Edward Jay Epstein. The work was originally the author's master's dissertation at Cornell University, and was thus at the time – and remains – one of the very few scholarly works by a Warren critic. Epstein's book highlighted the apparent discrepancy between the official claim about a single bullet striking both Kennedy and Connally, and autopsy evidence at the time. Epstein's doubts have been answered by photographs and other evidence released subsequently.[26] Epstein went on to write two other books on the assassination, *Counterplot: Garrison Against the World* (1968) and *Legend: The Secret World of Lee Harvey Oswald* (1978). He later became quite critical of the Warren critics.[27] 1967 saw the publication of Josiah Thompson's *Six Seconds in Dallas*, the first book to use the Zapruder film. Thompson concluded that Kennedy was killed in a crossfire from three different sites. Thompson is a careful writer, whose sober work, though wrong in its central assertions, is never sensationalist.

During the period from the late 1960s and the 1990s, a plethora of works appeared which marked out the case for the Warren critics. These included another 1967 work, by Sylvia Meagher, *Accessories After the Fact: The Warren Commission, the Authorities, and the Report*, based on detailed study of the Warren Report; Jim Marrs, *Crossfire: The Plot that Killed Kennedy* (1989); David A. Lifton, *Best Evidence: Disguise and Deception in the Assassination of John F. Kennedy* (1981), and dozens of others. Almost invariably, these books focus on the allegations that more than three shots were fired, making it impossible for Oswald to have acted alone; that these shots probably came from the so-called 'grassy knoll' to the right of Kennedy's car as it drove

Figure 2.2 The scene of the assassination: Dealey Plaza in Dallas, Texas. The Texas School Book Depository Building, where Oswald, hiding behind boxes on its sixth floor, shot President Kennedy, overlooks the motorcade route. Getty Images/Donald Uhrbrock/Time Life Pictures

through Dealey Plaza, or from the overpass in front of the motorcade; that Kennedy's autopsies and forensic x-rays were altered, or at least provide clear evidence that Kennedy was shot from the front as well as from the rear;[28] that Oswald, both a marine *and* a Marxist defector to Russia, was a double agent; and that Oswald and Ruby knew each other and were part of a wider conspiracy. These points have been repeated in one form or another in dozens of works by the 'Warren Critics', and are examined in a later part of this chapter.[29]

Since the main points made by the 'Warren Critics' are almost always similar, from a historiographical viewpoint some basic patterns about them are clear. At base, virtually all Warren Critics posit a *left-wing conspiracy theory*, usually involving the CIA, the FBI, right-wing anti-Castro forces, and Cuban exiles, often backed by organised crime, and Texas oil millionaires, often entailing the active involvement of Lyndon Johnson, J. Edgar Hoover, and H. L. Hunt, the mega-rich Texas oil baron. Some or all of these men and forces take centre stage in the denouements of virtually every anti-Warren tome, far more predictably than the butler on the last page of a classic English detective novel. Here are some typical examples, from well-known anti-Warren books:

> *By the beginning of 1963, serious talk against President Kennedy was circulating within many groups – organised crime, the anti-Castro Cubans, the CIA, business and banking, the oil industry, and even the military ... So the decision was made at the highest level of American business – banking-politics-military-crime power structure – should anything happen to Kennedy, it would be viewed as a blessing for the nation ... Once such a consensus was reached among the nation's top business-crime-military leadership, the assassination conspiracy went into action. Operational orders most probably originated with organised-crime chieftains such as Carlos Marcello and his associates Santos Trafficante and Sam Giancano – who already were involved with the CIA.*
>
> *As the true assassination plot began to come together, word must have reached the ears of J. Edgar Hoover, a power unto himself with plenty of cause to hate the Kennedy brothers. Hoover was in contact with his close friend Lyndon Johnson and with Texas oilmen such as H. L. Hunt and Clint Murchinson of Dallas.*[30]

According to Harrison Edward Livingstone and Robert J. Groden, both tireless writers on the assassination,

> *At the time of the assassination, the Secret Team – or the Club, as others call it – manipulated the affairs of state. This group is not a formal organisation. It is composed of some of the most powerful and wealthiest men in the United States ... The Secret Team runs the United States ... The Club, a loosely knit, informal organisation, has gradually established a shadow government with a secret, institutionalised covert action capability outside the official government ... How did the Secret Team bring about the death of President Kennedy? The plotters had only to let the right mechanics know that the President would not be well protected and they would take care of the rest ... How could it all have happened without someone finding out the truth? To begin with, the circle of conspirators was relatively small, but they had at their disposal all the apparatus of government and the underworld.*[31]

Noel Twyman's *Bloody Treason: On Solving History's Greatest Murder*

Mystery: The Assassination of John F. Kennedy (Rancho Santa Fe, Cal., 1997), a mammoth 909–page tome on the assassination, concludes that:

> *The combination of J. Edgar Hoover, H. L. Hunt, and Lyndon Johnson – all in the plot – had the blackmail, the money, and the political power to see to it that the crime would never be seriously investigated … The Mafia joined forces with a few Kennedy haters from the CIA, radical anti-Castro Cuban exiles, and others in the extreme right wing, both civilian and military … Extensive evidence leads to the inescapable conclusion that a combination of U.S. government intelligence operatives, radical Cuban exiles, and Texas right-wing extremists played a major role in the assassination …*[32]

Harrison E. Livingstone has more recently revised his opinion, since co-authoring *High Treason.*

> *Since writing and publishing* [High Treason] *I came to know more about Lyndon Johnson's involvement. I think it is a mistake to believe that he could have motivated* (sic) *the entire assassination … Johnson had major help from military allies and from J. Edgar Hoover. There were at least four gun teams, men from various groups, including the Dixie Mafia, two from each group in each gun team – CIA contract Cubans, FBI connected provocateurs, Texans …, Mafia hit-men controlled by Carlos Marcello … I am sure that [J. Edgar] Hoover had to have directed part of the assassination … [Lyndon] Johnson and his Texas friends contributed some of the hit men, and some members of the shooting team were imported. Others were supplied by the Mob, and that also meant the anti-Castro Cuban mafia …*[33]

And so on. Anyone familiar with the anti-Warren assassination literature will know that a rendition of these views can be found in virtually every such work. Since the Warren Critics believe, by definition, that Oswald did not act alone, they must therefore believe that there was a conspiracy, and some such theory is almost universally posited, despite the total lack of real evidence for their views.[34] Occasionally, however, one finds a Kennedy assassination theory not necessarily entailing the participation of dark right-wing forces. Such a work as David E. Scheim's *The Mafia Killed President Kennedy* (London, 1988) – which at least has the great merit that one need not open the book to know the author's conclusions – eschews the usual right-wing bogeymen in favour of an assassination conspiracy masterminded by the Mafia.[35] Oddly enough, one obvious conspiracy theory about Kennedy's assassination has seldom or never been made by anyone, namely that he was killed by the Soviet Union and Castro. Such a theory makes far more sense, surely, than positing a left-wing conspiracy: Oswald was, unquestionably, a committed and extreme Marxist who had lived in the Soviet Union, married a Russian girl, and worked voluntarily, upon his return to the United States, as a pro-Cuban activist. Many standard conspiracy theories allege that the CIA or some other government agency had got to Oswald before his flight to Russia and that he was working thereafter as a double agent. But suppose it was the KGB, in Russia, which had taken control of Oswald? The Soviet Union might well have wanted the clever, glamorous, internationally popular Kennedy, with his worldwide following of passionate supporters, who had got the better of the Russians during the Cuban Missile Crisis, replaced by Lyndon Johnson, a man with no ostensible experience or interest in foreign affairs and little charisma, who was despised by the influential East Coast liberal Establishment and might not even have been renominated in 1964. Do I think this theory likely? No, I don't, but it is genuinely surprising that so few have suggested that Kennedy was killed by a *left* wing conspiracy, although one can easily interpret the facts to build up a superficially attractive case. Lyndon Johnson in fact appointed the Warren Commission specifically to lay to rest rumours that the Communists were behind Kennedy's assassination.[36] More significantly for those who believe that the dark forces of the American right were responsible for Kennedy's assassination in order to overthrow Fidel Castro, the Warren Commission quite specifically and explicitly rejected the suggestion that Communists were responsible for the assassination. 'The Commission discovered no evidence that the Soviet Union or Cuba were involved in the assassination of President Kennedy.'[37] If the Warren Commission was instructed to camouflage a right-wing conspiracy intended to oust Fidel Castro, why did it conclude that he was not in any way involved? Why did it not claim that he was responsible for the assassination, a perfect pretext for an immediate American invasion of Cuba?

In fact, books *supporting* the conclusions of the Warren Report have been notable for their extreme rarity. By far the most important – and, in my opinion, by far the most important work on Kennedy's assassination – is Gerald Posner's *Case Closed: Lee Harvey Oswald and the Assassination of*

JFK, which appeared to much publicity and critical acclaim in 1993. Posner, a lawyer and more recently a professional writer, concluded a detailed and meticulous investigation of the lives of Oswald and Ruby, as well as the events surrounding the assassination, and examined every conspiracy theory. Posner's conclusions, that the Warren Report was absolutely correct in virtually all of its assertions, that Oswald and Ruby acted alone, and that all of the many theories of the 'Warren Critics' are unsubstantiated fantasy, seems to me to be totally compelling. It is difficult to see how any rational person can read Posner's work without being convinced that he is reading, at last, a true account of the assassination. As an academic historian, too, I can only express my regret that Posner's work was written by someone outside the profession, and that more of the 25,000 college and university historians in the United States have not examined Kennedy's assassination in the critical and expert way that Posner, a lawyer and writer, did.

Apart from Posner's work, however, only a handful of books have ever appeared whose aim is to support the Warren Report and its conclusions. William Manchester's *Death of a President* (1967) is by far the best known. It was the 'official' narrative account of the assassination, commissioned and endorsed by Jacqueline Kennedy and her family. Manchester's vivid work accepted the Warren Report, but did not attempt to refute the 'Warren Critics', most of whom wrote long after *The Death of a President* appeared. Jim Moore's *Conspiracy of One* was written in 1990, a few years before Posner's book, and, in many ways, anticipates several of his conclusions, although it is far less sophisticated. It was possibly the first book to take the various 'conspiracy theories' head on and attempt to refute them.[38] It is a valuable work, too little noted. Mel Ayres, a British schoolteacher, wrote a virtually unknown work, *Questions of Conspiracy: The True Facts Behind the Assassination of President Kennedy* (Warrington, Cheshire, 1999), which also fully supports the Warren Report, assessing the claims of the 'Warren Critics' and refuting them. In 2002 he published an updated version of this book, *The JFK Assassination: Dispelling Myths and Challenging the Conspiracy Theorists* (West Sussex, 2002). Dale K. Myers' *With Malice: Lee Harvey Oswald and the Murder of Officer J. D. Tippit* (Milford, Michigan, 1998), is a monumental 702-page work dealing exclusively with the murder of Tippit. Myers is a Detroit computer specialist producing radio and television documentaries and plays. As with *Case Closed*, it is impossible for any rational person to read his extraordinarily detailed book without becoming fully convinced that Oswald killed Tippit exactly as the Warren Report claimed. Larry M. Sturdivan's *The JFK Myths: A Scientific Investigation of the Kennedy Assassination* (St. Paul, Minn., 2005) is arguably the most important book on the assassination since *Case Closed.* Sturdivan, a wound ballistics expert, demolishes the supposed 'scientific' evidence against Oswald as lone killer. Posner and Sturdivan together constitute a knockout punch against the conspiracy theorists. So far as I am aware, however, this constitutes the meagre list of pro-Warren works. All of these, in my view, are vastly superior and more convincing than any work by a 'Warren Critic' with which I am familiar.

Belief in an assassination conspiracy took on renewed life, of course, in 1991, with the release of Oliver Stone's *JFK*, which introduced the assassination and the alleged conspiracy that carried it out to a new generation. *JFK* has many claims to being considered the worst and most offensive film ever made in Hollywood – no mean feat. Stone's film was based in large part on the discredited account by Jim Garrison, in *On the Trail of the Assassins* (1988), of his attempts to prosecute Clay Shaw, a prominent New Orleans Society figure, for the assassination of President Kennedy. Shaw allegedly worked with Guy Bannister and David Ferrie, two anti-Castro activists. Garrison's prosecution was a scandalous tissue of rubbish and nonsense; Shaw was acquitted by a jury in 1969 in forty-five minutes.[39] Shamefully, Stone resurrected Garrison's absurd farrago, making it, for tens of millions, a convincing account of the assassination. According to Posner, Stone's film was not originally about Garrison and Shaw at all, but was to detail another crackpot theory of the assassination, the claim by a man named Ricky White that his father, Roscoe White, a Dallas policeman, was the 'grassy knoll' assassin who actually killed Kennedy. Stone 'reportedly considered paying $750,000 for the White story but eventually decided to buy the rights to Garrison's 1988 book *On the Trail of the Assassins* for $250,000.'[40] In other words, in *JFK* Oliver Stone chose one of two entirely different (and both nonsensical) accounts of President Kennedy's murder simply because it was for sale more cheaply on the open market.

In 1970, owing to public disquiet at the Warren Report, the U.S. House of Representatives initiated its own Select Committee on Assassinations, which investigated the killings of President Kennedy and Martin Luther King Jr. This Select Committee was about to conclude that all credible evidence suggested that the Warren Report was absolutely correct when, at the last minute, it came to the view that there was probably a fourth bullet fired by a second gunman on the grassy knoll, and that the conspiracy to kill Kennedy was in all likelihood instituted by the Mafia. Soon afterwards, however, it became absolutely clear that its conclusion about the second gunman was based upon fatally flawed evidence derived from an alleged open microphone on a police motorcycle.[41] The National Academy of Sciences appointed a panel to examine the questioned evidence, concluding that there 'was no acoustic evidence' for the Committee's claims.[42]

In the past decade or so, and especially since Posner's *Case Closed* appeared, it is probably true to say that fewer works critical of the Warren Report have appeared than before, although these have arguably become more extreme. Although there are other central points, anti-Warren claims now centre, in particular, around the contention that the Zapruder film was tampered with if not faked. The Zapruder film is the celebrated twenty-seven second recording of the assassination filmed by Abraham Zapruder, a local businessman, and immediately sold to *Life* magazine. With its horrifying depiction of President Kennedy's brain being blown out by the third bullet, it is probably the central piece of direct evidence about the assassination, and has been termed the most famous home movie in history. Every frame of the Zapruder film has been poured over and minutely examined by Warren Critics to detect inconsistencies with the official version of the assassination, and many now claim that all or most of the film was faked. An entire volume of essays edited by James H. Fetzer, *The Great Zapruder Film Hoax: Deceit and Detection in the Death of JFK* (Chicago, 2003) has been published on this alleged fabrication, as have many other essays in recent anti-Warren works, especially those edited by Fetzer, a professor of philosophy at the University of Minnesota–Duluth, who is currently one of the leading anti-Warren activists and critics.[43] Yet it seems impossible that the Zapruder film could have been faked, since it was seen at 9 a.m. the next morning by many witnesses, including Richard Stolley of *Life* magazine, several Secret Service men, and Zapruder himself. It was exactly the same then as it is now.[44] Unless the 'conspirators' had managed to create a totally convincing inauthentic Zapruder film overnight, with America in chaos after the assassination, employing the technology available in 1963, the film must be genuine. When it was allegedly faked, Oswald was still alive, of course, and in order not to give the 'conspiracy' away, these filmmakers would have had to make the film consistent with Oswald's story – whatever that was.

It would obviously have been infinitely simpler to have destroyed the film, with Zapruder being told that his film or camera had failed to work properly. Other central claims made today by anti-Warren sources include the bizarre contention that there might have been 'two Oswalds', one an impostor planted, possibly as early as the mid-1950s, by the military and CIA, and that there was extensive tampering with Kennedy's posthumous x-rays and other medical evidence.[45] The internet has naturally given a renewed lease on life to the Warren Critics, as it has to many other unorthodox strands. At the present time, there appear to be two main websites by the Warren Critics, JFK Lancer and Assassination Science. The former (www.jfklancer.com) argues that Kennedy was killed as the result of a conspiracy, but rejects the more outlandish conspiracy theories. It holds an Annual Conference in Dallas which includes academic speakers (although these generally give presentations on ancillary topics such as Kennedy's relationship with intelligence agencies) as well as conspiracy buffs. Each conference concludes a memorial observance in Dealey Plaza. This site publishes an on-line journal, *Kennedy Assassination Chronicles.* Far more *outré* is Assassination Science (www.assassinationscience.com), edited by James Fetzer, whose site presents a range of full-on left-wing conspiracy theories with bells and whistles. Its extensive home page includes numerous attacks on the George W. Bush administration ('Was the 2004 election fixed?' is typical) and its policies, and several blogs alleging that the 9/11 attacks might have been an 'inside job'. (This view has quickly become a staple of the conspiratorial demi-monde.) It also includes a blog by Jack White (who has written extensively on the Zapruder film 'hoax') in which he states that 'grave doubts exist that the Apollo missions to the moon were anything other than the most incredible hoax of all time ... all photographs of the Apollo feats had to be forgeries.'

In addition to the usual theories of conspiracy, a number of lesser-known accounts of the assassination have been written over the years which ought to be considered. In 1992 Bonar Menninger, a journalist, published *Mortal Error: The Shot That Killed Kennedy.* In it, he suggested that the fatal bullet was fired from an AR-15 rifle in the Secret Service car following Kennedy's limousine. According to Menninger, it was accidentally fired by a Secret Service agent who picked up his gun in response to Oswald's initial shot and hit Kennedy by mistake when he inadvertently fell backwards.[46] This is certainly an intriguing theory, which cannot be dismissed, and certainly deserves more attention than the (virtually nonexistent) amount it has received. Nevertheless, it appears to contradict the fact that the three bullets were certainly fired from Oswald's rifle, and from the sixth floor of the Depository building.[47] Another possibly very useful theory was offered by John Luken in his booklet *Oswald's Trigger Films: The Manchurian Candidate, We Were Strangers, Suddenly* (Falcon Books, 2000). Luken speculates that Oswald might well have seen three films, the first in the movies, the other two on television, dealing with assassinations that acted to 'trigger' his destructive capacity. *The Manchurian Candidate* (1962), dealing with a 'programmed' former defector to Russia similar to Oswald, was playing in Dallas movie theatres at the time, while two forgotten films, *We Were Strangers* (1949) and *Suddenly* (1954), on similar themes, were presented on television while Oswald was in Dallas. As with Menninger's book, this potentially important insight has been virtually ignored. Luken admitted, however, that he has no direct evidence as to whether Oswald actually saw these films, let alone was influenced by them. Nevertheless, his interesting theory should certainly be noted by historians.

Finally, there is the theory that Oswald's real target was not President Kennedy but actually Governor Connally. This suggestion was made at the time and is discussed in the Warren Report.[48] There is, at least superficially, a surprising amount of circumstantial evidence that this might have been the case. Oswald apparently held a grudge against Connally who had, as Secretary of the Navy some years earlier, signed a letter to Oswald stating that his dishonourable discharge from the Marine Reserves would not be reviewed. Significantly, on 6 September 1964, Marina Oswald testified before the Warren Committee that she thought that he 'was shooting at Connally rather than President Kennedy'.[49] It would have been easy for Oswald to have aimed at Connally, hesitated for a fraction of a second, and shot the President, sitting two feet behind him in the same open limousine, by mistake. The Warren Commission rejected this possibility, believing Kennedy to have been the target. This was very likely the case, although the theory that Connally rather than Kennedy was the real target, ignored by virtually all writers on the assassination, should not be dismissed. Oswald's apparent *lack* of thought or planning given to his escape after the shooting might be more understandable if 'only' the local Governor rather than the President himself were the intended target. The 1960s also saw several other notorious assassinations in the United States which have given rise to great controversy, although certainly not on the scale of President Kennedy's murder. The most likely conclusion which might be reached about the 1968 murder of Senator Robert Kennedy, the President's brother, by Sirhan Sirhan, is that his assassin, like Oswald, acted alone, but the investigation was poorly handled by the Los Angeles police.[50] On the other hand, the killing of Dr. Martin Luther King Jr. shortly before Robert Kennedy's assassination was probably the result of a conspiracy. King's killer, James Earl Ray, a career criminal of low intelligence and few resources, could probably not have organised King's killing and his own subsequent flight overseas by himself. It seems likely that the conspiracy was organised by Ray's relatives and a few wealthy Southern racists, but certainly not by the FBI or the federal government. Such is the conclusion of Gerald Posner, who has shown that there was no conspiracy in President Kennedy's assassination.[51] The death of the famous Hollywood star Marilyn Monroe at the age of thirty-six in 1962, officially ruled a suicide (and regarded by some as the result of an accidental overdose of sleeping pills), is sometimes seen as a murder. According to Donald H. Wolfe in *The Assassination of Marilyn Monroe* (1999), the star may have been killed on the express orders of President Kennedy and Robert Kennedy, who – according to this critique – desperately wished the return of a notebook kept by the actress with details of the affairs she had been having with the two brothers, affairs which she threatened to make public and which would certainly have destroyed their careers. This lurid theory has been presented in a way which is much more convincing than most conspiracy theories, including those surrounding the death of President Kennedy.

Having read innumerable works on Kennedy's assassination, and having followed it literally since it took place in 1963, I am firmly convinced that Oswald and Ruby acted alone, in precisely the manner described in the Warren Report and Posner's *Case Closed*. Indeed, I am more convinced of this than of perhaps any other conclusion reached in the present work. It might be helpful to set out my views on Kennedy's assassination in question-and-answer form, with salient questions being followed by my own views.

Q. *How many bullets were fired at President Kennedy?*

A. Three and only three. Apart from the ear-witness evidence dismissed in the Warren Report and discussed in *Case Closed*, an extraordinary amount of reliable testimony by reporters on the scene has been published in two works written thirty and fifty years later. In these, reporters present in Dallas on the day of the assassination recalled what had happened. In contrast to the casual bystanders typically cited by Warren Critics, these reporters are professional journalists whose reputations depend upon their accuracy. All were pro-Kennedy, none was associated in any way with an anti-Kennedy conspiracy of any kind, and all enjoyed long and successful careers. *All* were in agreement that three and only three shots were fired. Bob Jackson, a photographer on the *Dallas Times Herald*, recalled in 2003:

> We had prearranged for me to drop off film that I shot along the route to a reporter … And that's when we heard the first shot, and then two more shots closer together.[52]

Merriam Smith, the well-known White House correspondent and Pulitzer Prize winner who died in 1970, was quoted in the same work as having said

> *Suddenly we heard three loud, almost painfully loud cracks. The first sounded as if it might have been a large firecracker. But the second and third blasts were unmistakeable. Gunfire.*[53]

Tom Dillard, the chief photographer of the *Dallas Morning News*, stated in a report written in 1964 that

> *My car had turned north on Houston Street and was at the county jail entrance when the first shot was fired. I said, 'They've thrown a torpedo.' At the second shot, 'No, it's heavy rifle fire,' and, at the third shot, 'They've killed him.'*[54]

Clint Grant was also a photographer with the *Dallas Morning News.* Thirty years later, in a November 1993 journalism symposium at Southern Methodist University, at which reporters and journalists recalled these events, Grant stated

> *… I hopped into the open Cadillac convertible with three White House photographers. We were the number two camera car behind the President. Twenty-five minutes later as we turned the corner at Main and Houston, I heard three shots ring out.*[55]

Bo Byers was then a reporter for the *Houston Chronicle*. He was on the White House press bus, with many other reporters, a few vehicles behind the President's car.

> *We were on Houston. I was looking across the plaza when we heard the shots. I remember three shots.*[56]

Hugh Aynesworth, a well-known reporter on the *Dallas Morning News*, recalled at this 1993 event, that although he was not specifically assigned to cover Kennedy's visit

> *I decided this was a special day and even if I wasn't involved I ought to go to watch it, so I went over to the area around Elm and Houston streets and was there when the three shots rung out. Three definite shots.*[57]

Finally, there is Mary Woodward Pillsworth, then also a reporter on the *Dallas Morning News.*

> *And then the motorcade came along ... They [President and Mrs. Kennedy] looked right at us, waved, and at that moment I heard a very loud noise. And I wasn't sure what it was at that point, and I turned to my friends and asked 'What was that? Some jerk shooting off firecrackers?', then I heard the second one, and this time I knew what had happened because I saw the president's motion. And then the third shot came, very, very quickly on top of the second one. And that time. I saw his head blow open, and I very well knew what had happened by that point.*[58]

Another direct witness who thought that only three shots had been fired was Nellie Connally, the wife of Governor John Connally, who was sitting directly in front of Jacqueline Kennedy in the presidential limousine. When she died at eighty-seven in 2006, Nellie Connally was the last survivor of the fatal car. In her memoir *From Love Field: Our Final Hours with President John F Kennedy*, published in 2003 but based on handwritten notes she made shortly after the assassination, she states (pp.7–8) that there were three shots: 'A moment later, a terrifying noise erupted behind us. Instinctively, I felt it was a gunshot … Then – a second shot … A third shot rang out … I no longer had any doubt that the President was dead.'

No reporter or journalist on the scene suggested that there were more than three shots. As Posner notes, almost every Warren Critic argues that there was more than one assassin, and more than three shots.[59] They are certainly wrong.

Q. Did the bullets aimed at Kennedy all come from Oswald's rifle in the Texas School Book Depository building?

A. Again, this appears incontestable. Posner has detailed many eyewitnesses who actually saw Oswald fire the rifle.[60] Harold Norman, who was working on the *fifth* floor of the School Book Depository building immediately below Oswald, recalled that 'when the first shot came, I heard boom, then click-click, boom, click-click, boom. I could hear the sound of the shells hitting the floor. I could hear everything. Three shots. No doubt in my mind.' He then shouted to two co-workers on the fifth floor: 'It's coming right over our heads.'[61] Bob Jackson, the photographer of the *Dallas Times Herald*, riding in the press car, said to Tom Dillard, another press photographer: 'There's a rifle in that open window [in the Depository building]'. Dillard noted that 'In the three or four seconds it took me to locate that particular open window and make a picture, the rifle had been withdrawn.'[62] Malcolm Couch, a television cameraman, stated 'We were right in front of the Texas School Book Depository and right about that time I looked up and saw about a foot of the rifle going back in the window.[63] James Worrall, a college student standing in front of the Depository, looked up when he heard the first shot: 'I looked up like that, just straight up. I saw the rifle, about six inches of it.' He saw the rifle actually fire, 'what you might call a little flash of fire and then smoke.' The gun was 'pointing right down at the motorcade'.[64] Oswald quickly became the prime suspect because an eyewitness, Howard Brennan, also saw the shooting and gave a good description of Oswald to the police.[65] Oswald's rifle was quickly found. Oswald's fingerprints were identified, in the 1990s, by new scientific methods, on the trigger guard of his rifle, and one bullet has been ballistically proven to have been fired from Oswald's rifle.[66] The trajectory of the bullets, scientifically traced, could come only from Oswald's 'sniper's nest' on the sixth floor of the Depository building.[67] All reports of other assassins, for instance on the 'grassy knoll', have been shown to be without substance, and are unable to counter the fact that only three shots were fired, all from Oswald's rifle.

Q. Were Oswald's actions suspicious?

A. They plainly were, and are grossly inconsistent with the actions of an innocent man. On 21 November 1963, Oswald asked a workmate if he could be driven to his wife's home in Irving, a suburb of Dallas (Oswald was living in a rooming house in Dallas itself) to take some 'curtain rods' to 'put in an apartment'. He spent the night there, but, unaccountably, left $170, virtually all of his cash, and his wedding ring, in his wife's house.[68] The following morning he drove to the School Book Depository with a paper bag allegedly containing 'the curtain rods'. Apart from the absurdity of bringing 'curtain rods' to work, no curtain rods were found in the Depository building.[69] Oswald was seen on the sixth floor of the Depository building at 11.40 a.m. or later by six co-workers. Oswald's job at the Depository was to fill book orders for school textbooks, which were listed on a personal clipboard. Oswald's clipboard was found, on 2 December, with three unfilled orders still attached to it.[70] Oswald then took a taxi to his rooming house. The impecunious Oswald had never taken a taxi there before.[71] Oswald was the *only* employee of the School Book Depository to leave the premises before the police arrived. At the rooming house, Oswald grabbed and loaded a revolver he kept hidden there in his room. About fifteen minutes later, he shot and killed Dallas police officer J. D. Tippit, who had stopped him because Oswald's appearance matched a description of the assassin sent out on the police radio. There cannot be the slightest doubt that Oswald shot Tippit.[72] The four shells discharged in killing Tippit have been matched to Oswald's gun to the exclusion of any other gun.[73] Appearing almost insane by this point, Oswald then ran to a row of shops, sneaking into a movie theatre without paying. Theatre officials informed the police, who were looking out for Tippit's killer. When they confronted Oswald in the theatre, he nearly shot and killed another policeman.[74] In custody, Oswald repeatedly lied to police interrogating him, even on trivial matters.[75]

Q. Could Oswald have been part of a wider conspiracy?

A. This seems highly implausible. First, Oswald was virtually broke. The Warren Commission cleverly investigated Oswald's finances from the time he returned from the Soviet Union in June 1962 until the assassination, liaising with every bank where he lived and with overseas sources. In this seventeen-month period, Oswald received only $3665 from all known sources. He had no other sources of income of which anyone was aware.[76] The Oswalds lived in virtual poverty. They possessed no major household appliances, owned no car, and used welfare clinics for medical and dental care. He invariably used buses to travel to work, or rode for free with neighbours.[77] It seems inconceivable that anyone who is the key member of a conspiracy to assassinate the President of the United States, a conspiracy allegedly well-funded by powerful and wealthy forces, would consent to continue living in poverty or have his wife and children do so. On the contrary, virtually any would-be assassin of the President would assuredly demand a substantial and secure payment for his efforts, presumably in a safe overseas bank account. The Warren Commission's clever and painstaking investigation of this point has *never* been cited – still less refuted – by any Warren Critic.

Secondly, Oswald was employed at the School Book Depository, and physically in a position to kill the President, only because of a series of coincidences which virtually rule out a conspiracy. Marina Oswald was befriended by a Quaker couple in Dallas, Michael and Ruth Paine, who took pity on her as a friendless Russian immigrant. In mid-October 1963 they were discussing Lee Oswald's difficulty in finding work with two neighbours. One of them, Linnie Mae Rundle, pointed out that her younger brother, Wesley Buell Fraser, had recently found work at the School Book Depository, and recommended that Oswald try to get a job there, since it 'was the busy season' there. Oswald applied, and was interviewed and hired by Roy Truly of the Depository, who was impressed by Oswald's respectful demeanour.[78] He was hired, and then only for a limited time, in part because Ruth Paine told Truly that Oswald's wife was expecting a baby.[79] Unless every one of these people was a part of the alleged conspiracy, Oswald's presence in the School Book Depository building was purely coincidental and fortuitous. Oswald did not know the route to be taken by the presidential motorcade until it was printed in a Dallas newspaper a few days before the assassination.

Thirdly, no assassin would agree to kill the President without having an elaborate and foolproof escape plan fully in place. Oswald plainly had no escape route in mind, apparently never giving his fate after the assassination any thought. He had $13.87 on him when he was arrested.[80] Nor would any well-placed conspirators use a presidential assassin without creating a foolproof mode of exit for him, presumably abroad. It should be noted, however, that Oswald did create the maximum possible confusion by shooting Kennedy from behind. Some commentators have wondered why Oswald did not shoot Kennedy from the front, as his car was driving down Houston Street before it made its sharp and hazardous left-hand turn into Elm Street. The answer, however, seems obvious: if Oswald shot Kennedy from the front, he would have been seen by the entire motorcade, whom he would have been facing as he fired. By shooting Kennedy from behind, Oswald gave himself a reasonable chance of emerging from the Depository building, as well as creating the endless controversy about the shootings which has persisted for over forty years.

Q. *Was Jack Ruby a part of a conspiracy?*

A. Again, there seems not the slightest doubt that he acted entirely alone. Ruby had no connection whatever with the Mafia, and all assertions that he did are false.[81] He had never set eyes on Oswald before the assassination. Oswald had never been in his nightclub, and they had never met or spoken. After Ruby's arrest, the Texas authorities tried as hard as possible to find some direct connection between Ruby and Oswald. Had such a connection existed, Ruby would have been guilty of premeditated murder, carrying the death penalty, rather than the spur-of-the-moment killing of a presidential assassin, for which he might well have been acquitted or convicted of a minor offence. They checked out every story or lead they received, but could find no credible evidence of any association whatever between them.[82] Oswald and Ruby occupied entirely different universes. Oswald was a young, intensely political, well-read autodidact, a committed Marxist who had lived in the Soviet Union. Ruby was a middle-aged fringe businessman, politically unsophisticated if not politically illiterate. The only qualities they had in common were well-documented histories of violence, maladjustment, and financial failure.

In addition, it is inconceivable that Ruby would have killed Oswald in the manner he did if he were part of a conspiracy. Ruby shot Oswald in a basement in which Oswald was guarded by dozens of armed police. It was overwhelmingly likely that Ruby would have been shot dead on the spot. If he somehow avoided this fate (as he did) he was certain to be convicted (as he was) and probably executed for murder. No sane man would agree to become part of a conspiracy under these conditions. Nor would any rational conspirators use Ruby, a middle-aged nightclub owner who had swallowed dozens of anti-depressant pills shortly before, for an operation as important as silencing Kennedy's assassin. They would obviously have used a professional hit man, and provided him with a foolproof route of escape. If Ruby was taken alive into police custody, the conspirators would merely have exchanged one likely source of information about them and their conspiracy for another. Logically, Ruby would have to be quickly killed just as Oswald was.

As has been pointed out by many recent supporters of the Warren Report, in more than fifty years since the assassination, a period in which hundreds of Warren Critics have conducted research or written on the assassination, the alleged conspirators have never been successfully identified or named, and the Critics sharply disagree among themselves as to who killed President Kennedy. It seems inconceivable that, in the contemporary United States, their identities could have remained a mystery for so long if a conspiracy had actually occurred. Either the real conspirators would have long since been identified by anti-Warren writers, or someone would have confessed, either for financial gain, or through feelings of remorse or guilt, or in the course of a deathbed or posthumous admission. None ever has, and vague but sinister-sounding finger-pointing at the CIA, the FBI, the Mafia, anti-Castro Cubans – and so on – have always taken the place of hard evidence and facts.

Q. Did Kennedy's Assassination Change the Course of American Foreign Policy and American History?

A. Most Warren Critics (and many others) argue that Kennedy's assassination changed the course of history, leading to the disastrous escalation of the war in Vietnam which began soon after Lyndon Johnson became President. The first point which ought to be made about the anti-Warren critique of American foreign policy is that it is based in a kind of sleight-of-hand. According to the Warren Critics, it was not Vietnam but Cuba which was the central driving force behind the assassination. According to them, the goal of the assassins was to remove Fidel Castro from power and replace him with a pro-American regime, similar to that in office in the 1950s, which would throw out the Russians and hand Cuba over, once more, to American economic domination and gambling interests which Castro had expelled. The aim of destroying the Castro government is central to virtually every anti-Warren theory.

The central problem with this critique has, amazingly, been ignored by everyone writing on Kennedy's assassination: his death did not bring about the overthrow of Fidel Castro, who, remarkably, still in a position of authority in Cuba, nine American presidents later. If Lyndon Johnson indeed became President to rid the world of Fidel Castro, the conspirators must have been sorely disappointed with his inertia. Indeed, by the time Johnson left office in January 1969, Fidel Castro was international politics' forgotten man, having been driven off the front pages by the Vietnam War and many other events.

Having obfuscated the Cuban situation as the central motivating factor in JFK's assassination, Warren Critics frequently turn, without further explanation, to Vietnam as somehow central to the killing. Their contention is that, had he lived, Kennedy would have withdrawn American military forces from Vietnam (then numbering about 10,000), and avoided the tragedy of the Vietnam War. President Kennedy was certainly a far more sophisticated and intelligent man than Lyndon Johnson, and it is difficult to believe that he would have escalated American troop involvement and military action in the war in the same bloody-minded way as his successor. It is quite possible that he would have removed all but token American forces from Vietnam, had he been reelected in 1964. Nevertheless, it is not a foregone conclusion that he would have ended American involvement in Vietnam, despite what Warren Critics (and others) maintain. Historians have been quite divided on this point. According to one recent Kennedy biographer, Michael O'Brien, President Kennedy never discussed American troop withdrawal from Vietnam either with his brother Robert F. Kennedy, his closest confidante, or with Dean Rusk, his Secretary of State, with whom he spoke on the Indo-China situation hundreds of times.[83] Nor should it be overlooked that Lyndon Johnson's main foreign policy advisers – Rusk, Robert MacNamara, Walt Rostow, and others – were almost always Kennedy appointees, who would presumably have given the same advice to Kennedy, had he lived, as they gave to Johnson. Nor could anyone have foreseen the disastrous results of American involvement in Vietnam, which led to serious and chronic opposition among much of American youth and among many American opinion-leaders. It is difficult to believe that right-wing forces in America would have favoured Lyndon Johnson's Vietnam policies had they foreseen its results.

Many commentators on Kennedy's assassination have pointed out that it seems incredible that so momentous a political change could have been brought about by a lone social misfit with a mail-order rifle, and that therefore much wider and deeper forces must surely have been responsible. As implausible as it might seem, this is precisely what happened, an ultimate example of the role of the accidental individual in history.

Chapter 3

The 'Jack the Ripper' Murders

The shocking and brutal murders of five prostitutes in London's East End in the autumn of 1888 by an unknown killer who came to be called 'Jack the Ripper' are probably the most famous unsolved crimes in history. They have inspired a vast, ever-growing body of historical accounts and theories by non-academic historians whose aim is almost always to set out a case for what they believe is the correct solution of these killings.[1] In this, the historians and theorists of Jack the Ripper murders differ markedly from many of the other subjects examined in this book. In most of the subjects discussed here, there is an officially-accepted sequence of events, from which these writers knowingly dissent. Thus, the official Warren Report verdict on the assassination of President Kennedy is that he was killed by Lee Harvey Oswald, acting alone, who in turn was killed by Jack Ruby, acting alone, and that no conspiracy of any kind was behind the President's assassination. All, or virtually all, so-called 'dissenters' from the Warren Report believe *ipso facto* that there was a conspiracy of some kind involved in Kennedy's assassination, and that Oswald did not act alone. The mainstream, commonly-accepted account of the works of William Shakespeare is that they were indeed written by the Stratford actor who was born in 1564 and died in 1616; those who believe in the 'Shakespeare Authorship Question' deny this, and argue that someone else wrote the works attributed to him. In contrast, the 'Jack the

Ripper' theorists do not have an officially-accepted theory to argue against: no one was caught and tried for the Ripper crimes in 1888, and the murders are just as mysterious today as they were then. In part for this reason, a large and ever-growing number of possible murderers, of varying degrees of plausibility, have been suggested over the years.

In recent years the 'Ripper industry' has (as with many other subjects examined here) mushroomed. It is likely, in fact, that more has been written on the Ripper in recent years than on any other subject dominated by 'amateur historians', and certainly as much as any other subject. The number of books published on the Ripper has escalated dramatically in recent decades, and has been added to by an ever-growing number of journals, conferences, websites, and documentaries. Virtually all Ripper theorists are driven, in my view, by the hope that he or she will finally solve the great mystery, making the crucial breakthrough with new evidence or a brilliant rearrangement of what is known, and thus besting a century of theorists and the police. This driving force is greater among 'Ripperologists' than with most of the other historical questions discussed in this book, since the case is unsolved, giving everyone an equal chance of success.

All discussions of the Ripper began by setting out, at least briefly, what 'Jack the Ripper' did during his murder spree, when five prostitutes were brutally killed. The first of the so-called five 'canonical' victims was Mary Ann (Polly) Nichols (1845–88).[2] The daughter of a London blacksmith named Edward Walker, she had married William Nichols, a London printer, in 1864, separating in 1880. She had had five children by him. Her life in the 1880s encompassed sleeping rough, the workhouse, and periodic bouts of temporary employment and cohabitation as well as prostitution. In August 1888 she was living in a doss house at 56 Flower and Dean Street. She was last seen, obviously drunk, at the corner of Osborn Street and Whitechapel High Street at 2:30 a.m. in the early morning of Sunday 30 August 1888. At 3:40 a.m. her body was found lying in Buck's Row, with her throat cut and her dress pulled up. An examination at the mortuary revealed that she had suffered horrible abdominal mutilations with a knife. Buck's Row (now Durward Street) is just north of Whitechapel Road, near the Whitechapel tube station, more than half a mile east of any of the other 'canonical' murders. The Inquest, which took place on 1 September 1888, drew a large crowd of journalists. The police suspected, first, a gang of criminals who demanded money from local prostitutes, and then, the slaughterers at a local abattoir, but could not identify the criminal and made no arrests.[3]

Whitechapel did not have long to wait for the next murder. At 6 a.m. on the morning of 19 September 1888 John Davis, a carman, discovered the mutilated body of Annie Chapman (1841–88) in the back yard of 29 Hanbury Street, about 400 yards north of Whitechapel High Street, near Brick Lane. Chapman, the daughter of George Smith, a lifeguardsman, had been married to John Chapman, a coachman, from 1881 until his death in 1886. She briefly lived with Jack Stivey, a sievemaker, but, at the time of her death, was an alcoholic prostitute. She was last seen at 1:35 a.m., attempting to stay the night at a lodging house adjacent to Hanbury Street, but lacked the fourpence fee. Visitors to the Hanbury Street area throughout the night noticed nothing unusual, although one witness, a carpenter named Albert Cadoche (or Cadosch), heard a scuffle and someone or something falling against the fence of the yard at about 5:20 a.m. (which seems unlikely to have been connected with the murder). Chapman, whose throat had been cut, had been dead for at least two hours at 6:30 a.m. She was covered in blood and her clothing was up to her knees. Her abdomen had been opened and her intestines severed from her belly and placed on the ground above her right shoulder. Her stomach, uterus, and genitals had been cut out. The post-mortem physician believed the mutilation had taken roughly an hour, and was probably done by someone with anatomical knowledge.[4] It was immediately realised, given the location of the backyard where she was found, that the murderer had had an amazingly lucky escape. Senior policemen also believed that she had been killed by the same man as had killed Mary Ann Nichols.

Large crowds gathered. Jewish immigrants were suspected because the crime was 'unEnglish', and, on 10 September, a Jewish immigrant boot finisher, Jack Pizer, known as 'Leather Apron' from his occupational outfit, and who was known to bully prostitutes, was arrested, but released after thirty-six hours. East Enders set up a Whitechapel Vigilance Committee, with George Lusk, a local builder, as its head, to assist the police.[5]

The third victim was Elizabeth Stride (1843–88), a Swedish-born prostitute known as 'Long Liz'. She had lived in London since 1866, and had numerous convictions for drunken behaviour. She had recently left her *de facto* husband, Michael Kidney, a labourer. Stride was apparently last seen around 11 p.m. on the evening of Friday, 29 September 1888. At 1 a.m.

on Saturday morning, Louis Diemschutz, a Jewish jewellery dealer, found Stride's body in Dutfield's Yard, behind Berners Street, which runs south of Commercial Road, Whitechapel. It is a considerable distance, about half a mile, to the south-east of Hanbury Street, the scene of the last killing. Her body was examined by police and the police surgeon, Dr. Bagster Phillips, almost immediately. Her neck had been cut, although she was not horribly mutilated. There was some doubt at the time that she was a Ripper victim, and her murder differs in some respects from the others. Newspapers and most senior policemen, however, accepted that she was the third victim.[6]

But there was more horror to come, for Jack struck twice that night. At about 1:45 a.m. on the same morning, the body of Catherine Eddowes (1842–88) was discovered in Mitre Square, a space behind Duke Street off Aldgate, just west of Whitechapel in the City of London and half a mile east of where Elizabeth Stride's body had been found. Eddowes, the daughter of a tinplate varnisher, lived with several men in the Midlands and the East End. Hers was the usual story of poverty, drink, and the street. Her throat had been cut, her whole body horribly mutilated.[7] By the time of the so-called 'double event', the Ripper murders had become a national sensation and had, indeed, been given their celebrated name. On 27 September 1888, a letter was posted to the Central News Agency from an East End address with the salutation 'Dear Boss'. Bragging about the killings, it was signed 'Yours truly, Jack the Ripper'. A second missive, received on 1 October 1888, a postcard also addressed to the Central News Agency, known as the 'saucy Jack' postcard because of its reference to 'saucy Jacky's work tomorrow double event', was also signed 'Jack the Ripper'. It is not clear whether either was genuinely written by the killer: the police thought they were written by a journalist, while the postcard might or might not have been written before the 'double event'.[8] Nevertheless, 'Jack the Ripper' the killer became, and has remained. From whatever source, the naming of 'Jack the Ripper' was a stroke of genius, lifting a gruesome series of slum murders to criminal, indeed historical, immortality. It is difficult to believe that if the killings had remained known as the 'Whitechapel Murders' they would have been remembered today, except to researchers of Victorian brutality, let alone become probably the most famous unsolved crimes in history, legendary and even, despite their sickening barbarism, romantic, and emblematic of late Victorian London. On 16 October, a letter was sent to George Lusk of the Whitechapel Vigilance Committee, with the writer's address given as 'from

Hell', containing half of a human kidney, which the (anonymous) writer claimed was from one of the victims – presumably Catherine Eddowes – and that he had 'fried and ate' the rest of it. The claim was assumed to be a hoax, but later researchers have concluded that it might have been genuine.[9] On the night of the 'double event' a message was found chalked on the doorway of the staircase of a tenement block on Goulston Street, Whitechapel, about 1500 feet from Mitre Square, along with a piece of an apron taken from the clothing of Catherine Eddowes. Known as the 'Goulston Street Graffito [Graffiti]' it apparently said 'The Juwes are the men that Will not be blamed for nothing', although it was soon erased by the police.

The last of the murders was the worst. At 10:45 a.m. on the morning of Friday 9 November 1888 the body of Mary Jane Kelly was discovered by a rent collector in the tiny partitioned-off back room at 13 Miller Court, where she lived. Miller Court was a back alley behind Dorset Street near Commercial Street, Whitechapel, a few hundred feet from where Annie Chapman's body had been found. She had been mutilated beyond description, in a manner which is still deeply shocking today, after a century of endless horrors. Kelly (*c.*1863–88), who was born in Ireland and lived in Wales, worked as a high-class West End prostitute before descending to the East End streets, where, until shortly before, she had lived with a fish porter named Joseph Barnett. She was probably seen alive at 2:30 a.m., and at 4 a.m. neighbours head a cry of 'Murder!' from the direction of her room. She was the only Ripper victim murdered indoors.[10] More has been written about Mary Kelly than the other victims. She was the only one with high-class West End connections, the last victim, and the most horribly mutilated. All sorts of theories have been proposed about her, for instance that she had some royal connection, or was the real target of the Ripper, the previous victims being killed to disguise the murderer's real intent in the manner of an Agatha Christie novel. There is no evidence for any of these theories.

By this time the truly terrible nature of these crimes, and the Ripper's apparent ability to escape capture as if by magic and to laugh at the police, were creating real panic in the East End, and there was genuine danger of mob violence, especially given the highly unsettled, even potentially insurrectionary, conditions among the London poor at the time. On 10 November 1888, the British Cabinet agreed to authorise a pardon to any accomplice of Kelly's murder who helped to catch the Ripper and, on the same day, Queen Victoria telegraphed Lord Salisbury, the Prime Minister, urging 'some very decided action'. The Ripper murders were now both a national and international sensation, probably the first crimes without an obvious political element to become renowned around the world. The police had by this time received 1400 letters about the crimes in five weeks.[11]

But then – assuming that the five 'canonical' victims were the Ripper's only victims – Jack the Ripper suddenly stopped killing. The horrible butchery of Mary Kelly was the end of Jack the Ripper's killing spree. No one knows why the murders stopped on 10 November 1888, and any successful solution to the mystery must explain why he stopped, and presumably never resumed, killing. There are many possible explanations. He could have been apprehended and incarcerated for another crime; he could have died; his mental or physical health could have changed or deteriorated; he might have fled abroad. If Mary Kelly was the intended victim, he might have stopped deliberately after finishing her off. Our knowledge of serial killers is primarily based on those in the twentieth century United States, where societal and psychological factors might well have been very different from those in late Victorian London, but in modern America serial killers seldom just stop, although there may be lengthy gaps between their crimes. As it happens, many of the leading Ripper suspects experience a traumatic change at just this time which could explain why they stopped, compounding the mystery still further.

A number of other points about the Ripper murders are worth noting. So far as anyone knows, the victims were selected unsystematically, and were randomly chosen prostitutes who had the misfortune to be in the wrong place at the wrong time. No researcher has ever demonstrated a pattern of association among the victims, who were probably all unknown to one another, and had no obvious friends, male or female, in common. They were of different ages, backgrounds, and physical appearance. All the murders took place on weekends, with the exception of Mary Kelly's, which occurred on the Friday of the Lord Mayor's Show, when many residents of the City and its adjacent areas would probably have had the day off. None of the murders occurred during the normal working week. It is difficult – as always – to know what might be reasonably inferred from this fact. Working men were traditionally paid their weekly wages on a Thursday: it is possible that this is relevant. The Ripper might have been otherwise occupied during the week, and able to lurk the streets late at night only on weekends. There were probably more prostitutes on the East End streets on weekends than at any other time but also presumably more potential witnesses and men who could apprehend the Ripper in mid-crime. The five murders took place at extreme ends of the Whitechapel area, first in the east, then in the north, then (on the same night) just west of Whitechapel and in the south central part of the borough, and finally again in the north. Some imaginative researchers have claimed that this was a deliberate attempt to carry out the killings in the form of (very roughly) a cross, although a more obvious explanation is that, to avoid the police, the Ripper carried out his next murder at a point furthest removed, in the Whitechapel area, from his previous killing. One might ask why the Ripper restricted himself to Whitechapel. Again, there is no ready explanation. It is likely that the killer was from Whitechapel, or, if not, certainly appears to have become familiar with its passages and byways, in order to facilitate his escape; it is also possible that he was simply very lucky. There were, of course, other slum districts in London, but these tended to have been built with more regular street patterns. Probably, too, fewer low-class prostitutes would have congregated in these areas, except around the railway terminals, where there would also have been fewer modes of escape and possibly more policemen. One final point is that the Ripper apparently did not engage in sexual intercourse with any of the prostitutes before killing them, presumably (one imagines) to get to the main business at hand without delay.

The police also obviously came in for a good deal of criticism, although most recent historians regard this criticism as unjustified. Nevertheless, police handling of the Ripper case left a lot to be desired. The Metropolitan Police Commissioner, Sir Charles Warren (1840–1927), was an engineer and professional soldier who had served throughout the Empire. Press criticism of Warren over the Ripper murder and other matters, including a personality conflict with Henry Matthews, the Home Secretary, led to his resignation on 9 November 1888, the day of the Mary Kelly murder. His main deputies, Dr. (later Sir) Robert Anderson (1841–1918), who was actually in charge of the Ripper case, was abroad on sick leave during part of the killing spree. He always claimed to have known the identity of the killer, apparently believing him to have been a Polish Jewish immigrant.[12] Warren's other deputy, James Munro (1838–1920), who succeeded him as Police Commissioner, was an effective police officer, who was much concerned with the 'Special Branch' which investigated political terrorism.[13] Additionally, one of the victims, Catherine Eddowes, was killed in the City of London, which had a separate police force apart from the Metropolitan Police. Since 'Jack the Ripper' was never caught, the bottom line is that the London police failed. Nevertheless, there were many extenuating circumstances. They had never before dealt with a serial-killing maniac of the Ripper's cunning. It was obviously impossible to police every square inch of the East End for an unlimited time period, and no one had any idea where the Ripper would strike next. The Ripper killed prostitutes, who specifically took their clients where they were unlikely to be seen or disturbed, and killed late at night in a slum area of London with minimal street lighting and many alleyways and passages. Drunken ribald shouting, periodical screams, and street noise throughout the night were a part of East End life, as were the presence of rough-looking thugs and petty criminals and crime. Any modern means of apprehending a dangerous criminal, for instance through mass fingerprinting, was far in the future. The Ripper's victims were chosen at random, from among streetwalkers whose clients must have regularly included criminals and violent men. For all of these reasons, it is probably not very surprising that the Ripper was never caught, although he almost certainly was also very lucky. In the 1970s, with all the criminological advances since 1888, it took the Leeds Police six years to apprehend Peter Sutcliffe, 'the Yorkshire Ripper', and many other serial killers have continued for years without being arrested.

The Ripper killings remained an enormous sensation for several years, with the active file on the case not closed until 1892.[14] The first book about the Ripper was the anonymously-written *The Whitechapel Murders, or the Mysteries of the East End*, published in London in 1888.[15] Three other books appeared in 1888, two published in the United States, and three more in 1889, one published in Italian and another in Danish.[16] Thereafter, however, no book appeared in English on the case until 1924, when Tom Robinson's *The Whitechapel Horrors, Being an Authentic Account of the Jack the Ripper Murders*, appeared. Only five other books were published on the Ripper between 1924 and 1959, at widely spaced intervals, one, Jean Dorsenne's *Jack l'Eventreur: Scenes Vecues* of 1933, in French. The Ripper case was given a lease on life by Mrs. Marie Belloc Lowndes' famous best-selling novel *The Lodger* (1913), based loosely on the Ripper case, which was made into a West End play and filmed several times, first in a silent version of 1926 directed by Alfred Hitchcock, which was remade in England in 1932 and in Hollywood in 1944 starring Laird Cregan, Merle Oberon, and George Sanders.[17] *The Lodger* is about a couple who suspect that a boarder in their house is Jack the Ripper. In general, however, what is striking is that, for many decades, the Ripper case gradually faded from view, although the name 'Jack the Ripper' had certainly passed into the language. By the 1940s other well-known murders of the late Victorian and Edwardian era, for instance the Crippen case of 1910, were almost certainly more famous.

There is general agreement that the main turning point in the study of Jack the Ripper came in 1959 with the discovery of the so-called MacNaghten Memorandum. Sir Melville MacNaghten (1853–1921) was an Eton-educated tea planter who became a friend of James Monro, later Assistant Commissioner of the Metropolitan Police. In June 1889, on Munro's suggestion, he became Assistant Chief Constable of the Criminal Investigation Department (the CID) at Scotland Yard, and then, in 1890, Chief Constable, holding the post until 1903, when he became Assistant Commissioner, retiring in 1908.[18] In 1959, Daniel Farson, a well-known television journalist, discovered a typescript from MacNaghten's handwriten notes in the possession of his daughter, Lady Aberconway.[19] Known as the 'MacNaghten Memorandum', it revealed that the 'Police held very reasonable suspicion about three suspects.'[20] They were 'M. J. Druitt, a doctor of about 41 years of age … whose body was found floating in the Thames on 31st Dec [1888]', 'Kosminski, a Polish Jew', who was 'detained in a lunatic asylum about March 1889', and 'Michael Ostrog, a mad Russian doctor'.[21] MacNaghten thought that Druitt was probably the Ripper, adding 'from private information I have little doubt but that his own family suspected the man of being the Whitechapel murderer'.[22] Another version of the MacNaghten Memorandum is known, saying much the same thing, as well as a third version, naming Thomas Cutbush, a paranoid lunatic, as the second possible killer, although this has only been seen by Philip Loftus, a friend of MacNaghten's grandson.[23] The MacNaghten Memorandum 'gave the impetus to serious modern study of Jack the Ripper'.[24] Farson's television programme of November 1959 on the Ripper case, which revealed Druitt's initials but not his full name, was arguably the starting point of the modern centrality of Jack the Ripper to British consciousness and to their world of the 'amateur historians'.

Another turning-point certainly came several years later with the naming of Prince Albert Edward, the Duke of Clarence (1864–92), the Heir Presumptive to the throne, as a possible Ripper suspect. This allegation first surfaced in print in a French work, *Edouard VII*, by Philippe Jullien, in 1962, but became well-known in an article by Dr. Thomas Stowell (1885–1970), 'Jack the Ripper – A Solution?' in *The Criminologist* in November 1970.[25] Stowell claimed to have seen this theory proposed in the confidential papers of Dr. William Gull (1816–90), Physician-in-Ordinary to Queen Victoria (who is also alleged to have been the Ripper).[26] The 'Royal Ripper' theory received further publicity in a well-known work by Stephen Knight (1952–85), a journalist, *Jack the Ripper: The Final Solution* (1976), which also brought in the Freemasons, Lord Salisbury the Prime Minister, an illegal Royal marriage, and the artist Walter Sickert, into the alleged conspiracy. (In a later variant, the main progenitor of the Ripper crimes was said to be Lord Randolph Churchill, the father of Sir Winston.) While easily dismissible as self-evident rubbish (Joseph Gorman Sickert, who claimed to be the artist's illegitimate son, later confessed that he 'made up' the Masonic link[27]), nevertheless anything somehow connecting the heir to the throne with Jack the Ripper was obvious dynamite and tailor-made to enhance and increase popular interest in the Ripper mystery.[28] To this day, if one asks an average British man or woman about Jack the Ripper, one is more than likely to be told 'Oh, he was a Royal Duke or some such, wasn't he?', as if murdering and dismembering prostitutes was an everyday pursuit of the British Royal Family, squeezed in between the State Opening of Parliament and another royal garden party.

Between 1959 and the 1970s, however, the flood of Ripper books began. Several forces gave it impetus: publishers' appreciation of the insatiable public appetite for Ripper books; the removal of censorship barriers to the frank discussion of the brutal details of the crime; the publication of the horrifying mortuary photographs of the victims, which first appeared in Daniel Farson's *Jack the Ripper* in 1972.[29] Heightened interest in Jack the Ripper, the ultimate unsolved murder mystery, also began at roughly the same time that the traditional 'classical detective story' *à la* Agatha Christie, Dorothy L. Sayers, and its dozens of other accomplished practitioners, definitely waned, with the more genteel 'body in the library' detective novel the killer invariably being the 'least likely person', being replaced by much more violent psychological thrillers and espionage novels. The Ripper case uniquely contained both a classical mystery with an endless cast of suspects and, as well, all the violence one could stomach, perhaps entailing well-placed conspiracies. While a few of those who have written on the Ripper case in recent decades, such as Martin Fido, were university academics, the overwhelming majority were not, being, rather usually, freelance and professional writers, journalists, broadcasters, professional researchers, or more occasionally, criminologists. Although most are best-known in the Ripper world, a number, especially Colin Wilson and Patricia Cornwell, are internationally known writers. Most are plainly highly intelligent, able to reason cogently and write clearly, with the wilder type of theory generally confined to the fringes. Perhaps because any writer on the Ripper case must start with the actual police and forensic evidence about actual events, far-fetched speculation found so often among the Baconian and other theorists on the Shakespeare Authorship Question, and among many of the 'critics' of the Warren Report on President Kennedy's assassination, are met with much less often among the 'Ripperologists', especially those widely regarded as the leading writers on the case. A work like *The Jack the Ripper A–Z* (1991; revised edition 1996), by Paul Begg, Martin Fido, and Keith Skinner, three of the most respected Ripper experts, and cited many times in this chapter, is the very model of the sober and intelligent expert presentation of the facts and theories of the case. Writers such as these are perfectly aware that obviously crackpot conspiracy theories about the Ripper Case are – to put it mildly – unlikely to be true, with the actual solution of a sordid and brutal series of murders in a London slum likely to be very mundane, although to be sure the Ripper case also presents some unique features and, while still unsolved, endless fertile soil for speculation. Outstanding general works, such as Donald Rumbelow's *The Complete Jack the Ripper* (1975), now appeared in number, as did the many essays and works of Colin Wilson, the well-known novelist and writer on the occult.

From the early 1970s, too, the number of Ripper books began to escalate in almost a straight line: nine in the years 1972–79, thirteen in the decade 1980–89 (eight in 1987 alone), 39 in the years 1990–99, with dozens appearing in the early years of the new century. Authors, too, are faced with the fact that the words 'Jack the Ripper' can appear in a book's title in only so many ways, so we have *Jack the Ripper Revealed* (1993), *Jack the Ripper Unveiled* (1994), to say nothing of *A Ramble with Jack the Ripper* (1996), *Jack the Ripper: A Reference Guide* (1996), and *Jack the Ripper: A Collector's Guide* (also 1996, by a different author). The 1990s, too, saw the birth of Jack the Ripper collegiality, Jack the Ripper magazines, and, inevitably, Jack the Ripper on the internet (as well as many 'History Channel'-type television documentaries). The first association devoted to studying the Ripper was the Cloak and Dagger Club, founded in London in 1994 by Mark Galloway. It usually meets five or six times a year in a pub in Whitechapel. The procedure at meetings which this author has attended in the early 2000s is an hour or so of drinking and discussion in small groups in the general pub downstairs, followed by the presentation of paper by a speaker on some aspect of the Ripper crimes or some associated topic (for instance, the London police in the 1880s) upstairs, in a private area. The 'Ripperologists' (as they are named) who meet at the Cloak and Dagger Club are probably the purest example of autodidactical amateur historians whom this writer has ever encountered. Many Club members certainly undertook no university degree in history or any other subject, yet they know by heart every last detail of the Ripper crimes – certainly far more than I do – and argue with a passion and knowledge which any professor would envy in his students or, for that matter, his colleagues. As mentioned in the Introduction, it might be imagined that a club devoted to studying the appalling murder and mutilation of five prostitutes, meeting in a East End pub, would contain many dubious, even dangerous, characters as members, but the 'Ripperologists' most certainly do not appear abnormal, let alone psychotic, and most are there, it would seem, simply because they are interested in the Ripper mystery. The Cloak and Dagger Club has produced a number of spin-offs, including an annual conference where participants sometimes dress up in period costume – again, in the interests of good-natured camaraderie not ghoulishness. 'Ripperologists' invariably distance themselves from their subject-matter, in a way which might well not be achievable with other notorious crimes of the past. Apart from the iconic and semi-legendary nature of the Ripper crimes, as already noted the driving force behind almost everyone in the 'Ripperology' world is the conviction that he or she is clever enough to arrive at the correct solution to the great mystery, outwitting all other investigators, as well as the 'experts' and the police.

The Cloak and Dagger Club engendered a high-quality magazine, *Ripperologist*, edited by Paul Begg (and now appearing in an on-line edition), which has published hundreds of high quality articles on the crimes, the suspects, the investigations, and related subjects. One might assume that, short of solving the case, there would be little or nothing left to say about Jack the Ripper, but the opposite appears to be the case: *Ripperologist* appears more frequently than in the past, and there are rival magazines, such as Nick Warren's *Ripperana*, and several American Ripper periodicals. In 2004 the Cloak and Dagger Club was reborn as the 'Whitechapel Society 1888', which is concerned with wider local history issues beyond Jack the Ripper. It publishes a well-produced *Journal of the Whitechapel Society*. An American publication, *Ripper Notes*, which is produced quarterly in Madison, Wisconsin, is a high quality journal with footnoted articles of lasting interest.

One positive effect of all this research is that social historians know far more about the Whitechapel working-class milieu of the time than ever before, while ancillary subjects such as the police, the press, charitable institutions in the late Victorian East End, and the like, have received much more scholarly and serious attention than they would otherwise have done. The five Ripper victims are probably the most thoroughly researched working-class women in late Victorian England, ironically enough. Websites also came into the picture in the 1990s, especially the genuinely excellent 'Casebook–Jack the Ripper' (www.casebook.org) an impressive and lengthy array of objective facts about the crimes, the main suspects, and all other aspects of the case.

Academic historians continue to treat the Ripper case at some remove, demonstrating little or no interest in the identity of the actual killer. Because of the iconic status of the Ripper crimes in the context of late Victorian history some scholarly works have appeared about the impact of aspects of the Ripper killings on wider society, for instance *Jack the Ripper and the London Press* by L. Perry Curtis Jr., published by Yale University Press in 2001, a study by a Brown University history professor of the response of London's newspapers to the Ripper crimes. Similarly, some professional criminologists such as Professor David Canter have investigated the Ripper crimes. Nevertheless, 'Ripperology' remains almost wholly a phenomenon of the amateur investigator or researcher. Academic historians of late Victorian England would be concerned not with the crimes themselves but with the wider social, cultural, and political implications of their killings, from poverty in Whitechapel to the organisation of the London police, and would not normally address or investigate the actual killings.

As noted, the 'Casebook–Jack the Ripper' website presents information on twenty-nine Ripper suspects, and allows anyone reading the site to vote on the most (and least) plausible candidates. (It is not possible to vote for or against some recently added suspects; voting is possible for only twenty-two of the twenty-nine persons listed.) This is indeed the voice of the 'amateur historian' in cyberspace if not in the flesh, and it is worth considering what,

Figure 3.1 Jack the Ripper: the identity of 'Jack the Ripper' remains unknown even after 120 years. Here is one of the leading suspects, Polish-born London barber George Chapman. Mirrorpix

vox populi believes about the identity of Jack the Ripper, bearing in mind that the Ripper might well have been someone else entirely.

First place belongs to Severin Klosowski, alias George Chapman (1865–1903), a truly fearsome-looking Polish-born barber who looks as if he might well have been Jack the Ripper when he was in a good mood, and then turned really nasty when he felt under the weather. Klosowski was born in Nagornak, Poland, and trained there as an Assistant Surgeon.[30] He came to England in June 1887, working as a hairdresser in West India Dock Road and later as a barber near Whitechapel High Street. He emigrated to New Jersey in 1890 with his common law wife, but returned to London in 1891 using the name George Chapman. Between 1895 and 1901 he poisoned three women with whom he had lived as their husband, and was hanged in 1903. Inspector Frederick George Abberline (1843–1929), in charge of detectives who were actually engaged in tracking the Ripper, reportedly stated after Chapman was hanged that Chapman was the Ripper.[31] In 1903, he was quoted as having said, when Chapman was arrested for killing three women, 'You've got Jack the Ripper at last.'[32]

Chapman is a strong candidate, but – as with so many other suspects – not a convincing one. Poisoning one's wife is very different from cutting the throat of and mutilating a prostitute. Chapman might have altered his *modus operandi* when he settled down with his first common law wife, May Baderski, but this may not have occurred until August or October 1889, a year after the Ripper spree. Further confusion also entered the picture with Wolf Levisohn, who himself had been suspected of being Jack the Ripper. At Chapman's trial, Levisohn, an acquaintance of Chapman, stated that he was not Jack the Ripper, but that a more plausible suspect was another barber's assistant living on Walworth Road. [33] This was an apparent reference to Dr. Alexander Pedachenko (*c.*1857–*c.*1908), an alleged Russian secret agent who looked strikingly like George Chapman. According to the writer William LeQueux (1864–1927), Pedachenko was the actual Ripper, planted in London by the Tsarist Secret Police to discredit the Metropolitan Police.[34] There is no known evidence for LeQueux's claim, and the confusion here is indicative of the Ripper case as a whole. Nevertheless, Klosowski/Chapman is a plausible if not convincing candidate, although it is hard to see why he should be the popular number one candidate, unless voters think that looks can indeed kill.

Number Two on the Ripper hit parade is James Maybrick. He will be discussed in more detail below. Number Three is Dr. Francis Tumblety (*c.*1833–1903), who was born in Ireland and lived for much of his life in North America, in Rochester, New York, Detroit, and Canada, and other places, working as a medical quack and 'electric doctor'.[35] Tumblety, who kept his private life a mystery, was certainly in London in 1888. On 7 November 1888 he was arrested and charged with eight counts of gross indecency and indecent assault against four men between 27 July and 2 November.[36] He fled to America, where local newspapers suspected that he was the Ripper. His whereabouts thereafter are unknown; he died in St. Louis in 1903. Tumblety was readily identifiable by his enormous moustache. He was apparently in custody in London at the time of the Kelly murder, although a number of researchers have speculated that he was out on bail. There is, however, really little or nothing to connect him with the Ripper killings; in particular he appears to have been an active homosexual. That might be the end of the matter, except for what is known as the 'Littlechild letter', a typewritten letter written in September 1913 by Chief Inspector John Littlechild, who had been head of the Secret Department of the Metropolitan Police, to G.R. Sims (1847–1922), a journalist. In it he stated that 'a very likely' suspect was an American quack named Tumblety, a 'sadist' whose 'feelings towards women were remarkable and bitter in the extreme'. He also noted that when Tumblety fled the country, the Ripper crimes ceased.[37] While obviously Littlechild's opinion must be respected, most Ripper researchers discount his views. Littlechild had little direct connection with the Ripper case; his views contradict MacNaghten's and other senior policemen's. There is no evidence that Tumblety was violent towards women, although he was an extraordinarily unsavoury character, who owned a collection of preserved uteruses.[38] Littlechild claimed that he had committed suicide, but he died of natural causes. Britain was certainly fortunate when Tumblety went home to America, although almost certainly not because Jack the Ripper had fled.

In fourth place is Joseph Barnett (1858–1926), a former Billingsgate fish porter who had lived with Mary Jane Kelly, the last and most atrociously mutilated victim. Barnett had lived with Kelly until 30 October 1888, when they had a dispute and he left. He had apparently also seen her on the night before her murder.[39] Barnett was also questioned for four hours by the police following Kelly's murder, but was released. He engaged in no further crimes and died nearly forty years later. The case for Barnett was put forward independently by the novelist Mark Andrews in *The Return of Jack the Ripper* and by Bruce Paley, an American living in London, in *Jack the Ripper: The Simple Truth*, published in 1995, long after he first proposed the theory. According to Paley, Barnett murdered the first four victims to scare Kelly into abandoning prostitution.[40] Barnett knew the East End well and fitted the description of the Ripper given by alleged eyewitnesses.

Apart from ingenuity and supposition, however, there is nothing to suggest that Barnett was the killer. One can think of less drastic ways of frightening a prostitute than serial murders and mutilation, which, in any case, apparently failed to persuade. The idea of either 'warming up' or disguising one's motive and identity by killing a series of randomly selected victims before dispatching the real victim sounds too much like the plot of an Agatha Christie novel – which, in fact it is – and very unlikely, to say the least, to happen in real life since, plainly, the killer stands every chance in the world of getting caught before achieving his real aim. The likelihood of being apprehended, high in any sequence of murders, was vastly greater in the Ripper killings, when every policeman and possible eyewitness in east

London hoped to pounce. While clearly not impossible, Barnett's candidacy seems highly unlikely.

Fifth on *Casebook*'s popularity list is 'the Lodger', an unknown, possibly unsuspected resident in or near the East End who is perhaps (as in Belloc Lowndes's novel) a religious fanatic. Without further evidence or an identity, there is little more which can be said about him. In sixth place is a much more serious candidate, Aaron Kosminsky (*c*.1864–1919), a Polish Jewish hairdresser who migrated to Britain in 1882 (and is not to be confused with Klosowski/Chapman). There were a great many immigrant eastern European Jews in Whitechapel in 1888, their number swelled by the Tsarist pogroms. As with most waves of migrants, many were young single men. Alone in a strange country, without families or familiar moorings, their number unquestionably included a share of criminals and psychotics. Traditional Orthodox Judaism, in which most had been raised, was sexually puritanical and emphasised the desirability of young men marrying and fathering children as early as possible. The unavoidable presence of hundreds of prostitutes in Whitechapel, their ready availability, the dangers of sexually transmitted diseases and of considerable psychological guilt engendered among Jews from traditional backgrounds by resorting to them, might well have sent a demented Jewish immigrant over the edge. (Of course, much the same might be said about men from virtually any background.) A Jew, 'Leather Apron', was arrested and released, and the clear possibility, if Jack turned out to be an immigrant Jew, that antisemitic rioting would ensue, was always apparent to London's Jewish leaders. Kosminski was first mentioned as a suspect in the MacNaghten Memorandum, and the distinct possibility that the Ripper was an immigrant Jew was asserted by Sir Robert Anderson and also by Chief Inspector Donald Swanson (1848–1924), who was in charge of the investigations from 1 September to 6 October 1888.[41] At some stage before his death Swanson wrote a note in the endpapers of his copy of Anderson's autobiography, which came to light in 1987. Known as the 'Swanson Marginalia', it claimed that the main suspect was 'a Jew' named 'Kosminski', the same man whom Anderson had indicated without naming him, in his book.[42] He had also been named in the MacNaghten Memorandum. Kosminski's life has, however, been investigated in some detail, and it is clear that many of the assertions made by the three police officers about his life were factually inaccurate. Kosminski was sent to a workhouse in July 1890, where it was noted that he had been insane for years. He was released after two days, but then sent to Colney Hatch Lunatic Asylum in 1891, where he was apparently suffering from aural hallucinations and was 'reticent and morose'.[43] He remained in Colney Hatch until his death in 1919.

There is, however, nothing concrete to associate Kosminski with the Ripper murders. It has also been argued that the immigrant Jew mentioned by Anderson was not Kosminski but another man entirely, Aaron Davis Cohen (1865–89), also known as David Cohen.[44] Cohen was arrested on 7 December 1888 as a lunatic wandering at large and sent to a workhouse, where he was violent and noisy, and attempted suicide.[45] Sent to Colney Hatch, he died in October 1889 of 'exhaustion of mania and pulmonary phthisis.'[46] Martin Fido, a well-known Ripper researcher, argued that his life history was much more like that of the suspect indicated by Anderson and Swanson.[47] Again, however, there is nothing concrete to suggest that he was the Ripper. Some witnesses apparently thought that a man seen with Catherine Eddowes before her murder was an immigrant Jew, but other alleged witnesses did not suggest that he was Jewish. As with so many other suspects, there is tantalisingly little to go on. One possibly relevant consideration here is the role of the respectable leaders of the Anglo-Jewish community, especially the M.P. for Whitechapel, Samuel Montagu (1832–1911; later Sir Samuel and still later Lord Swaythling). Montagu and other Jewish leaders were, as noted, only too well aware of the latent antisemitism certain to manifest itself if the Ripper turned out to be an immigrant Jew, and would assuredly have moved heaven and earth to have had any actual Jewish Ripper quietly and efficiently placed in an asylum as swiftly as possible. Montagu, although a wealthy banker, was a widely respected figure in the Jewish East End, and the founder of the very Orthodox Federation of Synagogues favoured by many immigrant Jews. He and his colleagues had innumerable contacts in the Jewish East End and it seems unlikely that any plausible rumours of a Jewish killer would not soon have come to their ears. The fact that Montagu apparently knew nothing of Kosminski or Cohen may well be relevant, suggesting that neither was likely to have been guilty.[48]

The 'Royal Conspiracy' is, somewhat surprisingly, in seventh place. In the popular mind one might have expected it to rank much higher; perhaps it is simply too implausible for many voters to take seriously. By the normal rendition of this theory, Prince Albert, the Duke of Clarence is supposed to have conducted an illegal marriage with one Annie Elizabeth Crook, and was being blackmailed by Mary Jane Kelly. The Prince brought in the government to deal with this unpleasant situation; they allegedly used the Freemasons and Sir William Gull (1816–90), the seventy-two year old Physician-in-Ordinary to Queen Victoria, to dispose of Kelly.[49] There are other variations of this theory, naming other alleged conspirators. This theory is, needless to say, utter nonsense from beginning to end. The whereabouts of senior royals is known on a daily basis; the Duke of Clarence is known to have been in, respectively, Grosmont, Yorkshire, and Abergeldie, Scotland – where Queen Victoria recorded in her diary that she had lunched with him about ten hours after the Stride and Eddowes murders – and at Sandringham when four of the five murders were committed.[50] The Freemasons do not commit murder, and alleging they do is the equivalent of claiming that the murders were committed by a Zionist or Jesuit conspiracy. The Duke of Clarence had not married illegally, and was not being blackmailed by Mary Kelly or anyone else. If Kelly were indeed the target, it is difficult to see why the Duke or the conspirators previously murdered and mutilated four other women. If Kelly was indeed proving to be seriously annoying to the Duke, she would have been given £500 and a one-way ticket to New South Wales, with a stern warning never to return to England and never to open her mouth. It seems incredible that any normally intelligent person could swallow the nonsense of the 'Royal Conspiracy', although to be sure anything involving the British Royal Family quickly becomes the stuff of conspiracy theories. The 'Royal Conspiracy' over Jack the Ripper is part of a long line of such allegations stretching from the fate of the princes in the Tower to Princess Diana, several of which are discussed in this book.

Following the Royals in eighth place is Francis Thompson (1859–1907), the poet and author of 'The Hound of Heaven' and other poems. Thompson was an opium addict living in London, but there is literally nothing to connect him with the Ripper murders. He is not even remotely a serious candidate.[51] In ninth place is a much more plausible candidate, Montague John Druitt. Druitt (1857–88) was named as the leading candidate in the MacNaghten Memorandum, first published in 1959 and was probably regarded as the leading candidate for the next fifteen years or so. Druitt was a gentleman who was educated at Winchester and Oxford, and was called to the bar at the Inner Temple in 1885.[52] Although he was in practice as a barrister on the Western Circuit, he was also a schoolteacher at a private school in Blackheath, but was dismissed from the school for 'serious trouble' around 30 November 1888.[53] The nature of this 'serious trouble' is unknown, but the implication is that it involved either homosexuality or financial chicanery. Another theory, popularised by the researcher Donald McCormick, is that Druitt was being blackmailed by someone who knew he was the Ripper.[54] In any case Druitt was last seen alive around 3 December 1888. On 31 December his body, dead for about a month, was found in the Thames at Chiswick. Druitt left apparent suicide notes for his brother and for the proprietor of the Blackheath school, and was declared a suicide 'whilst of unsound mind' at the Inquest.[55] MacNaghten believed that he was the Ripper and, moreover, 'that his own family suspected this man of being the Whitechapel murderer'.[56]

Druitt is plainly a very strong candidate, and it is surprising that he does not rank higher in the 'Casebook's' poll. Nevertheless, there are – as with every suspect – many difficulties in fully accepting the case for Druitt. Druitt was apparently playing cricket in Dorset on 1 September 1888, making it virtually impossible for him to have killed Mary Ann Nichols, who was seen alive at 2:30 a.m. on 31 August and whose body was found at 3:40 a.m.[57] On 8 September 1888 Druitt was playing cricket in Blackheath at 11:30 a.m., meaning that 'if he was the killer he was changed, cleaned, and enjoying his cricket game just six hours after butchering Annie Chapman.'[58] Apart from the MacNaghten Memorandum, there is really no concrete evidence to connect Druitt with the Ripper murders, although in many respects he seems a likely candidate.

In recent years a number of new candidates have been proposed who, although not included in the 'Casebook' poll, ought to be considered. The famous artist Walter Sickert (1860–1942) was first proposed as a candidate in 1973 by Joseph Gorman Sickert (b.1925), who claimed to be the artist's illegitimate son, although he was born when his alleged father was sixty-five.[59] Joseph Sickert claimed that Walter was part of the Royal-Masonic conspiracy, a theory which was given wider credence in Ripper circles by Jean Overton Fuller in her 1990 book *Sickert and the Ripper Crimes.*[60] The Sickert theory was given worldwide publicity by the well-known crime writer Patricia Cornwell in her book *Portrait of a Killer: Jack the Ripper – Case Closed* (2002). The novelty of Cornwell's work lies in her claim that both the paper and DNA evidence from letters written by Sickert were identical with letters purporting to have come from 'Jack the Ripper'. Her claim was extended by an independent paper expert to the assertion that several letters written by Sickert were from the same batch of stationery as two Ripper letters.[61] Few Ripperologists, however, accept the Sickert theory. He was almost certainly in France when the Ripper crimes were committed, and there are no known links between Sickert and the Ripper crimes. The so-called DNA evidence is also very questionable, proving no more than (at most) that Sickert was one among perhaps 400,000 men in England in 1888 who might have had DNA in common with the author of several 'Ripper' letters to the police. Nor is there any real evidence that the Ripper was the author of these letters.[62]

In 2005 there appeared Tony Williams' *Uncle Jack*, which alleges that Sir John Williams (1840–1926), a distant relative of the author's, was the Ripper. In the 1880s Williams was a gynaecologist at the Whitechapel Workhouse Infirmary, and apparently treated several of the victims, including Mary Anne Nichols. Most researchers dismiss Williams as a possible suspect, although the knife he allegedly used to kill some of his victims is among his effects at the National Library of Wales in Aberystwyth. Williams was a scholarly man and renowned bibliophile whose private collection of historic Welsh books and manuscripts forms the basis of the National Library of Wales. His known lifestyle seems wholly inconsistent with his being a demented serial killer. (A negative critique of this work by Jennifer Pegg, '*Uncle Jack* Under the Microscope', appeared in *Ripper Notes*, October 1005 (No.24), pp.12–22.)

One should also certainly mention another candidate although he was only fourteenth in the 'Casebook's poll: Robert Donston Stephenson (1841–after 1904), a chemist, customs official, and journalist who, in 1888, was a voluntary patient in the London Hospital. Stephenson reportedly reenacted his crimes in front of hospital witnesses.[63] Blood-encrusted ties were also allegedly found in a box in his room in 1890.[64] Stephenson was at this time reportedly an Occultist and Black Magician, but in 1893 was converted to Christianity. If Stephenson was the Ripper, in 1904 he published what is surely the least likely work imaginable by the Whitechapel fiend, *The Patristic Gospels*. Stephenson *could* have been the Ripper, although it seems highly improbable that he could have been living in a hospital at the time without his nocturnal comings and goings, and his presumably bloodstained clothing, being noticed by hospital staff.

A number of other candidates on the website's list are worthy of comment. These include the convicted murderers James Kelly (d.1929) and Frederick Deeming (1853–92), the Hungarian-Argentinian possible murderer Alois Szemeredy (1844–92), and Michael Ostrog (*c.*1833–after 1904), the Russian-born conman named in the MacNaghten Memorandum, but for whom no real evidence exists. The theory that Jack was *au contraire* Jill the Ripper surfaced remarkably early, first proposed by Rev. Lord Sydney Osborne in a letter to the *Times* during the killing spree, and taken up soon after by Sir Arthur Conan Doyle, no less.[65] 'Jill' proponents suggest that she was a demented midwife or abortionist. Against this, it is difficult to see what possible motive a midwife or abortionist might have to kill, while no woman would, surely, be allowed to stand directly behind a prostitute in the dead of night in the manner of a male client. There have been few women serial killers, and it seems a very safe bet that none was active in Whitechapel in 1888. Other candidates include such absurdities as Lewis Carroll, the author of *Alice in Wonderland*.

In my view the balance of evidence is that James Maybrick (1835–89) was Jack the Ripper, a view which I have held since the late 1990s. Maybrick was

Figure 3.2 Another leading suspect, Liverpool cotton broker James Maybrick. Getty Images/ Hulton Archive

a successful Liverpool cotton broker who was never, before the early 1990s, mentioned in connection with the Ripper. He was, nevertheless, already well-known in the annals of crime because in May 1889 he died, apparently of arsenic poisoning. His wife, the American-born Florence Maybrick (*née* Chandler, 1862–1941), was arrested for the crime, tried, convicted, and sentence to death, reprieved, and spent fifteen years in prison before she was pardoned. She returned to America, dying in obscurity in Connecticut in 1941. Many thought her innocent, her conviction chiefly the result of the fact that she was unquestionably having an affair at the time.[66]

Maybrick became a prime Ripper suspect only in 1992–93. In that year, a sixty-three page handwritten Journal, allegedly by Maybrick, came to light, in the possession of Michael Barrett and his wife Anne Graham, both of Liverpool. The Journal – invariably known as the 'Maybrick Diary' – was purportedly written by Maybrick as Jack the Ripper between April 1888 and May 1889 and signed at the end 'Jack the Ripper.[67] Everything about the Diary – its authenticity, provenance, handwriting, contents – have been matters of the most intense controversy, certainly not yet resolved, which have been discussed in several books.[68] This debate remains unresolved. Remarkably, however, all efforts to prove it fraudulent have failed: if it is indeed a hoax, it is a rather good one. Maybrick lived at 'Battlecrease', a large villa at Aigburth, in Liverpool, although he frequently travelled to London. According to the 'Diary' Maybrick embarked on his killing spree to secure vicarious revenge on his wife who was having an affair with another Liverpool cotton merchant, Alfred Brierley. Maybrick was a long-term arsenic addict. In small doses, arsenic produces a 'high' similar to other addictive substances. By the time of the Diary's conclusion, Maybrick had repented of the Ripper crimes and contemplated suicide.

In many respects the 'Diary' is highly unsatisfactory, containing no dates and written in a boasting, stream-of-consciousness style. The provenance of the 'Diary' is also unclear. Allegedly, it was seen by Anne Graham's father, William Graham, in 1943 when he was on leave from the army. At the time it was allegedly kept in a black tin box in his mother's house in Liverpool. Anne Graham claimed to have seen it in a trunk in her house in Liverpool in the 1960s. She took possession of it in the mid-1980s when her father moved house. In marital difficulties, she allegedly gave the 'Diary' to a friend of her unemployed husband Michael Barrett, hoping that friend would then give it to her husband, to keep him intellectually occupied. In 1993

Michael Barrett – apparently for reasons related to his marriage breakdown – claimed to have forged the 'Diary', but his claim is not now accepted by even sceptical researchers.[69]

The key question is the whereabouts of the 'Diary' between Maybrick's death in 1889 and 1943. Among believers in its authenticity, the most popular theory is that it was taken away following Maybrick's sudden death by a servant, Alice Yapp, who gave the 'Diary' to William Graham's stepmother before her death in 1938.[70] William Graham, who was a manual worker in a Dunlop tyre factory, took no interest in the 'Diary'.

There are good reasons for believing that the 'Diary' is not a *recent* forgery. A 'Diary of Jack the Ripper' forged *c.*1990 might be expected to contain pornographic descriptions of sexual arousal during his encounters with prostitutes. However, while it does contain descriptions of mutilation and cannibalism, the 'Diary' has no explicit sexual content.[71] No forger has come forward to smirk at the gullibility of the public, and any forger was taking an enormous risk. Maybrick's daily life was virtually unknown in 1992–3, and evidence might quickly be found – in an obscure trade journal, for instance – that he was irrefutably elsewhere at the time of a Ripper murder. (No such disconfirming evidence has been found.)

Perhaps the most interesting feature of the 'Diary' is that it appears to contain information which no forger could know. Throughout the 'Diary' Maybrick often referred to himself as 'Sir Jim' or 'Sir Jack'. In 1993 Feldman found that the Maybricks had as their houseguest an American girl, Florence Aunspaugh, the daughter of a business friend of James. In 1941–42, after Florence Maybrick's death, Trevor Christie, a New York journalist, conducted a correspondence with Aunspaugh, then a lady in her sixties living in Dallas, as background material for a book he was writing on the poisoning case.[72] Neither Christie nor Aunspaugh had any idea that Maybrick might have been the Ripper. In 1970 Christie's widow deposited their correspondence at (of all places) the University of Wyoming, where it remained unread until Feldman sent Keith Skinner, an eminent Ripper authority, to photostat the file. Aunspaugh recalled that Alice Yapp had said 'she certainly would be glad when that damned little American left Battlecrease ... she did not see why Sir James (Mr. Maybrick) ever brought me there any way.' (Aunspaugh also recalled in 1941–42 that 'a current of mystery seemed to circulate all around' at Battlecrease, and that Maybrick, though charming, had a 'morose, gloomy disposition and extremely high temper' and was an 'arsenic addict [who] craved it like a narcotic fiend'.) It seems highly improbable that anyone would have hit upon the nickname 'Sir James', the unusual nickname actually used in Maybrick's household, who was not familiar with Maybrick, and it seems impossible to see how a forger from *c.*1990 – who had certainly *not* read the Aunspaugh correspondence – could have hit upon it.

Some critics of the 'Diary' also contend that it is an old forgery, contrived in the Edwardian period, perhaps by James's brother Michael Maybrick (1844–1913), a talented composer who wrote under the name 'Stephen Adams', Michael Maybrick almost certainly knowing more about his brother's activities than he ever stated in public.[73] There are, however, objections to this theory as well. The forger must have had precise knowledge of both Maybrick's Liverpool household and of Whitechapel. Had the 'Diary' become public knowledge in the Edwardian period, any factual mistake would have been found immediately by contemporaries of Maybrick. More importantly, the 'Diary' apparently contains information which did not become public knowledge until much later. It refers to a 'tin box' which was 'empty' and which was found and left by Maybrick at the murder of Catherine Eddowes. There was indeed '1 tin match box, empty' among Eddowes' effects, but this fact did not appear in print until 1987. It is also sometimes suggested that Maybrick might have written the 'Diary', but as a Walter Mittyish fantasy. But the 'Diary' contained information not known at the time. At its end, Maybrick sincerely repented and it is clear that there would be no more Ripper crimes. But if he was not the Ripper, he could not have known, prior to his death in May 1889, that there would be no more Ripper crimes. For all these reasons, it seems difficult to accept that the 'Diary' was either an old forgery, or a recent forgery, or a fantasy by Maybrick himself.

The case that Maybrick was the Ripper is very strong even without the 'Diary'. Indeed, Maybrick would still be a leading candidate if the 'Diary' proves fraudulent. Perhaps the most striking evidence for this is to be found in a number of unknown letters discovered by Feldman in Liverpool sources. On 9 October 1888 the *Liverpool Echo* newspaper published a story (based on a letter it received) that the Ripper was about to strike in Dublin. The following day this newspaper published the following, written on a postcard:

> *I beg to state that the letters published in yours of yesterday are lies. It is somebody gulling the public. I am the Whitechapel purger. On the 13th,*

at 3pm, will be on Stage, as am going to New York. But will have some business before I go.

Jack the Ripper *DIEGO LAURENZ*
(genuine)

Feldman asks, 'What does Diego Laurenz mean? I have no idea. Is it a clue?'[74] In my opinion, it most assuredly is a clue – an extremely important one. 'Diego' is the Spanish equivalent of 'James', while 'Laurenz' is surely meant to rhyme with 'Florence'. If this is what is meant – and what else could it possibly mean? – then the letter constitutes virtual proof that James Maybrick was Jack the Ripper. There was, indeed, an inexplicable gap of five weeks between the two murders of 30 September and the Kelly killing on 9 November, which has always puzzled researchers. Maybrick himself was known to have made frequent trips to America throughout his career.[75]

Why the Ripper stopped killing after 9 November 1888 is one of the central mysteries of this subject. With Maybrick there is a good explanation. On 19 November 1888 he changed doctors, employing Dr. J. Drysdale, who treated him with homeopathic remedies, and saw him, with increasing success, five more times before his death.[76] This provides an explanation as to why Maybrick slowly but surely lost interest in killing; obviously after his death in May 1889 there would be no more killings, ever.

The 'Diary' also states that, just before he died, Maybrick confessed to his wife that he was Jack the Ripper. A letter written just before Maybrick's death from his wife to her lover Alfred Brierley figured prominently at her trial. In this Florence noted that her husband was 'delerious', but mysteriously stated that 'The tale he told me was a pure fabrication and only designed to frighten the truth out of me.'[77] This remark occurs abruptly and is not elaborated upon. It is possible that a clever 'Diary' forger might have noted this sentence buried in a long letter in a published account of Mrs. Maybrick's trial, but it does not answer the question of what this 'tale ... designed to frighten' her might have been or why Maybrick would tell her such a frightening tale.[78]

In another episode suggesting a link between Maybrick, Liverpool, and the Ripper, William Graham told Feldman that as a boy (he was born in 1913), he lived near Battlecrease House and that he and his friends would run past it 'pretending we were Fred Archer, the jockey, smack our backsides and shout, "Look out, look out, Jack the Ripper's about ..."'[79] Archer, the most famous jockey of the nineteenth century, committed suicide in 1886, only two years before the Ripper killings. If authentic, this story seems incomprehensible unless there was something to connect Battlecrease with the Ripper, presumably whispering from the servants to their friends. No connection between the Ripper and Liverpool had ever been made before the 1990s.

Furthermore, the name 'Jack the Ripper' may itself have a Liverpool origin. Between 1884 and 1886 Liverpool's local newspapers ran many stories about the alleged existence of a murderous 'High Rip Gang' which, it claimed, terrorised passers-by in the Scotland Road slums. There was considerable debate about whether such a gang actually existed, and mention of the 'High Rip' seems to have ceased in early 1887.[80] However, the 'High Rip' and its association with street violence would have been well-known to any Liverpudlian in 1888.

On top of all this, in 1992 a watch (made in 1846) was found in Liverpool by a local man named Albert Johnson. Scratched on the inner case Johnson found the signature 'J. Maybrick', the words 'I am Jack', and the initials of the five Ripper victims![81] Examination with a scanning microscope revealed that the scratchings were almost certainly not made recently, but are compatible with being made in 1888–89.[82]

As things stand, Maybrick it certainly appears to be, notwithstanding the obvious difficulties in accepting the 'Diary' as genuine without an enormous amount of further evidence. If not Maybrick, however, then who? Probably a demented sailor on shore leave is the most likely explanation, one which accounts for the gaps between killings. Such an explanation was first put soon after the killings, but all attempts to identify a particular sailor in a convincing manner have failed. Recently, the theory has been revived by Trevor Marriott, in his *Jack the Ripper: The 21st Century Investigation* (London, 2005). Marriott believes, after much research, that the Ripper might have been a merchant seaman on one of a number of German merchant vessels sailing between London, Bremen, and Hamburg, but records do not exist allowing him to identify a likely suspect.[83] Once more, the Ripper seems to have slipped through the net, unless, as seems likely, Maybrick is the man. Research and speculation about the Ripper will, of course, continue indefinitely, fanned by human curiosity and by the chance that one of hundreds of researchers will somehow make the crucial breakthrough and solve the great mysery.

Chapter 4

The Shakespeare Authorship Question

The Shakespeare Authorship Question probably has a longer *continuing* history as the subject of debate by 'amateur historians' than any other.[1] It is by now nearly two centuries old and, rather than dying down, it has in recent decades assumed new vigour and popularity on both sides of the Atlantic and elsewhere. The Shakespeare Authorship Question asks whether William Shakespeare, the actor who was born in Stratford-upon Avon in 1564 and died there in 1616, actually wrote the plays and poems bearing his name. On the face of it, this is an extremely unusual question to debate, perhaps one without any other real parallel. No one asks whether Ben Jonson, or John Donne, Shakespeare's contemporaries, actually wrote the works attributed to them, or whether the *Divine Comedy* was actually written by someone other than Dante Alighieri. Famous writers known to us as Voltaire, Mark Twain, and George Eliot are actually the fictional pseudonyms of real persons with different names, but their actual identities are well-known and have never been questioned by anyone. In this, Shakespeare is unique. One may point to the major reasons for this state of affairs. First, William Shakespeare stands apart, He is not merely universally regarded as the greatest of English-language writers, but, given the hegemony of the English language as the

Figure 4.1 Shakespeare: William Shakespeare is regarded as the greatest writer in history, but virtually nothing is known about many aspects of his life. The famous painting of Shakespeare shown here may or may not be authentic. Mary Evans Picture Library

world's preeminent cultural medium, the greatest of all the world's writers. His status is, indeed, far above that of a mere playwright and poet and is very much like a spiritual figure who has founded a major religion: in our secular age, Shakespeare has assumed the role of a semi-divinity. Just as all intelligent Christians want to know much more about the 'lost years' of Jesus, so virtually anyone with an interest in Western culture wishes to know about the 'lost years' of Shakespeare and, indeed, about every other aspect of his life and career. This takes us to the second reason for the Authorship Question: astonishingly little is known about Shakespeare's life, especially his intellectual career, despite the heroic efforts of generations of scholars and researchers. For William Shakespeare is probably the most deeply-researched man in history, a fact which makes the oceans of blankness and obscurity about most aspects of his life all the more mysterious.

At the heart of the Shakespeare Authorship Question is the extraordinary – many would say, unbelievable – gap between the meagreness of Shakespeare's background and the magnitude of his achievement. Shakespeare's parents were illiterate. He grew up in a small provincial town, three days' travelling time from London, with only a handful of educated men and, in all likelihood, very few books. His schooling ended at thirteen. There is no direct evidence that he owned a book. No manuscript definitely known to have been written by him exists. The only examples of Shakespeare's handwriting which survive are six signatures, all on legal documents: three are written on pages in his will, and these may have actually been penned by clerks. Of the seventy-five known contemporary documents in which Shakespeare is named, not one concerns his alleged career as an author. Most are legal and financial documents which depict him as a successful and, it seems, rather rapacious local businessman and property developer. What William Shakespeare was doing between his 'shotgun marriage' to Anne Hathaway in 1582 and his emergence as an actor and presumed writer nearly ten years later is a complete mystery, the so-called 'lost years'. Biographers of Shakespeare have credited him with all manner of employment and activities, as an apprentice butcher, a law clerk, schoolmaster, tutor in wealthy households, soldier, traveller on the Continent, and apprentice actor. No direct evidence exists to support any of these theories. At the age of about forty-seven, after a quarter-century at the centre of one of the world's greatest cultural renaissances, Shakespeare – it appears – permanently retired from London to Stratford, a provincial village of 1300 people with virtually no educated men, living quietly as a local businessman until his death at the age of only fifty-two. Shakespeare's two surviving daughters were illiterate, and were unable even to read their father's plays and poems. His will, while it often provides extremely detailed instructions concerning his personal effects and land (such as the 'second best bed', which he notoriously left to his widow), contains no mention of his books or manuscripts, any direction he might have had concerning the rights in his plays, or any orders about the publication of his works. In 1623, seven years after his death, an enormous and very expensive memorial volume appeared, produced by several of his former theatre associates, and containing introductory poems and other material by Ben Jonson, the *de facto* poet laureate, and others. This work, the *First Folio*, contained nearly all of Shakespeare's plays, many printed for the first time. The *First Folio* does not mention or acknowledge his family in Stratford, although it seems inconceivable that the editors of the work would not have contacted his widow (who died in August 1623, shortly before the *First Folio* was published) or daughters to see if Shakespeare had not left some publishable works with his family. There is no evidence that any member of Shakespeare's family ever owned a copy of the *First Folio*, although his sister Joan Shakespeare Hart had descendants who survive to this day. While, as noted, William Shakespeare is arguably the most closely and deeply studied man in history, no one knows whether he was a lifelong conforming Anglican or a secret Catholic, and there are now two contradictory accounts of how he first came to London.[2]

One of the main reasons for this vortex of ignorance and supposition about Shakespeare is that he did not become the English National Poet until the mid-eighteenth century, over 200 years after his death. This point is probably not as widely understood or appreciated as it should be: one reason that there was no Shakespeare 'Authorship Question' before the nineteenth century is that he was not regarded as the King of Kings, the English National Poet, until the mid-eighteenth century.[3] Shakespeare was regarded as a good and widely-known playwright and poet, but nothing more. During Shakespeare's lifetime, and for many decades thereafter, no one took the slightest real interest in his life or biography in any sense recognisable today, and innumerable opportunities to learn the most crucial facts of his life and alleged writing career were lost, presumably forever. In September 1634, for instance, a Lieutenant Hammond visited Stratford, where, in the Church, he noted a 'neat Monument of the famous English Poet, Mr. William Shakespeare'. Had he wished, Hammond might have stayed long enough to visit Shakespeare's two daughters, Joan and Susanna, or his sister Joan Shakespeare Hart, and their families, all of whom were still living in Stratford, as were dozens of people who would certainly have known William Shakespeare well. Had he done so, in a day or two Hammond could have learned, and recorded, more about William Shakespeare than have all of his biographers since then. But it never occurred to Hammond to do this, and his sight of Shakespeare's monument was the only part of his visit to Stratford he bothered to note. Nor did anyone else journey there to set down the recollections of those who had known the greatest writer in history. In fact, the first person to collect alleged anecdotage about Shakespeare's life did not do so until the years *c.*1657–1681, when Thomas Plume (who recorded, probably in 1657, that Shakespeare was a 'glover's son'), John Ward (who claimed that Shakespeare 'spent at the rate of £1000 a year') and, in particular, John Aubrey, in 1681 made cursory attempts to write down some recollections of his life, between forty-one and sixty-five years after he died, when virtually no one alive could have remembered him.[4] The first biography of Shakespeare, by Nicholas Rowe, appeared only in 1709, nearly a century after he died. It contains the first claim that Shakespeare attended Stratford Grammar School 'for some time', but also states that the impoverished condition of Shakespeare's father forced him to 'withdraw him from thence', a point often omitted by Shakespeare's biographers, who credit the playwright's erudition to the education he received at the local school.[5] Rowe's life also contains the familiar story that Shakespeare was forced to 'shelter himself in London' after poaching deer from Sir Thomas Lucy, a claim generally accepted by all biographers until recently, when this account was superseded by the yet more improbable story that Shakespeare went to London after working as a youth in two Catholic households in Lancashire.[6] Shakespeare's will, with its celebrated bequest of his 'second best bed' to his wife Anne Hathaway, was not read by anyone until *1747*, when it was first seen by one Joseph Greene (1717–90), the school master at Stratford Grammar School and later an Anglican vicar. The will was not published *anywhere* until *1763*, nearly 200 years after Shakespeare's birth, when it was printed in a reference work called *Biographia Britannica*.[7] In other words, there was such meagre interest in Shakespeare's life in the modern, biographical sense that no one bothered to look up the most important surviving document about his worldly status for more than 130 years after his death. Five or six generations of notable writers and 'biographers' of Shakespeare, from Ben Jonson to Alexander Pope (who died in 1744), thus remained ignorant of the fact that Shakespeare's will contained no reference of any kind to any books or manuscripts he might have owned, or to any requests of any kind to preserve or publish his plays. The first attempt to produce a chronology of Shakespeare's works was not made until Edward Malone (1741–1812), a friend of Dr. Johnson, wrote his *Attempt to Ascertain the Order in Which the Plays of Shakespeare Were Written,* in George Steevens' edition of the plays in *1778*.[8]

Essentially, it was the period from about 1769 – the date of the Stratford Jubilee, a celebration organised five years late by David Garrick – until the early Victorian period which saw Shakespeare enshrined forever as the English National Poet.[9] 'Bardolatry', as it became known, coincided with the Romantic era, as well as the rise of affluent gentlemen of leisure who had the resources and interests to comb the archives in search of more facts and evidence about Shakespeare's lives. Much, perhaps most, of our knowledge of Shakespeare's life and milieu derives from this period. It also coincided with England's industrial revolution and the Age of Reform, when Shakespeare's

Warwickshire and Elizabethan London seemed to many to be a lost utopia. These years also saw Britain's ascendancy, following Trafalgar and Waterloo, as arguably the greatest power in the world, requiring a National Writer to place beside Homer, Virgil and Dante, a role which Shakespeare fitted marvellously well.

But this period also saw the first stirrings of doubt about Shakespeare's authorship. So far as is known, the first person to doubt that Shakespeare wrote the works attributed to him was Rev. James Wilmot (1726–1808), a Warwickshire clergyman who lived a few miles from Stratford. Wilmot attempted to find Shakespeare's books, reasoning that many would have been acquired by members of the local gentry and would be retained in their libraries.[10] In due course he examined every private library within fifty miles of Stratford, libraries owned, in many cases, by families who had been in place since the Elizabethan era. He found precisely nothing. Wilmot was also puzzled by the lack of local references in Shakespeare's works, and – like many other subsequent Doubters – by Shakespeare's lack of education. He came to the conclusion that Sir Francis Bacon actually wrote Shakespeare's works, seeing Bacon as well-qualified to write them and his lifespan as – in his view – coinciding with the trajectory of Shakespeare's writing career. Wilmot kept his heretical opinions to himself, revealing them only to a literary man from Ipswich, James Corton Cowell, who presented his account of Wilmot's efforts to the Ipswich Philosophical Society in 1805. Cowell's own paper was unknown until it was published in the *Times Literary Supplement* in 1932.[11] From the mid-nineteenth century, a virtual tidal wave of anti-Stratfordian theories emerged. Most proposed that Sir Francis Bacon wrote Shakespeare's works. The first well-known published work making this claim was probably *The Philosophy of the Plays of Shakespeare Unfolded*, published in 1857 by an American woman, Delia Bacon (whose surname was a coincidence). In the same year an Englishman, William Henry Smith, published a lengthy pamphlet making the same argument, *Bacon and Shakespeare*.[12] By the end of the Victorian period, innumerable pro-Baconian works appeared, many arguing that the *First Folio* concealed a secret code or cryptogram. Identifying this code became a stock-in-trade of late Victorian Baconians such as Ignatius Donnelly and Sir Edwin Durning-Lawrence, giving the anti-Stratfordian enterprise a well-deserved reputation for the crackpot from which it has, essentially, never recovered. Baconianism in fact became part-and-parcel of the crackpot world: Donnelly (1835–1901), known as the

Figure 4.2 One of the alternative 'candidates' put forward as the actual author of Shakespeare's works is Edward De Vere, seventeenth Earl of Oxford (1550-1604). Getty Images/Hulton Archive

'King of Crackpots', an American lawyer and political radical who wrote the famous Platform of the People's Party (the 'Populists') of 1892, was also known for his account of the destruction of Atlantis and his 'funny money' currency theories. Donnelly's anti-Stratfordian work is entitled *The Great Cryptogram: Francis Bacon's Cipher in the So-Called Shakespeare Plays*, published in 1888.[13]

Although a variety of other Authorship 'Candidates' have been proposed over the years, at the present time by far the most popular is Edward De Vere, seventeenth Earl of Oxford (1550–1604), who has certainly eclipsed Sir Francis Bacon in popularity among anti-Stratfordians. Today, a range of so-called 'Oxfordian' societies, conferences, and journals exist which support De Vere's claims to be the actual Bard of Avon.[14] Numerous books have appeared in recent years arguing the case for De Vere, including a 598–page biography by Mark Anderson, *Shakespeare By Another Name: The Life of Edward De Vere, Earl of Oxford – The Man Who Was Shakespeare*, published by Gotham Books, New York, a mainstream publisher, in 2005 with Foreword by Sir Derek Jacobi, the famous actor (who, like Mark Rylance and other distinguished actors, does not believe that Shakespeare of Stratford wrote the works attributed to him). *Hundreds* of well-read and well-educated people currently believe that De Vere wrote Shakespeare's works, and their numbers have certainly grown markedly in recent years.

De Vere was first proposed as the real Shakespeare in 1918–20 by a Gateshead schoolmaster who rejoiced in the name of J. Thomas Looney (pronounced 'Loney'). His book, *'Shakespeare' Identified*, appeared in 1920.[15] One early, celebrated supporter of 'Oxfordianism' was Sigmund Freud, who believed that in *Hamlet*, De Vere was writing about his own relations with his step-father.[16] Looney *claimed* that he hit on De Vere as the real author after he made a list of eighteen characteristics which the real author of Shakespeare's works *must* have had. Some of these are reasonable enough, for instance his suppositions that the real author was 'of superior education – classical – the habitual associate of educated people' and 'an enthusiast for Italy'.[17] Others, however, are highly tendentious and simply cannot be inferred from any of Shakespeare's writings, for instance that the real author was 'apparently eccentric and mysterious', 'unconventional', 'one of the higher aristocracy', 'loose and improvident in money matters', and 'doubtful and somewhat conflicting in his attitude to women'. There is nothing whatever in any of Shakespeare's plays from which any of these characteristics may be inferred; indeed, in some cases it is reasonable to draw precisely the opposite conclusion. For instance, far from being 'eccentric' – whatever that might mean, in the context of Elizabethan England – the author of Shakespeare's works was, surely, unusually businesslike, producing his thirty-seven plays with the regularity of clockwork. Shakespeare's attitude towards women appears unusually progressive, with his female characters always depicted in three-dimensional terms. There is nothing whatever in Shakespeare's writings from which the conclusion that he was 'one of the higher aristocracy' or 'improvident in money matters' might be drawn. In any case, Looney found De Vere's well-known poem 'Women', which begins 'If women could be fair and yet not fond …' in a poetry anthology, looked him up in *The Dictionary of National Biography* and decided that Edward De Vere was the man, although it looks to me very much as if Looney had decided on De Vere, and then devised a list of his personal characteristics which might have fitted Shakespeare. Looney also had to overlook the inconvenient fact that De Vere's dates simply do not fit the life of any putative Shakespeare: Shakespeare's works were written between *c.*1589–91 (when De Vere was aged around forty) and 1613 (when De Vere had been dead for nine years). De Vere *was* known to be a writer of stage comedies which were highly regarded (although none survive), and Oxfordians argue that *these* were his juvenilia. Wrong, too, are his surviving poems, which are manifestly nothing like Shakespeare, entirely lacking the latter's habitual complexity and metaphor, and which always fail utterly any computer stylistic comparison with Shakespeare, whatever one might think of such tests. That works like the three parts of *Henry VI* and *Titus Andronicus*, written while William Shakespeare was in his mid-late twenties, might be Shakespeare's actual juvenilia, just as they seem, is a conclusion rejected by Oxfordians. Supporters of De Vere have an even greater problem with Shakespeare's late works, especially *The Tempest*, usually dated to 1611, which is invariably seen to be based in significant measure on the so-called 'Strachey Letter', an account of the famous shipwreck of 1609 written in 1610 by William Strachey, the London Virginia Company's secretary on the voyage of the ill-fated *Sea-Venture*, the Company's ship. By 1610 De Vere had been dead for six years. Looney's explanation of this was that *The Tempest* was actually written by someone else. Recent Oxfordians have denied that *The Tempest* was influenced by the Strachey Letter, or that any of Shakespeare's supposed late works were actually written after 1604 (as, of course, they must). Some Oxfordian writers have created a novel chronology of Shakespeare's *oeuvre* in which many of his works were written before 1589–90. For instance, many Oxfordians date *Hamlet* to the early 1580s, pointing out that an earlier *Hamlet* (known as the *Ur-Hamlet*) was certainly performed on stage no later than 1589.[18] *Macbeth*, normally dated to 1605–06, might have been an anonymous lost play performed in 1567–68, or perhaps written just after the execution of Mary Stuart in 1587 – and so on.[19] The most important positive element in the case for De Vere as Shakespeare revolves around the many features of his life which are, apparently, mirrored in Shakespeare's works, both in his plays and in many of the Sonnets. According to Oxfordians, these clear-cut autobiographical echoes plainly reflect De Vere's life but can in no way, shape, or form be applied to William Shakespeare, the Stratford actor. These claims will be considered below.

Many other Authorship 'Candidates' have been posited: R.C. Churchill lists twenty-one such claimants as of 1958, and more have been added since.[20] Probably the best known are Christopher Marlowe (1564–93), the great playwright, Shakespeare's exact contemporary. According to all historical accounts, Marlowe was killed in a tavern brawl in Deptford on 30 May

1593 (possibly as a spy, secret agent, or double agent) aged twenty-nine, a fact which would make it difficult for him to have written the thirty-one Shakespeare plays which are conventionally dated as having been written between 1594 and 1613. 'Marlovians' (advocates of the Marlowe theory) argue that Marlowe survived and moved to France, where he continued to write plays. Other Authorship 'Candidates' including William Stanley, sixth Earl of Derby (1561–1642) and Roger Manners, fifth Earl of Rutland (1576–1612), who would thus have been aged around thirteen or fourteen when Shakespeare's first works appeared. Yet another possibility often encountered is that Shakespeare's works were written by a group of authors, probably headed by Sir Francis Bacon, which might have included De Vere, Marlowe and others.[21] Against this so-called 'Groupist' view are the facts that all Shakespeare's works appear to have one 'voice'; that some evidence must surely survive among those highly literate writers if such a far-reaching collaborative effort actually occurred; and that no evidence of any kind exists to support this theory. New 'candidates' are still encountered. This writer co-authored a work with Brenda James, *The Truth Will Out* (2006), in which we set out our view that Shakespeare's works were written by Sir Henry Neville (*c.*1562–1615), with what we regard as convincing evidence. This will be discussed below.

Despite the deficiencies of the Stratfordian case, the anti-Stratfordian view has made little or no impact on the contemporary mainstream. There are two principal reasons for this state of affairs. In the past, no genuinely credible alternative 'Shakespeare' has been discovered. At least as important, however, is the attitude of the Shakespeare 'Establishment' to any discussion of the Authorship Question, and especially the attitude of university English Literature departments around the world. As this attitude is not clearly understood by many, it is worth setting out the situation in some detail.

Until well into the twentieth century, virtually *all* eminent and important scholars of Shakespeare were 'amateurs' in the sense denoted in this book, that is, writers holding no university teaching position. Edward Malone (1741–1812), Shakespeare's first real biographer, and the editor of a fifteen-volume edition of Shakespeare's works, was a barrister; Howard Staunton (1810–74), editor of a three-volume edition of Shakespeare and the first to publish a photographic reproduction of *The First Folio*, was a journalist who also managed to find the time – and achieve lasting fame – as the world's strongest chess player of the 1840s. Even in the first half of the twentieth century some important Shakespeare scholars were to be found outside of university quadrangles. E. F. Halliday (1903–82), author of the extraordinarily useful work *A Shakespeare Companion* (originally 1952, revised edition 1964), was a teacher at Cheltenham until he became a full-time writer. Most significantly, the man who was, and arguably remains, the most eminent of all Shakespeare scholars, Sir Edmund Kerchever Chambers (E. K. Chambers, 1866–1954), was a senior civil servant in the Department of Education, who, until he retired in 1926, undertook research in his spare time. Down to the First World War and even beyond intellectual journals such as *The Fortnightly Review* published article after article about Shakespeare by intelligent 'amateur' writers, often deeply learned and certainly enthusiastic, who had something novel or important to say about the Bard. The development and evolution of the Authorship Question ought to be viewed with these facts in mind: nearly all writers who doubt that Shakespeare of Stratford wrote the works attributed to him have been 'amateurs' – but, for many generations, so were all significant writers on Shakespeare who fully accepted the orthodox account of his career. Possibly the earliest eminent writer on Shakespeare who was a university academic in the modern sense was Ernest Dowden (1843–1913), who was Professor of English Literature at Trinity College, Dublin (Dublin University) from 1867 until his death. His 1875 work, *Shakspere [sic]: A Critical Study of His Mind and Art*, originally delivered as a series of university lectures, was the first work to set out the familiar division of Shakespeare's writing career into evolutionary phases.[22] Since the 1920s, however, and emphatically since 1945, virtually *every* significant writer on Shakespeare has been a university academic. There are, of course, some exceptions – Eric Sams and Ian Wilson, two of the best-known recent writers on Shakespeare's life, did not hold university positions, and nor do Clare Asquith, the author of *Shadowplay* (2005), a widely-discussed and controversial explication of why Shakespeare was a secret Catholic, or Irvin Leigh Matus, whose *Shakespeare, In Fact* (1994) is often cited as one of the better defences of the orthodox view of Shakespeare's life. Nevertheless, it is safe to say that 95 per cent of men and women who have produced books or articles on Shakespeare during the past forty years or so are university academics, generally publishing in scholarly journals or with academic presses. Certainly the best-known Shakespeare scholars of the past generation – Samuel Schoenbaum, Stanley Wells, Gary Taylor, E. A.J. Honigman, Stephen Greenblatt, Jonathan Bate, Jonathan

Shapiro, and others of similar repute, are university professors whose scholarly milieu permeates their approach.

There is, however, another important consideration about the contemporary academic domination of Shakespeare studies which should be kept squarely in mind in considering the Authorship Question: virtually none – indeed, perhaps none at all – of those university academics is an historian. Probably without exception, all recent academic writers on Shakespeare's life and works have been employed in university English Literature departments, while in all likelihood none has been employed in a History department. To the layman, this distinction might seem of little importance, but it is arguably crucial, since academics in English Literature and academics in History are trained to do quite different things in quite different ways. Historians work from a variety of primary and secondary sources, treated objectively, critically, and in a wider context, to build up a picture of the most plausible sequence of events via the best available evidence. Clashes of opinion about the best evidence of an event in the past or its best interpretation comprise the very heart of academic history. Academic historians frequently engage in such debates and generally relish it, with academic history seen as consisting of such debates and clashes of opinion. Self-evidently, such disputes must be founded on real evidence: without salient evidence, historical debate cannot take place.[23] Although I am a History professor, I have never heard of any debate or discussion about the Shakespeare Authorship Question among academic historians, possibly because it is too specific an issue for them to debate, but also because it is deemed to be a literary matter to be discussed in literature departments. Yet, I am fairly sure that the attitude of academic historians towards this question would be markedly more flexible and disinterested than among academics in English Literature. *Probably* the attitude of most academic historians at the conclusion of an academic conference about the Authorship Question would be that it is likely, given the fact that Shakespeare's name is on the title page of his works and that no one seems to have questioned the identity of the real author for 200 years after Shakespeare's death, that he was the actual author, but that the real paucity of evidence about his life, and the lack of congruence between his life and background and the works he wrote, strongly imply that the Authorship Question is an open one, to be discussed again if new evidence is found. In all likelihood, this debate would be regarded by academic historians as interesting and intriguing but would not generate great heat or emotion, and would certainly not be regarded as *per se* taboo or as evidence of dementia on the part of those who questioned the orthodox viewpoint.[24]

This likely tolerant attitude of academic historians ought to be contrasted with the probable attitude of academics in English Literature departments towards those who might question the Stratfordian orthodoxy. What this attitude is likely to be has been set out bluntly by Professor Alan H. Nelson, formerly Professor of English at the University of California – Berkeley, who has, ironically, devoted much of his career to undermining the anti-Stratfordian view in every possible way, especially Oxfordianism, and is the author of *Monstrous Adversary* (Liverpool, 2003), a comprehensive biography of Edward De Vere, seventeenth Earl of Oxford, the leading anti-Stratfordian Authorship 'candidate' which attacks this 'myth created by his apologists'.[25] After noting that 'I myself do not know of a single Professor of English in the 1300–member Shakespeare Association of America who questions the identity of Shakespeare', Nelson concedes that 'there exist indeed professors of law, mathematics, medicine, psychology, sociology and even theatre among the ranks of the unbelievers,' but then frankly states that:

> *Anti-Stratfordians attribute this lop-sided alignment to internal professional discipline: anyone who expresses a reservation [about Shakespeare as author] will be denied tenure, drummed from the ranks, returned to civilian life. I agree that antagonism to the authorship debate from within the profession is so great that it would be as difficult for a professed Oxfordian to be hired in the first place, or to gain tenure, as for a professed creationist to be hired or gain tenure in a graduate-level Department of Biology ...*[26]

Accounts of the iron wall of hostility not merely towards debating the 'Authorship Question' among English Literature academics, but of admitting that there is a 'Question' are legion and legendary among anti-Stratfordians. On the leading academic website discussion group, 'Shaksper' [*sic*], any issue relating to William Shakespeare, his works, or his cultural milieu may be freely discussed, with one glaring exception. The 'Authorship Question' is *verboten* and taboo, and no messages relating to it will be posted. Attempts by university academics simply to post announcements of anti-Stratfordian conferences, at which most speakers were university academics in disciplines other than English Literature, have also automatically been turned down. Scholarly papers relating to the Authorship Question have, time and again, been rejected, often with contempt.

Academics in university English Literature departments are seldom (or, indeed, probably never) trained historians. They are primarily trained to read and analyse texts, and *most* mainstream literary criticism has, during the past seventy years, specifically tried to detach the 'text', which enjoys a self-sufficient independence and integrity, from its historical context. English Literature academics are also notorious for jumping on every egregious, precious, and self-inflated intellectual bandwagon which rolls along – Marxism, feminism, 'post-colonialism', and whatever School is next vouchsafed to us. Most academic historians regard English Literature departments as a world apart, as incomprehensible as the University's department of quantum physics, and about as useful to their historical research. It is safe to say that *most* mainstream English Literature academics have, essentially, no real interest in William Shakespeare as an historical figure or in any possible dimension of the 'Authorship Question'. While this is not necessarily a bad thing, it does detach the Author and his life from his works, and precludes most research on Shakespeare unrelated to questions of the text of the works and their meaning.

To be sure, the reluctance of academics in English Literature seriously to consider the possibility that anyone other than William Shakespeare actually wrote the works attributed to him is enormously compounded by the jejune and often utterly naïve nature of most anti-Stratfordian writings by obvious amateur writers, which is often unrelentingly awful and worthless. No one can read widely in the anti-Stratfordian corpus, either that from the past or from the present, without concluding very quickly that the great majority of such writers are grossly ignorant crackpots. Secret codes in the Shakespearean Canon, hidden histories often involving the secret, illegitimate child of Queen Elizabeth, alleged autobiographical references throughout the plays and Sonnets, and disguised clues as to the real identity of the author, are familiar stocks-in-trade among anti-Stratfordians. Some important points, however, can be made even here: within the past few decades, the level of anti-Stratfordian writings from Oxfordians and other sources has obviously improved, and there is now little or nothing to be found in well-edited anti-Stratfordian sources such as *The Oxfordian: The Annual Journal of the Shakespeare Oxford Society* in the way of obviously nonsensical material that was the case in equivalent sources two generations ago. Secondly, one must distinguish between the raising of doubts between William Shakespeare as the author, an area where the actual evidence is so meagre that doubts can surely arise and questions be asked, and the evidence provided in favour of a particular candidate such as De Vere, which often includes a strong measure of special pleading and a failure to mention or explain the embarrassing and inconvenient facts about one's candidate. The case against Shakespeare as the author is much stronger than the case for any of the well-known Authorship candidates.

While some of today's anti-Stratfordian writers are academics – although almost always in fields apart from English Literature – the great majority are 'amateur historians' of the type encountered throughout this book – often intelligent, often well-read, almost always enthusiastic, indeed obsessive – but not academics in the fields of English Literature or history. Most, indeed, are entirely outside of academic life altogether. This fact points to a crucial reason for the wall-to-wall disdain on the part of English Literature academics towards the anti-Stratfordians: giving any legitimacy to non-academics enunciating a non-academic view often associated with crackpots delegitimates the academic Shakespeareans. Not merely does it admit amateurs as equal participants in an important discussion with university academics, but it undermines the very professional status of English Literature academics, a threat compounded by the growing marginalisation of English Literature and other Arts disciplines within the University structure, elbowed aside in the battle for student numbers and tertiary resources, by practical, pre-professional disciplines and the Sciences. Fear of the loss of professional status is one of the motivating factors in the refusal of most English Literature academics even to discuss the possibility that someone else wrote Shakespeare's plays. The situation today is thus wholly different from that in the nineteenth century, when intelligent and learned men felt no stigma in discussing the Authorship question in intellectual journals of opinion. The situation today is that a growing, but still marginal, body of researchers – often 'amateur historians', increasingly academics in other disciplines – question whether William Shakespeare of Stratford wrote the works attributed to him, while, in adamant opposition to this, the academic world of university English Literature departments is totally hostile not merely to their conclusion, but even to the very discussion of the Authorship Question. The Authorship debate remains largely outside the academy because of the attitude of academic insiders, a situation reinforced by the lack of a genuinely credible alternative candidate and by the very dubious history of anti-Stratfordianism, especially during the Victorian period.

Each of the well-known alternative 'candidates' has much to be said in their favour, and it is worth looking at the claims made on their behalf by their proponents. The case for Edward De Vere, seventeenth Earl of Oxford rests fundamentally on two props: his personal qualifications for writing Shakespeare's works, and the similarity of many characters and events depicted in Shakespeare's works to incidents in De Vere's life – so many that they must surely be intentionally autobiographical. De Vere was well-born, well-educated, and visited most of Europe on an extended basis. He was known to have been a playwright and poet of note under his own name, and was a highly-regarded patron of the arts. Oxfordians argue that *Hamlet*, the most intense and introspective of Shakespeare's plays, is largely an autobiographical account of De Vere and his family. 'The king who poisoned Hamlet's father and then married his mother is an exaggerated version of Oxford's stepfather [Sir Charles Tyrrell]. Polonius, Lord Chamberlain in the court of Denmark and Hamlet's tedious counsellor, is a caricature of Queen Elizabeth's chief minister, Lord Burghley, who was Oxford's guardian. The daughter of Polonius was Hamlet's Ophelia, while Burghley's daughter, Anne Cecil, was a partner in Oxford's troubled marriage,' John Michell has summarised their arguments.[27] There *are* parallels, although to be sure there are differences. Oxford did not kill Burghley, unlike Hamlet and Polonius. More importantly, Oxford's stepfather Sir Charles Tyrrell did not murder his real father, the sixteenth Earl (who died in 1562 when De Vere was twelve) unlike the play. Since the *point* of *Hamlet* is the ghostly injunction for Hamlet to seek revenge for his father's murder by his stepfather, one might expect this glaring incongruity to weigh heavily on any interpretation of the work as De Vere's autobiography. In fact, Tyrrell is hardly mentioned in recent Oxfordian biographies of De Vere or accounts of their theory.[28] More promising, perhaps, are the *Sonnets*, which Oxfordians (and many others) regard as highly autobiographical. Many apparently autobiographical lines in the *Sonnets* appear difficult to reconcile – to put it mildly – with what is known of Shakespeare's life. For instance, most critics believe that the *Sonnets* were addressed to Lord Southampton, to whom Shakespeare had dedicated his two long poems in 1593–94. Sonnet 10 asks the man addressed to marry and 'make thee another self for love of me'. It is simply inconceivable that, in Elizabethan England, the actor son of a provincial tradesman could urge a powerful earl to marry and beget children 'for love of me', an invitation to be made shorter by the head. Other Sonnets speak of the poet as 'old' and 'lame'. Many critics believe they were written in 1592–94, when Shakespeare was aged between twenty-eight and thirty; there is no evidence that he was lame. The homo-erotic nature of some (not all) of the *Sonnets* is difficult to reconcile with what we know of Shakespeare, who married after a 'shotgun' wedding and had fathered three children before he was twenty-one. In contrast Oxfordians thus argue that the material in the autobiographical *Sonnets* show the absurdity of believing that Shakespeare of Stratford wrote them; only someone who was Southampton's social equal and who had De Vere's biographical and personal characteristics (he was accused of being a homosexual pederast) could have written them.

This is at first glance a strong case, and it is easy to see why the Oxfordian theory is now so popular, especially when it is realised that De Vere was something of a tempestuous Elizabethan swashbuckler, a 'Renaissance man' of wide culture, and a kind of anti-hero of a type frequently lionised in the Western world since the mid-1950s. Nevertheless, it is also a case which is deeply flawed, and its flaws – some of which have already been described – are too readily passed over by Oxfordians. It is one thing to assert that Shakespeare the actor did not write the works attributed to him, a proposition which might well be true, but quite another to maintain that De Vere was the actual Author. There is not a shred of direct evidence proving that De Vere wrote any of Shakespeare's works, or had any connection of any kind with William Shakespeare. Since Looney wrote in 1920, his supporters have had nearly a century to locate evidence for De Vere's authorship but have failed to do so. With a highly literate, well-connected man like De Vere, some written evidence surely *must* exist, but none has ever been found. There is one partial exception to this in the copy of the English translation of the 'Geneva' Bible of 1569–70 once owned by De Vere and now held by the Folger Library in Washington D.C. This Bible contains 1028 markings of passages. It was carefully examined by Dr. Roger Stritmatter in a 2001 doctoral dissertation, who found that about one-fifth of the marked passages appear in Shakespeare's works, either directly or theatrically.[29] Thirty of 81 Biblical passages (37 per cent) in Shakespeare's works that he had used four or more times were marked in De Vere's Bible. Many of these marked passages – according to Oxfordians – reveal hitherto unsuspected Biblical origins for passages in Shakespeare. This is clearly interesting and arguably important, although it should certainly be treated with caution. Eighty per cent of the marked passages do *not* occur in any of Shakespeare's works. Some books of the Bible heavily used by Shakespeare were hardly marked at all.[30] The markings in the Bible appear to be in more than one hand, strongly suggesting that some were not written by De Vere. The provenance of this copy of the Bible after De Vere's time is unclear. In short, this is interesting but hardly conclusive, especially given that it is the Bible which has been marked, a book ubiquitously owned, read, and drawn upon. No other piece of direct evidence to support the Oxfordian case is known.

As well, there is an obvious and gaping problem with the dates of De Vere's birth, career, and death: he was born in 1550, and thus was 25–30, the age when one might have expected him to first produce masterful works, in 1575–80. More importantly, he died in 1604. The writing of Shakespeare's works is dated by all reputable scholars as between 1589–91 and 1613. It is *possible* that Shakespeare wrote earlier works, but since he was born in 1564, he would have been only sixteen in 1580 when De Vere was thirty. And unless the King's Company was in contact with the spirit world, it must have premiered many plays written before De Vere's death in July 1604 years later.

Oxfordians attempt to get around this glaring problem by inventing a new chronology of Shakespeare's works as they go along: many, they claim, were actually written much earlier than in the conventional chronological schema, and all were written by 1604, even *The Tempest*, which is invariably seen as dating from 1611 and based in part on accounts of the famous Bermuda shipwreck of 1609–10. The first thing one might say about any such alternative dating schema is that if one invents a chronology of Shakespeare's works as one goes along to fit the life of one's candidate, one can prove that anyone wrote Shakespeare's works: it can't be hard. The dating and chronology of Shakespeare's works has been calculated in a sophisticated way by a range of evidence including publication and performance dates, references by contemporaries, the percentage of rhyme to verse, colloquialisms (much greater in the later plays), the use of rare words, verbal parallels, and metrical tests.[31] These all reinforce each other with considerable consistency. According to Oxfordians, however, many of Shakespeare's plays were written far earlier than thought and are actually revised versions of plays known to have been performed earlier but never credited by orthodox scholars to Shakespeare. For instance, Oxfordians argue that *Love's Labours Lost* is actually a revised version of a court play entitled *A Maske of Amazones and A Maske of Knights*, performed in January 1579 (when Shakespeare was fourteen).[32] There is, of course, no evidence whatever for this view. Moving the start of Shakespeare's career back by perhaps fifteen years also presents some insuperable difficulties about dating. The earliest Shakespeare plays to be published appeared in 1594–95. These comprised what certainly appear to have been Shakespeare's juvenalia, such as *Henry VI Part 2*, *Henry VI Part 3*, and *Titus Andronicus*. Yet by this date, according to Oxfordians, De Vere had already written *Hamlet* (dated by them to 1581), and it is unclear why De Vere chose to publish his second-rate works but not, until much later, his masterpieces (*Hamlet* was first published in 1603). Oxfordians also must maintain that, by definition, all of Shakespeare's works need to have been written by his death in July 1604. There is abundant evidence, however, that many of Shakespeare's plays were written well after that date. *Macbeth* contains apparent references to the Gunpowder Plot of 1605–6, *Coriolanus* to the great frost of 1607–08, *King Lear* to an anonymous play called *King Leir* which was registered in May 1605, while, above all, *The Tempest* relies upon the account of the Bermuda shipwreck of 1609–10 in many varied ways. When the King's Company began performing in the indoors Blackfriars Theatre in 1608–09, Shakespeare's works, written then and later, changed in nature, adding more special effects, scene breaks, and music. Oxfordians have to deny (or ignore) all of this and, in particular, deny any linkage of the Bermuda shipwreck to *The Tempest*. There is also the question of how De Vere's plays, written before July 1604, were 'released' to the King's Company. Who owned them and on what basis were they drip-fed to the theatre? Oxfordians cannot answer this either, maintaining that they were in the hands of the so-called 'grand possessors' (as mentioned in the introductory Epistle to the 1609 edition of *Troilus and Cressida*), although no evidence has been found for the existence of 'grand possessors'.

There is, as well, another very major problem which strongly affects the viability of Oxfordianism. It is their constant theme that De Vere had an intimate relationship of some kind with Lord Southampton, the man to whom 'Shakespeare' dedicated the two long plays and to whom many of the Sonnets were probably addressed.[33] Yet there is no evidence that the two ever met or spoke to each other, let alone had a close relationship. Both were, as minors, royal wards of Lord Burghley (Sir William Cecil), but many years apart, as De Vere was twenty-three years older than Southampton. The only time the two men were known to have been in the same room at the same time was in 1601 when De Vere was the foreman of the jury of Peers which condemned Southampton to death for his role in the Essex rebellion. No correspondence between the two men exists, nor is one even mentioned in the surviving records of the other, and no contemporary reports remarked on any association whatever between the two.[34] As seems so often to be the case, Oxfordians appear to be advancing a far-reaching thesis which is wholly lacking in evidence or plausibility. While the Oxfordian case has a certain superficial attractiveness about it, the closer one examines it the weaker it seems, and in nearly nine decades its supporters have failed to provide any real evidence for their thesis. Given that Oxfordianism has certainly been the most popular anti-Stratfordian theory for the past half-century or more, it is easy to see why orthodox Stratfordians have dismissed it, and have then, regrettably, gone on from its inadequacies to dismiss any discussion of the Authorship Question as *ipso facto* pointless and wrong.

For decades, the leading alternative Shakespeare was Sir Francis Bacon (1561–1626, later first baron Verulam and first viscount St. Albans). Bacon was an acknowledged genius and a major writer, a man of the widest knowledge, who was certainly intellectually capable of writing Shakespeare's works. His birth date is right, as was his education at Cambridge and his profound legal knowledge – he became Lord Chancellor – with many anti-Stratfordians maintaining that 'Shakespeare' must have been legally trained. There are a number of distinct points in his favour. In 1985 workmen renovating a fourteenth century inn at St. Albans, Hertfordshire – Bacon's home town – found a concealed mural behind some panelling apparently depicting a scene in Shakespeare's *Venus and Adonis*.[35] As Michell points out, if this mural had been discovered in an old inn in Stratford-upon-Avon, it would be trumpeted in every subsequent biography of Shakespeare as proof positive that he wrote the works attributed to him. Because it was discovered in St. Albans, however, it has been ignored (or dismissed) by orthodox Stratfordians and, for that matter, by Oxfordians and others. Even more interesting, perhaps, are the parallels between a manuscript collection of Bacon's own notes, aphorisms, and pithy sayings, known as *The Promus* [Storehouse] *of Formularies and Elegancies, by Francis Bacon*, written around

1594–95. *Many* of these later appeared, although often in a different form, in a Shakespeare play.[36] Like De Vere's Geneva Bible, this is a point to be taken into account, although many of the sayings in Bacon's *Promus* are not exactly like Shakespeare's use of them (e.g. 'At length the string cracks' in *Promus* becomes 'The strings of life began to crack' in *King Lear*), while others are simply time-honoured clichés (e.g. 'Every Jack would be a Lord', which appeared in *Richard III* as 'Every Jack becomes a gentleman'). Other aphorisms found in *Promus* were used by many Elizabethan writers in their works.[37] Finally, there is the Northumberland Manuscript. This was the folder, discovered in 1867 in the London mansion of the Duke of Northumberland, and originally used as a wrapper for Elizabethan pamphlets, that contains innumerable scribblings. It was apparently written around 1596.[38] Among its many, almost indecipherable, scribblings are 'By·mr. Ffrauncis Bacon / Essaies by the same author / William Shakespeare' and the names of several of Shakespeare's plays. The mysterious words 'honorificabil- etudine', found in *Love's Labours Lost*, is also there. No one knows who wrote it or why, although finding the names of Bacon and Shakespeare together is obviously striking, given that they ostensibly had no known connection.[39] *Probably* the Northumberland Manuscript was simply a wrapper in which Bacon held quarto copies of several of Shakespeare's plays, but it remains a considerable mystery.

As with De Vere, there is a good deal one might say against Bacon as the author. His elephantine style was appropriate for a philosopher or an eminent lawyer, which he was, but completely unlike the style of Shakespeare. Bacon had no known connection with the theatre. He was the chief *prosecuting* barrister against Essex and Southampton in 1601, although he appears to have been an acquaintance of Southampton – they were both directors of the London Virginia Company.[40] (Nevertheless, this relationship is certainly far closer than any known connection between Southampton and De Vere, or Southampton and Shakespeare.) Bacon (in direct contrast to De Vere) lived too long, dying ten years after Shakespeare's last work. He had no traceable connection with the *First Folio*.[41] Ben Jonson was, however, an admirer of Bacon and wrote an Ode on his sixtieth birthday in January 1621.[42] Although Baconianism has manifestly declined in importance, it still has its followers, who have produced a number of interesting works in recent years.[43] As an alternative Authorship theory, it seems clearly more plausible than Oxfordianism, and it is rather surprising that it has declined in popularity.

There are also other Authorship candidates, of varying degrees of credibility. Christopher Marlowe would certainly be the strongest alternative author if he had not inconveniently died in 1593. His supporters argue that he wasn't killed but went to France, where he continued to write Shakespeare's plays. This view received a good deal of publicity in 1955 with publication of Christopher Hoffman's *The Murder of the Man Who Was Shakespeare*. In 1956 Hoffman opened the Walsingham family vault in Chislehurst church, where he expected to find Marlowe's manuscripts. He found nothing.[44] *If* real evidence ever came to light that Marlowe was alive after 1593, the case for him as author would have to be taken seriously, bearing in mind that Marlowe's surviving plays, although unquestionably great works of literature, lack Shakespeare's broad humanity and universal empathy. Nor is there any known direct connection between Marlowe, a Cambridge graduate who wrote for the Admiral's Company (rivals to Shakespeare's Chamberlain's Company) and William Shakespeare. There is no reason to suppose that they ever met, although Shakespeare did cite one line from Marlowe's *Hero and Leander* in *As You Like It* (normally dated to 1599–1600 after Marlowe had died). The strongest of the previous remaining candidates is probably William Stanley, sixth Earl of Derby (1561–1642), who was known to have been a playwright and who visited the Court of Navarre in 1582, a journey which, his supporters claim, found its way into *Love's Labours Lost*.[45] Derby was a friend and political ally of Southampton, and actually married the daughter of Edward De Vere, seventeenth Earl of Oxford, the woman pointedly rejected as a wife by Southampton. The case for Derby has other evidence in its support, and also seems a good deal stronger than the case for De Vere.[46] But there is no direct evidence of any kind that Derby was Shakespeare, while the fact that Derby lived for nearly thirty years after Shakespeare wrote his last play must count against it.

Today, nearly all of the periodicals, newsletters, websites, and conferences putting the anti-Stratfordian view are pro-Oxfordian. Virtually extinct in the 1960s, Oxfordianism has expanded enormously in influence and popularity over the past generation. Its growth has been fanned by long-established Oxfordians and by new converts. Charlton Ogburn's lengthy *The Mystery of William Shakespeare* (1984 and 1988) had a considerable impact, as did a 1992 PBS-TV debate on American public television on the Authorship Question. A range of societies now exist in the English-speaking world and Europe. In America the Shakespeare Oxford Society publishes a well-produced quarterly, *The Shakespeare Oxford Newsletter*, as well as an excellent, very valuable annual journal of nearly 100 pages, *The Oxfordian*, with eight or ten long articles based on impressive scholarship. 'Rival' Oxfordian societies occur, such as the Shakespeare Fellowship. In Britain, Oxfordianism is represented by the De Vere Society, which also publishes a quarterly, *De Vere's Society Newsletter*, and holds annual conferences. Individual activists are of key importance, for instance Professor Daniel Wright of Concordia University in Portland, Oregon, who has hosted ten annual conferences on the Authorship Question – these almost invariably presenting the Oxfordian viewpoint – while Mark Rylance, the well-known actor and recent head of the Globe Theatre in London, has, remarkably, allowed the Globe to host several conferences on the Authorship Question. (Rylance was a Baconian but is now neutral as regards Authorship claims.). The Shakespeare Oxford Society of the United States has also hosted thirty annual well-attended conferences; the Shakespeare Fellowship website, which includes a contributors' forum, is one of a number of anti-Stratfordian internet sites. Concordia University's annual conference takes place over three or four days, and features many academic speakers, although seldom or never from English Literature departments. I would say that the level of presentations is as high as at any academic conferences I have attended, although inevitably some papers by well-intentioned independent researchers seem somewhat unsophisticated. The two Concordia University conferences I attended (in 2003 and 2006) each had over one hundred registrants, among them many obviously highly intelligent persons from a range of professional activities outside of the university academy. It was clear, however, that the great majority were convinced Oxfordians who were not pleased by rival anti-Stratfordian theories, although to some extent welcoming them as allies. Oxfordianism has mushroomed to such an extent in recent years that other brands of anti-Stratfordianism have been reduced to individual activists such as the veteran pro-Baconian campaigner Francis Carr of Brighton, England, and the Marlovian writer and website master Dr. John Baker of Washington state, and to low circulation newsletters. The near-total dominance of Oxfordianism is, in many respects, a mixed blessing. It has generated enormous publicity for the anti-Stratfordian cause, especially for the very real case to be made against Shakespeare as the author, but has produced a single rival claimant, Edward De Vere, whose own case is full of deficiencies and lacking in evidence. Above all, there is no genuinely neutral venue or website about the Authorship Question, and virtually nothing exists in the way of a forum where pro- and anti-Stratfordians can exchange views – chiefly if not entirely because of the taboo imposed by orthodox English Literature academics. It may be, as some anti-Stratfordians claim, that the orthodox view of Shakespeare's life is a paradigm about to shift dramatically, but only dramatic new evidence, or a much more plausible alternative candidate, is likely to bring this about.

Despite the many inadequacies of the case that William Shakespeare of Stratford wrote the works attributed to him, we may well have to conclude that, in the absence of another plausible candidate for whom real evidence exists, Shakespeare must be given credit for his own work. There are clearly very powerful and compelling reasons to arrive at this conclusion. Shakespeare's name is on the title page of his works, including the posthumous *First Folio.* No one in Shakespeare's lifetime, or for many decades afterwards, appears to have questioned whether he wrote his works, while some contemporaries may seem to have acknowledged his authorship. His dates are completely consistent with the accepted chronology of his works. Whoever wrote Shakespeare's plays must have known a great deal about the theatre, and Shakespeare was assuredly a man of the theatre. All of the supposed anomalies of his career, from his supposed knowledge of Italy to his apparent lack of books, can be explained away, however unsatisfactory and meagre the resulting biography may seem.

These are powerful arguments, which will be persuasive to many, probably to most. Nevertheless, each is far more problematical than may seem at first glance. Even in Shakespeare's lifetime, some people seem already to have questioned his identity. In 1610–11 John Davies of Hereford (*c.*1565–1618), who knew Sir Francis Bacon and was a member of the literary Mitre Club, published a book of epigrams and poems, *The Scourge of Folly.* One poem was entitled 'To Our English Terence Mr. Will: Shake-speare,' and reads.

Some say (good Will) which I, in sport, do sing
Hadst thou not plaid some Kingly parts in sport,
Thou hadst bin a companion for a King;
And, beene a King among the meaner sort.
Some others raile, but raise as they thinke fit,

Thou hast no rayling, but, a raigning Wit:
And honesty thou sow'st, whch they do reape;
So to increase their stocke which they do keepe.

Rightly described by E.K. Chambers as 'cryptic' and 'obscure', the poem seems inapplicable to Shakespeare of Stratford.[47] He did not 'play some Kingly parts in sport', but professionally, as an actor. Shakespeare was not a 'companion for a King' (what 'king'?). He was not 'a King among the meaner sort'. This might, one supposes, have been the attitude of the 'groundlings' who inhabited the Globe's cheaper seats, but Shakespeare was supposed to appeal not to the uneducated but to 'the wiser sort', as Gabriel Harvey put it in the early seventeenth century. The title's reference to 'Terence' seems rather curious. Terence was a famous Roman author of comedies (not of tragedies or histories) but was also an author whose works were believed to have been written by others, Scipio and Laelius.[48] Terence's reputation was well-known at the time that Davies wrote.[49] This passage is simply not what one might expect in a tribute to Shakespeare of Stratford as we know him. In the *First Folio* and elsewhere, Ben Jonson certainly appeared to be praising Shakespeare of Stratford, although below the reasons to be deeply suspicious of this will be examined. In truth, to reiterate a point made before, there are *no* unambiguous statements in Shakespeare's lifetime clearly and plainly identifying him, the man who was born in Stratford in 1654 and died there in 1616, as the author of his supposed works. If some contemporary had merely noted in his diary, 'I saw Master Wm. Shaksper coming from ye theatre with ye MS. of his newe play, Macbeth, whiche he was carrying', or the like, the Authorship Question would have been settled forever, but *no* such statement exists. William Shakespeare, the Stratford man, was often identified in his lifetime as a 'player' but never as an author, and centuries of the most intensive research have simply failed to identify anything of the sort, regardless of how hard we look.

And while, clearly, there continues to be a strong *prima facie* case that William Shakespeare wrote the works attributed to him, nevertheless, there remain remarkably strong reasons for questioning whether the Stratford actor wrote his supposed works. Earlier in this chapter, a long list of such points was presented, but it would be well to set out some other strong considerations here. The first is that it seems inconceivable that Shakespeare the actor had the time, energy, or resources to write plays, let alone the prodigious number he actually produced, for Shakespeare was, for much of his career, a full-time actor and theatre-manager. The situation has perhaps been best summarised by Professor James Shapiro, ironically a strict believer in the orthodox view and the author of *1599: A Year in the Life of William Shakespeare*:

> *Shakespeare and his fellow [theatre] sharers spent their mornings rehearsing and their afternoons performing alongside hired men and boys who were needed to fill out the cast of approximately 15. Except for a break during Lent and the occasional closing of the theatres due to scandal or plague, performances went on all year round. As Elizabethan audiences expected a different play every day, actors had to master a score of new roles every year – as well as recall old favourites needed to flesh out the repertory ...*[50]

Shapiro neglects to add that the Chamberlain's/King's Men, Shakespeare's acting company, also went on lengthy, exhausting tours to the provinces. He also fails to note that Shakespeare was maintaining two households, a semi-permanent one in London and a permanent one in Stratford, three days' travelling time away, where he had a family and increasingly significant business interests, which he must have visited several times each year. Shapiro does point out that '... new plays were acquired from a score of freelance dramatists who were paid on average £6 a play (at a time when a schoolmaster might earn £20 a year).'[51] Despite all this, Shapiro sees no incongruity in espousing the orthodox claim that 'what little free time Shakespeare had at the start of his working day must have been devoted to reading and writing ... [and] providing his company with, on average, two new plays a year.

That Shakespeare actually did this – needless to say – beggars belief. It seems beyond the capacity of any human being to engage in the exhausting daily drudgery of being a jobbing actor on the Elizabethan stage *and* also write at least thirty-seven plays, most of which were certainly deeply researched in an extremely wide range of sources. And who on earth would do this, if he could make a reasonable income from writing alone? To claim that Shakespeare did this is rather like claiming that a former manual worker on Ford Motors' factory floor, promoted in his mid-thirties to an executive position, nevertheless insisted on continuing to work night shifts on the factory's assembly line three or four times a week. This simply would not happen. (Yet, according to Shapiro, 'we know that Shakespeare was still acting alongside his fellow sharers as late as 1603 … and there is little evidence that he took time off to write'!) No one *besides* Shakespeare, it seems, either then or more recently, has lived in this way. Other *former* actors – Ben Jonson is the most famous – of the Elizabethan period *became* playwrights after leaving the stage, although *most* of Shakespeare's famous playwrighting contemporaries – Marlowe, Kyd, Beaumont, Fletcher *et al* – were never actors at any stage of their careers, so far as we know. It is perhaps worth considering the careers of Shakespeare's contemporaries in more detail. The on-line edition of the recently-published *Oxford Dictionary of National Biography*, which can be searched by a variety of categories, contains entries on seventy-seven persons deceased between 1590 and 1640 – Shakespeare's contemporaries – who are listed under the heading 'theatre and live entertainment'. Six of these are described as 'playwrights and actors'. Robert Armin (1563–1615), the clown in the King's Men, wrote one play, *Two Maids of Moreclack*. Thomas Drewe (*c.*1586–1627) wrote two plays in all, as did Nathan Field (1587–1620). Samuel Rowley (*d.*1624) was an actor from 1597 until 1613. He wrote one play during this period, with perhaps three more long after he retired from the stage. William Rowley (*d.*1624), no known relation, apparently collaborated on up to sixteen plays, but only two or three were his unaided work. Robert Wilson (*d.*1600) wrote up to twenty plays, but only two in the period (1572–88) when he was an actor. Other playwrights such as Ben Jonson were actors briefly at the start of their careers, but certainly left the stage by the time they wrote the great bulk of their work.

From this, it will be seen that if Shakespeare was both a full-time actor *and* wrote thirty-seven plays – with probably *twenty-seven* being written in the years up to 1603 when he was still apparently a full-time actor – he must have been both unique among playwrights of his era, a man of super-human energy as well as a super-human genius. The anomalousness of this claim as well as its utter implausibility seems to me to be *prima facie* evidence that we are dealing with two distinct men, the Author and the actor. In modern times, it is difficult to think of any playwright of the first rank in Britain or any other country – Ibsen, Strindberg, Chekhov, Shaw, O'Neill, Arthur Miller, Edward Albee, Harold Pinter – who combined acting with writing for more than a small part of their careers, if at all. Moreover, there was one period in Shakespeare's life when we know that London's theatres were closed, in June 1592–June 1594 (with very brief interludes), because of disagreements with the civic authorities followed by a severe outbreak of the plague.[52] Shakespeare apparently did *not* put this unexpected enforced spare time to good use by writing a lengthy sequence of plays, but instead produced his two long poems, *Venus and Adonis* and *Rape of Lucrece.*

Few writers on Shakespeare's life, either Stratfordians or anti-Stratfordians, have seriously considered the implications of these all-important time constraints on the Authorship Question. It surely seems *a priori* improbable in the highest degree that Shakespeare could have combined being a full-time actor *and* a prodigiously fertile writer, or would have wished to. Equally, this seems *a priori* to suggest that the actual author was someone else, a man with time, leisure, and ready access to the many sources on which Shakespeare's plays are well known to have been based.

The second important point which might be made is that Shakespeare's works appear to show a clear evolutionary trajectory which bears little or no relation to the known facts of Shakespeare's life. On the contrary, they indicate that we are dealing with two different men, the Author and the Actor. The author killed off Falstaff, his most popular character, for no apparent reason in 1598–99, rather than milk him in five more plays, to the financial advantage of the Chamberlain's Company. Centrally, the author appears to have suffered a traumatic experience of some kind in 1601, leading to a comprehensive change in the nature of Shakespeare's works: out went the Italianate comedies and triumphalist Histories, in came the great tragedies and the 'Problem Plays'. The author was apparently pleased when Queen Elizabeth died in 1603 ('The mortal moon hath her eclipse endured ... In certainties now crown themselves assured, / And peace proclaims olives of endless age', from Sonnet 107, taken by most critics to refer to the Queen's death) and was one of the few notable poets of the time not to write a memorial tribute to the Queen. The author's plays from the 1600s are, it has often been argued, part of the post-Essex rebellion's oppositionist politics. The author was apparently keenly interested in the London Virginia Company and had access to the 'Strachey Letter', a confidential document about the Bermuda shipwreck circulated only to directors of the Company. The author was evidently a friend of Lord Southampton, since he dedicated two long poems to him, while Southampton is widely believed to have been the 'onlie begetter' of *Shake-speares Sonnets.*

In contrast, the actor was none of these things. He had no reason to kill off Falstaff in 1598–99, an act detrimental to his own financial interests. He suffered no traumas in 1601. Most orthodox scholars attribute the great break of 1601 either to the death of Shakespeare's son Hamnet – although this occurred five years earlier and in the interim Shakespeare wrote the Falstaff plays – or to the death of Shakespeare's father in 1601, although the former was thirty-seven at the time and there is no evidence that he was close to his father. The actor had absolutely no reason to be pleased when Queen Elizabeth died and no reason to refrain from writing a memorial tribute. The actor had no known political profile but, instead, apparently avoided all political involvement, presumably because of the extreme dangers Elizabethan politics presented to a nobody in a marginal profession. The actor had no conceivable connection with the London Virginia Company; he was not among the 570 men who spent twelve pounds to buy a share in the Company. He had no access to its confidential documents, such as the 'Strachey Letter' and appears to have been living almost full-time in Stratford at the time of the Bermuda shipwreck. There is no reason to suppose that Southampton ever set eyes on Shakespeare (there is no mention of Shakespeare in Southampton's surviving papers or any mention of any connection, however remote, by contemporaries) unless Southampton saw Shakespeare act on stage.

It seems as clear as anything can be from all this that – once again – we are dealing with two separate and distinctive men, the Author and the Actor, whose life trajectories were quite different. In the case of Shakespeare the actor, we know a great deal about his life trajectory and aims: centrally, to use the money he made in London to become a recognised 'gentleman' and man of property in Stratford, and to found a dynasty. He appears to have pursued these aims almost single-mindedly. He had no known literary or cultural aims of any kind, and, despite allegedly being the greatest writer in history, remarkably little interest in the London intellectual world once he retired – aged forty-seven or so – to Stratford. The Author and the Actor must, however, have been contemporaries or near-contemporaries. If not, there would have been an inexplicable mismatch in the life of the actor and the chronology of his works, such as bedevils the Oxfordian theory.

In August 2001 I wrote an article in the British monthly *History Today*, 'Who Was Shakespeare?', examining the Authorship Question with the information which was known to me at the time. I concluded that it was not absurd to claim that someone else wrote Shakespeare's works, and that De Vere appeared to be the strongest candidate, but that the case for him was not convincing and, in the absence of any new evidence or better candidate,

Figure 4.3 Sir Henry Neville (c.1562–1615), another alternative 'candidate' to being the actual author of Shakespeare's works. Mary Evans Picture Library

we may well have to return to the orthodox view that William Shakespeare of Stratford wrote the works with which he is credited. I had no reason to suppose that my conclusion – perfectly reasonable to a historian if not to an academic in English Literature – would ever be altered. But it has been.

I received a large volume of correspondence about my article, including perhaps a dozen enunciations of new (or old) Authorship theories, all without real merit. Early in 2003, however, I was introduced to an entirely new Authorship theory propounded by Brenda James, an independent scholar in Sussex. Brenda James is a cultural historian with a first-class honours degree who was prevented, for health reasons, from pursuing an academic career. In due course, I was initiated into the view, never previously put in the long history of anti-Stratfordian theories, that Sir Henry Neville (*c.*1562–1615), a well-born, well-educated Elizabethan member of Parliament and, briefly, Ambassador to France in 1599–1601, wrote Shakespeare's works. In common with the great majority of people, I had first imagined that I had never previously heard of Sir Henry Neville, but it seems that I had actually mentioned him in my *History Today* article, citing Michell's claim that his name was on the top of the Northumberland Manuscript, and Michell's (inaccurate) statement that he was Bacon's 'nephew and close associate'.[53] I had actually looked Neville up in the *Dictionary of National*

Biography and noted the closeness of his dates to Shakespeare's, but his rather misleading description as a 'diplomat' – which he was for less than two years – meant that I did not pursue his career more carefully. I soon met Brenda James and read her original manuscript setting out her case. The more I read of the case for Neville, the more I became convinced that she had, miraculously, found the truth, that Sir Henry Neville was indeed the author of Shakespeare's works, and was unquestionably the strongest Authorship 'Candidate' who had ever been put forward. (Indeed, the obvious question is how on earth he had been missed.) I collaborated with Brenda James on a cogent book, setting out the case for Neville, which was published in 2005 by Pearson Longman of London as *The Truth Will Out: Unmasking the Real Shakespeare* and was published in the United States in 2006 by HarperCollins.

While that book, of course, makes the case for Neville in detail, it is worth summarising the main facts of his life and why we believe that he wrote Shakespeare's works. Sir Henry Neville's paternal descent was from the illustrious Neville family; he was a descendant of John of Gaunt and of the brother of 'Warwick the Kingmaker'. His mother, however, was the niece of Sir Thomas Gresham, the great London merchant and founder of Gresham College. Neville lived chiefly at Billingbear Park, about six miles from Windsor. He was educated at Merton College, Oxford, his mentor there being Sir Henry Savile, the renowned scholar. Between 1578 and 1582 Neville accompanied Savile and others on a four-year trip to the Continent, including Italy, where they collected manuscripts and met leading scholars; Neville was already well-known for his impressive learning. He was elected to Parliament in 1584 and served as an M.P. until his death, with the exception of a three-year period when he was imprisoned in the Tower. William Shakespeare's mother's property was owned by the Neville family, which may be how they came to know one another. As a member of Parliament and the scion of a family with royal connections, Neville could not openly produce his early History plays under his own name, and came to use and rely upon the provincial nonentity William Shakespeare as his frontman and producer-director. Neville killed off Falstaff, his most popular character, in 1598–99 when he became Ambassador to France. In 1601, while still Ambassador, Neville became involved in the Essex rebellion and was condemned to indefinite confinement in the Tower and a huge fine. He spent 1601–03 in the Tower with his close friend Lord Southampton, to whom many of the Sonnets are plainly addressed. He wrote *Hamlet* early in his confinement in the Tower; it is 'about' the Essex rebellion.[54] Neville and Southampton were released by James I early in 1603. Neville increasingly became a leader of the parliamentary opposition to James in the 1600s. He also became a director of the London Virginia Company, publishing *Shake-speares Sonnets* in 1609 on virtually the same day as the Company's charter was officially granted. It was clearly dedicated to Southampton, its Dedication actually written by Neville himself. Neville felt deeply the loss of the *Sea Venture* on Bermuda in 1609–10, and based *The Tempest* in part around it. In his last years he was a close friend of Jonson, Beaumont, and Fletcher, and died in 1615. Ben Jonson was apparently resident at Gresham College when he wrote the introductory material to the *First Folio* in 1623; we believe that he was given his post there by Neville's family to produce the *Folio* material. This brief account only skims the surface of a remarkable amount of material about Neville examined in *The Truth Will Out*.

One question which is invariably asked of the Shakespeare Authorship debate is 'Why does it matter?' 'Who cares who wrote Shakespeare's works?' and 'What difference does it make?', are constant refrains of those only slightly familiar with this question. On one level, it makes no difference: the plays are still the same and would still be enjoyed and admired. On another level, however, it matters very greatly indeed. If the identity of the actual author were known with certainty, virtually every line in Shakespeare's works would have to be reinterpreted to place in the social, political, and historical context of the real author's life. One assumes, too, that many mysteries about the plays would be resolved, something which the largely inadequate and unsatisfactory life of William Shakespeare, the Stratford actor, precludes us from doin.

Chapter 5

Richard the Third and the Princes in the Tower

Did King Richard III murder the princes in the Tower? This enduring puzzle has been termed 'history's greatest unsolved mystery' and 'the most famous mystery in the annals of England'.[1] It is unarguably the most famous mystery involving English royalty, and owes some of its lasting renown to this fact. It is, moreover, still highly controversial and still able, after more than 500 years, to arouse considerable and even heated debate. 'Richard III is still capable of arousing strong feelings, as anyone rash enough to give public lectures on him soon discovers', the historian Rosemary Horrox wrote in 1989.[2] Societies and periodicals, as well as the inevitable websites, continue to multiply, some to debate the mystery, some explicitly to defend Richard's character. The mystery of Richard and the princes does differ, however, from the other subjects considered in this work in a number of ways. Although Richard III's life and reign are matters of historical record, it is fair to say that continuing popular interest in the fate of the princes in the Tower derives from two works of fiction, Shakespeare's celebrated play *The Tragedy of Richard III,* and from an enormously popular English detective novel written 460 years later, Josephine Tey's *The Daughter of Time*, which was published in 1951.[3] Tey's work came towards the end (perhaps after the end) of the 'golden age of the detective story' of the first half of the twentieth century. Characteristically, a 'golden age' mystery, normally a murder, is solved by a talented amateur detective (or, occasionally, a Scotland Yard man) based on clues and evidence fairly presented, eschewing excess violence, sexuality, psychological undertones, or espionage. It is genuinely surprising that *The Daughter of Time* appears to be the only classical detective novel of that era, and certainly by far the best known, which attempts to solve an actual historical mystery. Tey's book remains widely and popularly known to this day: again and again, when I have mentioned to academic historians and others that I intend to discus Richard III and the princes in the Tower in this book, I have been referred to *The Daughter of Time*, as if I were somehow unaware of it. Many of those who have mentioned Tey's novel to me have certainly not read it themselves, are often surprisingly rusty about the facts of Richard and the princes, and know nothing or almost nothing about the non-fiction and academic literature on Richard III. Nor have they read any of Josephine Tey's six other detective novels: such are the vagaries of fame. In Tey's book, her detective, Inspector Grant, recuperating in a hospital, sees a copy of the famous portrait of Richard III in the National Portrait Gallery and, through a mixture of boredom and growing fascination, tries to solve the case by employing researchers and reading many books. He concludes that Henry VII, not Richard, murdered the princes. Tey's information is apparently derived chiefly from Sir Clements R. Markham's *Richard III: His Life and Character* (1906), one of the first books to view Richard in a more favourable light and one of the first to point the finger of guilt at Henry Tudor. Tey acknowledges 'someone called Markham', and two of his pro-Richard predecessors (Sir George Buck and Horace Walpole) in two sentences (p.179) without further explanation.

Another factor which sets the mystery of Richard III and the princes apart from the other subjects considered in this book is that much, perhaps most, writing about the fate of the princes during the past sixty years has been produced by university academic historians, including the most eminent of authorities with international reputations. It is probably fair to say that they have raised the level of discussion about this subject among non-academic writers. Works on Richard III and the princes by non-academic historians tend to be very good indeed, with a relative absence of crackpot theories; non-academic historians of this subject in general have a detailed knowledge of the historical context of the fate of the princes, and also tend to write well. Academic experts and authorities who write on the life of Richard III necessarily have to discuss the fate of the princes, one of whom was Richard's predecessor as king, and thus have to weigh and assess the various theories and possibilities about the demise of the princes and Richard's involvement in their end. The situation here is thus quite different from, say, the subject of the identity of 'Jack the Ripper' or the assassination of President Kennedy, which academic historians almost invariably avoid discussing or debating. It is almost the precise opposite of the situation of English literature university academics and the 'Shakespeare Authorship Question', which is regarded as literally taboo. The probable reason for this is because academic writers on Richard III are historians, and the fate of the princes is a matter of legitimate historical debate, however much non-academic historians have figured prominently in shaping this debate. One might add that *most* recent academic historians clearly believe that the weight of evidence strongly points to Richard III's guilt.

Apart from his supposed murder of the two princes, Richard's image has, for centuries, been coloured by the 'black legend' which surrounds his life, beginning with the purported two-year pregnancy of his mother, and his (quite apocryphal) hideous appearance as a hunchback. It is thus important to set out a brief account of his life.[4] Richard was born at Fotheringay Castle, Northamptonshire, in October 1452, the fourth surviving son of Richard Plantagenet, third Duke of York, and Cecily Neville, daughter of Ralph Nevill, first Earl of Westmoreland and cousin of Richard Neville, 'Warwick the Kingmaker'. His elder brother Edward (1442–83) reigned as King Edward IV from 1461 until his death (with the exception of a brief period when the former Lancastrian king, Henry VI, was restored to the throne). There is no evidence that he had a withered arm or a hunchback – none whatever. Richard spent much of his childhood at Middleham Castle, Yorkshire – not London – under the supervision of his uncle, 'Warwick the Kingmaker', and later married his daughter Anne, by whom he had one son, Edward Plantagenet (or Edward of Middleham, 1473–84). He also had a number of illegitimate children. Richard was instrumental in assisting his elder brother Edward IV to defeat 'Warwick the Kingmaker' at the Battle of Barnet in 1471. As a result he received most of Warwick's vast holdings in the north of England and, as well, the hand of Anne, whom, according to Shakespeare in Richard III, he subsequently poisoned. (There is no evidence that her death

Figure 5.1 Richard III: King Richard III, depicted here, certainly killed many on his way to the throne, but did he have his two nephews murdered? Some think not. Getty Images/ Hulton Archive

was anything but natural.[5]) He was created Duke of Gloucester. Edward IV also had Henry VI, the deposed, restored, and deposed Lancastrian king, murdered in the Tower in 1471. In 1477 Richard's irrational older brother George, Duke of Clarence, was indicted for treason, condemned by Parliament, and murdered in the Tower, allegedly by being drowned in a butt of malmsey wine. In the meantime Richard built up a vast empire in the north of England as successor to 'Warwick the Kingmaker'; he also acquired the confiscated lands of other nobles.[6] There, he built up a coterie of loyalists from the north and became a virtual sovereign there, continuing to enjoy his brother's favour. Richard lived chiefly at Middleham Castle and other northern estates, visiting London only infrequently. He successfully fought the Scots and was given the headship of a new county palatine to be created in the north of England and southern Scotland. In the north, he was regarded as a hero and champion, and helped the region economically and in other ways. Then, as later, the north of England was something of a poor relation to London and the more prosperous south, and Richard held something like a unique status as a great champion of the region.

On 9 April 1483 Edward IV unexpectedly died at the age of only forty, and, at the age of twelve his son became Edward V. Edward V's mother, the widow of Edward IV, was Elizabeth Woodville (or Wydeville, *c.*1437–92), the daughter of a minor gentry knight (but the granddaughter of a duke). Elizabeth Woodville, as queen, had become enormously powerful. Her father, Sir Richard Woodville, had been made Earl Rivers; her son by a previous marriage to Sir John Grey was made Marquess of Dorset; a sister had married Henry, Duke of Buckingham, a royal relative and descendant of John of Gaunt. Power in Britain quickly became the subject of an intense conflict between the Woodvilles, who expected to continue ruling under the new King, and Richard, who immediately organised an anti-Woodville coalition consisting of himself, the Duke of Buckingham, and William, Lord Hastings, another powerful magnate.[7] A royal council meeting agreed to name Richard as 'Lord Protector' of the kingdom, holding *de facto* executive authority, until Edward V was deemed old enough to rule by himself, within no more than about three years. Richard feared, probably with good reason, that at that point the young king's mother and her family would assert their authority and remove Richard from all of his power and wealth, almost certainly hastening his journey into the next world as well. Over the next few months, April through July 1483, Richard engaged in a war to the death with the Woodville faction on which his reputation as a monster is largely based. His behaviour during this brief period has been compared by anti-Ricardians with the thuggery of Don Corlione, the Mafia don in *The Godfather*.[8] It would not be too far-fetched, perhaps, to compare it with the actions of Joseph Stalin who, in the period 1934–40, killed all his rivals for supreme rule in Russia, starting with Kirov, continuing with the Old Bolsheviks, and ending with Trotsky, his exiled arch-rival. On 1 May 1483 Richard, as Lord Protector, with Buckingham's help, intercepted the new king's progress from Wales, where he had been staying, to London, arresting at Stony Stratford, the King, his guardian, the second Lord Rivers, as well as Elizabeth Woodville's son by her first marriage, Sir Richard Grey, and a loyal chamberlain, Sir Thomas Vaughan. The young King was taken to the Tower of London, never to emerge. Declaring that a treasonable conspiracy existed, Richard then (13 June) arrested and executed his former ally, Lord Hastings. He next (16 June) seized control of Edward IV's younger brother and heir presumptive, Richard of York, and had him taken to the Tower as well, also never to be seen again outside that place. On 25 June, he had Rivers, Grey, and Vaughan executed without trial. Three days earlier (22 June), the original date of Edward V's Coronation, he had Friar Ralph Shaa [Shaw], brother of the Lord Mayor of London, preach a sermon at St. Paul's Cross (just outside the Cathedral) in which he made the startling claim that Edward IV's marriage to Elizabeth Woodville had been illegal, as he had been pre-betrothed to another woman, Lady Eleanor Butler. Hence, argued Shaa, the two sons of Edward IV were illegitimate and ineligible to succeed to the throne, and Richard, Edward IV's brother, was the rightful King. On 25 June, the date of the execution of Lord Rivers and two others, a group of lords, knights, and leading citizens assembled at Castle Baynard in London to proclaim Richard the rightful king. Richard's northern army of 4000 men then (2 or 3 July) arrived in London, and on 3 July Richard was crowned as King. In the meantime, Elizabeth Woodville had taken sanctuary in Westminster Abbey. It was in the summer of 1483 that the two princes apparently disappeared from sight and, according to most writers, were murdered.

Before turning to the apparent deaths of the two princes in the Tower, something should be said, very briefly, of the rest of Richard's reign. In October 1483 a rebellion broke out to put Henry Tudor, the Lancastrian royal candidate, on the throne. It was led by Richard's former ally the Duke of Buckingham. Richard easily suppressed the rebellion and put Buckingham to death. In April 1484 Richard's son and heir, Edward, Prince of Wales, died suddenly, causing great sorrow to him and his Queen, Anne Nevill, who herself died in March 1485. Many, including Shakespeare, believed that Richard had poisoned her. In the meantime Richard gave many prominent positions to his northern associates, leading to his increasing unpopularity in the south of England. His unpopularity is well-known to us from the famous doggerel verse about Richard's reign by William Collingbourne, 'The Cat, the Rat, and Lovell the Dog / Ruleth all England under a Hog', allusions to three of Richard's deputies, William Catesby, Sir Richard Ratcliffe, and Francis, Viscount Lovell, and to Richard's personal emblem, a Boar. In fairness, however, it should be noted that Richard enacted much useful legislation during his reign, and was certainly popular in the north of England and with much of the ruling elite.[9]

In August 1485, however, Henry Tudor, with the *de facto* backing of French forces and the support of both the resident Lancastrians and the Woodville faction, landed at Milford Haven and at Bosworth on 22 August 1485, somewhat unexpectedly defeated Richard and his forces, helped crucially by the defection to his side of some key noblemen. Richard was killed, apparently demanding a horse, but certainly not promising his kingdom in exchange. Henry Tudor was proclaimed Henry VII, married Elizabeth Woodville's daughter as promised, and founded the Tudor dynasty. His reign (1485–1509) is often seen by historians as the first of 'modern' or 'early modern' as opposed to 'medieval' history. He greatly improved the royal and governmental finances, weakened the chronically seditious nobility, ended the 'War of the Roses' between Lancastrians and Yorkists, and put in place the conditions which, under his son Henry VIII and his granddaughter Elizabeth I, would lead to the Protestant Reformation and England's emergence as a great power with a worldwide empire.

In spite of the dark side of Richard III's reign, it is important to keep in mind that, despite appearances, he was not, in normal circumstances, a murderous, sadistic psychopath. Virtually all historians agree that his years as *de facto* viceroy in the north of England, and the brief period of relative stability during his reign, were almost models of constructive achievement in the context of late medieval English society. It is, indeed, the very incongruity between Richard the constructive ruler of his country and Richard the merciless assassin of all who stood in his way, which makes it so difficult to offer a fair or reasonable assessment of his character. It is also important to keep in mind that the fifteenth century was an age of dynastic violence, when the heads of royals and noblemen rolled like apples falling from a tree. While Richard might well have been the worst of his kind, he was far from unique. On the other hand, the murder of children, let alone those one was pledged by oath to protect and to whom one was closely related, was certainly regarded as beyond the pale, even by the brutal standards of the time.

Our evidence for what might or might not have happened to the princes comes from a number of key sources by contemporaries and near-contemporaries. Crucially, however, there is no known primary, eyewitness evidence concerning the supposed killing of the princes. These sources have also helped to form our understanding of Richard's reign as a whole. They include, especially, the *Croyland Chronicle*, written at an abbey in

Figure 5.2 The two princes. Mary Evans Picture Library/Douglas McCarthy

Lincolnshire by anonymous authors. Its so-called 'second continuer' wrote one of our most important accounts of these events. He was evidently well-informed, and greatly disliked Richard. The most popular candidate as its author is John Russell, Bishop of Lincoln, who held senior governmental offices under both Edward IV and Richard III.[10] Several foreign visitors and commentators of the time also left accounts of Richard III and his reign. One was Philippe de Commeynes in his *Memoirs*, dictated about 1490. Commeynes was a major figure at the court of Louis XI. Another was Dominic Mancini, an Italian monk resident in France who was in London for three months in 1483, between the death of Edward IV and the Coronation of Richard III, when he returned to France.[11] Mancini left a Latin account of English royal politics at the time, translated as *The Occupation of the Throne of England by Richard III.* This important work remained unknown until 1934, when it was discovered in a library in Lille.[12] Mancini was also a well-informed and probably reliable source. Because Mancini's work was unknown until the 1930s, it was of course not used or taken into account by the first historians, such as Horace Walpole and Sir Clements R. Markham, who attempted to revise the traditional black depiction of Richard and his deeds. While other much briefer relevant accounts of or remarks on the fate of the princes also exist, two works, both written a generation later, are primarily responsible for forming the 'black legend' of Richard's wickedness. These were Polydore Vergil's *Anglica Historica* (1533) and the *History of Richard III* by Sir Thomas More, Henry VIII's famous Chancellor, who was executed in 1535. More's work was first published in an altered form in 1549 and in an authentic form in 1557.[13] Vergil, an Italian monk, lived in England from 1502 until 1551 (he died in Italy in 1555). His work was commissioned by Henry VII and dedicated to Henry VIII; Vergil came to England seventeen years after Richard's death. He was, thus, not a reporter of events he witnessed at first hand and his work, though regarded as thorough and reliable, was, by definition, given its origins and dedication, highly biased. To an even greater extent, More's work (which some historians do not believe was written by him) is an unrelieved anti-Ricardian account, bordering on open propaganda, and was essentially the basis of the 'black legend' of Richard's wickedness taken over by Shakespeare. More was born in 1478, and was thus seven years old at the time of the Battle of Bosworth. Between about 1515 and 1532 he worked for the Tudor monarch and, however honourable, can hardly be described as a neutral historian. The seal was placed on the 'black legend', probably for all time, by Shakespeare's *Richard III*, usually dated to 1591. By the orthodox dating of his works, Richard III was arguably Shakespeare's first truly memorable stage character, the archetypal villain. The Bard's depiction of Richard should be seen as a step in his progress as a dramatist, between the discursive characterisation of his very early plays and the equally memorable but much more ambiguous central characters in such works as *The Merchant of Venice*, *Hamlet*, and *Macbeth*. Arguably Shakespeare never depicted as unambiguously evil a character in his plays again until Iago in *Othello*, generally dated to 1604. Shakespeare's *Richard* must surely have been an unquestioned crowd pleaser and draw card, as his play has remained to this day.

A reaction to the 'black legend' did set in with such works as Sir George Buck's *History of Richard III*, written in 1619, giving an emphatically favourable view of the king.[14] The first attempt to write a coherent 'revisionist' account of Richard's life and reign is usually said to have been made by Horace Walpole (son of Sir Robert Walpole, Britain's first Prime Minister) in his *Historic Doubts on the Life and Reign of King Richard the*

Third of 1768. Walpole focused on the inadequacies and outright errors of previous anti-Ricardian historians. Walpole did, however, make his own share of mistakes, in particular his misreading of a Wardrobe account for Richard's Coronation which in his view related to Edward V, allegedly proving that Edward was still alive in mid-1483. It is now generally believed that this is not a reference to Edward V.[15] During the nineteenth and early twentieth centuries a major outpouring of 'revisionist' works appeared, especially Caroline Halstead's two-volume *Richard III as Duke of Gloucester and King of England* (1844) and Sir Clements R. Markham's *Richard III: His Life and Character* (1906), both of which frankly attempt to refute the 'black legend'. As noted, the 'revisionist' school broke through to generate widespread popular publicity with *The Daughter of Time.* Most recent historians, both academic and popular, have attempted a more balanced view than in the past. Few historians now accept the 'black legend' in its entirety, although the majority, as noted, reach the conclusion that Richard probably killed the princes. The various pro-Ricardian works of modern times did lead to the development of the Richard the Third Society and other groups devoted to restoring his good name.

With these historiographical traditions in mind, the question of the killing of the princes in the Tower can be brought into closer focus.[16] It might be useful to present a time-table of the events surrounding the boys' disappearance:

9 April 1483 – Edward IV dies; Edward V succeeds.

1 May 1483 – Richard and Buckingham seize Edward V and his entourage at Stony Stratford

By 8 May1483 – Richard recognised as 'Lord Protector'.

13 May 1483 – Richard seizes and executes Lord Hastings.

16 May 1483 – Richard gains protection of Prince Richard (Edward V's brother) and sends him to the Tower.

22 June 1483 – The sermon by Ralph Shaa proclaiming the two princes illegitimate and Richard the rightful King.

25 June 1483 – Execution of Rivers, Grey and Vaughan.

25–26 June 1483 – Richard proclaimed King.

6 July 1483 – Richard III's Coronation.

8 September 1483 – Creation of Richard's son Edward as Prince of Wales.

2 November 1483 – Execution of Buckingham.

These dates should be kept in mind when considering the precise dates when the alleged killing or disappearance of the two princes was first known to various contemporaries or near-contemporaries:[17]

'Not long after' 13 June 1483 ('before [Richard] claimed the throne') – George Cely, a London merchant, heard that Edward V might be dead. He was reporting frequently-heard rumours in London.

Around 20–25 June 1483 – The princes 'smothered about five weeks after they were imprisoned' (Jean Molinet, writing in 1500). This must be around 20–25 June 1483 as Prince Richard was seized in 16 May 1483.

'Late July or August 1483' – Sir Thomas More's date of the murders.

Before mid-July 1483 – Mancini, before he left England in mid-July 1483, stated that the princes 'were withdrawn into the inner apartments of the Tower proper and day by day began to be seen more and more rarely behind the bars and windows, till at length they ceased to appear altogether.'

Before September 1483 – The *Croyland Chronicle* (1486) stated that a rumour arose in September 1483 that the princes were dead.

By 30 July 1483 – John Rous (1489) stated that the princes had been killed within three months of Richard gaining control of Edward V on 30 April 1483.

22 June 1483 – The precise date of Edward V's death, according to the Anlaby family cartulary (written after 1509).

By 30 August 1483 – King Louis XI of France reportedly knew about the princes' death by this date, when he himself died.

By 15 September 1483 – The two princes were put to death before this date, according to Robert Ricard, recorder of Bristol.

Other, similar dates are also given in contemporary or near-contemporary sources. A number of points are evident from this array of citations. There was, clearly, a widespread belief that the princes were dead by the second half of 1483. Reports to this effect were noted throughout England and overseas. The belief that the princes were dead certainly had gained wide currency well before Richard III was deposed, and well before they could have been the product of 'Tudor propaganda'. On the other hand, although there was, apparently, a common belief that Richard had killed his nephews, he was not universally accused of murdering them, and there are no known eyewitness accounts of their murder. The 'confession' by Sir James Tyrell in 1502, reported by More, has never been found, and More's work is apparently our only source which claims he confessed.[18] Richard, however, had assuredly engaged in a ruthless and illegal plot to seize the throne, and the killing of the princes at this time would have been consistent with his other actions. If Richard had indeed had the princes killed (no one, of course, suggests that he killed them with his own hands), a date just before or just after his proclamation as King on 25–26 June 1483 seems most likely. 22 June 1483, the date given in the Anlaby family cartulary, might well be accurate. The most likely conclusion from all this is that Richard probably killed the princes, as part of his blood-stained plot to gain the throne, just before or just after he was proclaimed King. However, the evidence is not crystal clear, and, while very strong, is probably not enough to convict Richard beyond a reasonable doubt. Nevertheless, the evidence suggests a strong presumption of his guilt. Compared with the variety of contemporary and near-contemporary sources which assert that the princes died at this time, there is almost nothing of a credible nature which claims that they died at another time. In 1486 a Spanish merchant, Diego de Valera, asserted that Richard poisoned the princes while Edward IV was still alive.[19] This is plainly false. No one seriously asserted *at the time* that Henry VII found the princes alive and murdered them. This theory, the basis of *The Daughter of Time*, was not propounded until centuries later. In Henry VII's reign, two impostors came forward claiming to be one or another of the princes, Perkin Warbeck and Lambert Simnel. It is *possible* though most unlikely, that Perkin was Prince Richard, spared by the murderer and secretly taken abroad. Few historians, however, accept this any more than they accept the veracity of the claims made about Lambert Simnel, who was put forward as a claimant to the throne by the Earl of Lincoln in his rebellion of 1487.[20] Some contemporaries thought that the princes were still alive (see below).

The case for and against Richard III being the murderer of his nephews might be set out in the following way. First, the case for his being the killer:

1. The princes disappeared from public sight in 1483 while in the Tower, under Richard III's direct protection and supervision, and were never seen again. Richard gave no explanation of their fate, nor ever produced them in public, although they had been declared illegitimate, and hence ineligible for the throne, by Parliament. In 1483, they simply vanished, after certainly being held hostage in the Tower of London.
2. Virtually every contemporary and near-contemporary source known to us at the very least suggests that the princes disappeared at this time, while many claim frankly that they were murdered at Richard's behest. Some of these claims were made by well-informed foreign sources, who could not plausibly have been enunciating 'Tudor propaganda'. *No* serious contemporary or near-contemporary source known to us claims that the princes were still alive at the time of the Battle of Bosworth in 1485.
3. If the princes were killed at Richard's behest, this was consistent with an unquestioned and extraordinarily brutal campaign by Richard to kill off his enemies and potential rivals. Most of these were members of the Woodville family or their associates, as were the princes.
4. Richard in fact became King in June 1483, but his mandate was not universally accepted. If Edward V (the older of the princes in the Tower) ceased being King and Edward's brother Richard ceased being Heir Presumptive, they would cease forever to be the clearest and most direct threat to his continued reign as king. Alive, they could readily act as the fount of discontent and sedition, at any time.

5. It is difficult to see how, in the period 1483–85, anyone could have secured immediate and personal access to the princes in the Tower of London without Richard's knowledge and consent. Indeed, it is difficult to see how anyone, apart from immediate and trusted retainers, could possibly have met with or spoken to the princes without Richard's knowledge and consent.
6. If, in 1483–85, the princes died of natural causes or were murdered by someone not acting at Richard's behest, it is difficult to see why Richard would conceal this fact or fail to make it public knowledge. If someone murdered the princes without Richard's approval, it is difficult to see why Richard would not have them immediately tried and executed.
7. Elizabeth Woodville, the mother of the princes, would not have supported Henry Tudor as king, or agreed to have him marry her daughter, if she thought the princes were still alive. At Rennes in late 1483, Henry Tudor promised, if placed on the throne, to marry Princess Elizabeth, the sister of the princes. His promise came, it is believed, as a result of negotiations between his mother (Margaret Beaufort) and Elizabeth Woodville, the former Queen and mother of the princes.[21] There are contemporary accounts of Elizabeth Woodville's grief at hearing that her sons were dead. Quite plainly, Elizabeth Woodville would not have entered into negotiations with Henry Tudor, whose claims to the throne were to say the least remote, unless she believed, in late 1483, that her sons were dead.
8. Richard's behaviour after the apparent murder of the princes in mid-late 1483 is consistent with his feeling guilt and remorse at his deeds, especially after the death of his own son. His guilt and remorse might well have contributed to the apparent incompetence which marked the closing phase of his life.
9. *Most* academic historians writing during the past sixty years have concluded that, on the balance of evidence, it is likely that Richard ordered the murder of the princes. So, too, have many excellent recent non-academic historians, nearly all of whom have consulted all the relevant extant sources.
10. In 1674, two skeletons were discovered buried in the Tower of London; they were immediately supposed to have been the two princes, and were reburied in Westminster Abbey as such in 1678. The two skeletons were of youths (whose sex cannot be definitively identified) of the same age

as the two Princes. In 1933 two eminent physicians reexamined the skeletons and concluded they were indeed those of the two princes.[22] Ideally, one would wish for another examination of these remains using today's forensic techniques; Westminster Abbey has not, thus far, allowed another exhumation. But if these are not the skeletons of the two princes, whose could they possibly be?

While this seems compelling, there are certainly some arguments which might be made against the proposition that Richard killed his nephews:

1. Once Richard was officially proclaimed King in mid-1483, he had no reason to fear, let alone kill, the princes, whom Parliament had officially declared to be bastards ineligible for the throne.
2. No eyewitness account or other plainly authentic and trustworthy report of the killing of the princes exist. All supposed accounts of their deaths either report contemporary rumours or were written after Henry VII became King, when anything other than heaping villainy on Richard III's reputation was extremely dangerous, let alone blaming Henry Tudor for their deaths.
3. Once Henry Tudor became King as Henry VII, he manifestly had every reason to blacken Richard III's name and reputation in every possible way. It seems reasonable to conclude that he, and subsequent Tudor monarchs, encouraged slurs and defamations of Richard's reputation. Yet it is noteworthy that in enumerating Richard's crimes and deficiencies, he was never *officially* accused of murdering the princes. It is also reasonable to suggest that, for many years, anyone offering a 'revisionist' view of Richard's character would have been made shorter by the head.
4. Almost as a matter of course, the common view of Richard's character has derived, in modern times, from Shakespeare's play. Yet its depiction of Richard as a murderous arch-fiend without parallel in English history is assuredly a grotesque pastiche. Virtually no modern historian would accept it as an accurate view of Richard's character, and virtually all modern historians would give a much more balanced and positive view of his character. Many of the incidents depicted in Shakespeare's play (beginning with his depiction of Richard as a hunchback) are, in fact, pure fiction or unarguable factual distortions. Richard, moreover, suffered during his lifetime and in the period following it as being a

northerner (and highly regarded in the north of England) who did much to offend and dismay England's dominant southern elite.

5. Richard, both as Duke of Gloucester and as King, was, on the contrary, an enlightened nobleman and ruler who was highly religious, encouraged learning and charity, and introduced useful reforms. Almost everything known of his actual behaviour as a leader is inconsistent with the Shakespearean portrayal of his character.
6. Much about Henry VII's behaviour in regards to the question of the killing of the princes is deeply suspicious. He gave two pardons to Sir Henry Tyrell in 1486 (on 15 June and 17 July).[23] Some pro-Ricardian writers have speculated that the second pardon was specifically for killing the princes in mid-*1486*. Tyrell's 'confession' to the crime of killing the princes, while assisting executions in May 1502 for treason (for aiding the Yorkist rebel the Duke of Suffolk), is very difficult to accept at face value. No written copy of it exists and we know of it through the writings of Sir Thomas More.[24] *Why* would Tyrell confess to killing the princes nineteen years after their purported deaths if he was already going to be executed for treason? And why did Henry VII not publicly announce Tyrell's confession in 1502, if there actually was one? Even beyond Henry Tudor, there are other candidates, especially Richard's kinsman, Henry Stafford, second Duke of Buckingham (1455–83) who might conceivably have killed the boys. This possibility was asserted by contemporaries.[25] Even apart from the two impostors, it is also just possible that they were still alive, as was actually believed at the time.[26]
7. The 'skeletons of the two princes' (as they have been described) found in the Tower in 1674, might well have been of the princes, but the medical examination carried out of these remains in 1933 is now widely seen as quite inadequate in the light of more recent scientific advances, while it is important to note that the cause of death of the two persons (of indeterminate sex, although probably of a similar age to the two princes in 1483) was not determinable from the remains.
8. The belief that Richard did *not* murder the princes effectively originated only in the late nineteenth century, when an objective and dispassionate examination of Richard's life and the primary sources for the period became possible. Since then, a steady stream of obviously intelligent and careful historians and writers have concluded that it is unlikely that Richard had the princes killed.

On balance, to reiterate, it seems highly likely that Richard killed the boys, probably just before he was proclaimed King. Nevertheless, his guilt is not unarguable and self-evident, especially in the light of most, but not all, modern research, and the mystery continues. It will doubtless continue for ever, unless some totally unexpected document comes to hand which ends the controversy.

The continuing fascination of Richard and the princes has also been recognised in the twentieth century with the establishment of the Richard III Society and other groups devoted to restoring his memory and, as well, popularising the era of the War of the Roses. The Richard III Society has as its 'Mission Statement' the 'belief that many features of the traditional accounts of the character and career of Richard III are neither supported by sufficient evidence nor reasonably tenable', and that the society will 'promote, in every possible way, research into the life and times of Richard III, and to secure a reassessment' of his career.[27] This might well have been interpreted as entailing a one-sided effort to find Richard innocent, but – to its credit – the society has been scrupulously fair in presenting all the evidence surrounding his supposed misdeeds. Even more significantly, it has published or republished a veritable library of new and old scholarly and serious writing on Richard III and his times in the manner of an academic historical society. The society was founded in 1924 by a Liverpool surgeon, Saxon Barton, and some of his friends who were 'enthusiastic amateur historians ... [with] a belief that history had not dealt justly with the king's posthumous reputation and they wanted to promote a more balanced view.'[28] It was originally named 'The Fellowship of the White Boar' (named for Richard's emblem), but declined over the next few decades. It was revived in the 1950s as a direct result of the influence of Josephine Tey's novel.[29] The society continued to grow and in 1980 acquired H.R.H. the Duke of Gloucester – Richard's title when he became king – as its patron. It now has 3500 members around the world, and engages in a remarkably wide range of activities.[30] It is composed of no fewer than twenty-eight local branches in Britain, and overseas branches in America, Canada, New Zealand, and five Australian states.[31] Since 1974 the society has published *The Ricardian*, an excellent quarterly journal, and the *Ricardian Bulletin*. *The Ricardian* is particularly notable in that its articles are seldom tendentious defences of Richard's character, but scholarly and semi-scholarly articles, often deeply researched and highly objective.[32] The society has also published or republished many classic works on Richard and his times, and holds a triennial conference which includes papers by leading academics as well as non-academic historians. The society also has endowed two bursaries (scholarships) at York University and the Institute of Historical Research in London, and hosts a range of other activities.[33] This remarkable organisation clearly represents the best and most valuable face of 'amateur history', and is a model of its kind. It is, regrettably, almost impossible to imagine that Stratfordian and anti-Stratfordian authors and academics, or orthodox Christian theologians and advocates of unorthodox theories about Jesus, would ever cooperate n this manner.

Chapter 6

Did Jesus Marry and Survive the Crucifixion?

Had this book been written thirty years ago, it is most unlikely that a chapter on whether Jesus Christ had married, produced offspring, and possibly survived the crucifixion would have been included.[1] The tremendous interest in and outpouring of non-academic works on these subjects, several of which have become international best-sellers, is almost wholly a product of the period since about 1980. Although some relevant predecessor works (such as Hugh Schonfield's *The Passover Plot* of 1965) predate 1980, world-wide interest in this topic can be dated fairly precisely to the publication of *The Holy Blood and the Holy Grail* by Michael Baigent, Richard Leigh, and Henry Lincoln in 1982. Baigent (b.1948) is a New Zealand-born teacher and writer; Leigh (b.1943), an American-born novelist; and Lincoln (b.1930), a London-born writer and television presenter. In 1969, Lincoln purchased by chance a French paperback book, *Le Trésor Maudit* [*The Accursed Treasure*] by Gérard de Sède, which told of secret documents found and decoded in the 1890s by Béranger Saunière (1852–1917), a French priest who became curé of Rennes-le-Château in the French Pyrenees. Rennes-le-Château is a tiny, almost inaccessible village near Carcasonne in an area associated in the Middle Ages with the heretical Cathar sect. The book in

Figure 6.1 Abbé Bérenger Saunière. Mary Evans Picture Library

question hinted at the meaning of these mysterious documents, but did not reveal them.[2] Lincoln thought that the story of Rennes-le-Château might be worth a television script, and met with its author, who declined to reveal the secret, insisting that Lincoln discover it himself from the coded messages in the book. The French book revolved around the fact that Saunière, hitherto living in poverty, had become enormously wealthy as a result of his possession of secret documents, apparently dating from the Middle Ages, which he had unearthed and deciphered while carrying out repairs to his old, remote church. Discovering these allowed him to find a secret treasure. Lincoln presented a television documentary on this, *The Lost Treasure of Jerusalem?* In February1972, three years later, Lincoln began to collaborate with Richard Leigh, who had a long-standing interest in Rennes-le-Château and its mysteries; from 1977, the pair also collaborated with Michael Baigent, who was researching the Knights Templar, the medieval crusading order apparently also connected with the Cathars and Rennes-le-Château. After his 1972 documentary, Lincoln received a large volume of correspondence. The strangest and most important came from a retired Anglican priest (not

Figure 6.2 Rennes-le-Château in southern France, now central to most unorthodox theories about Jesus of Nazareth. Getty Images/Roger Viollet

named in *The Holy Blood and the Holy Grail*, although later revealed to be Rev. Douglas Bartlett) who stated that the 'treasure' found by Saunière was not a material one, but was rather 'incontrovertible proof' that Jesus did not die on the Cross but was alive as late as 45 A.D.[3] Over the next few years, the three collaborators produced two more television documentaries and, with much effort and research, discovered the existence of a secret society, the Priory of Sion, allegedly founded in 1090 by Godfrey de Bouillon, who were guardians of the secret of Jesus's survival. (It allegedly separated from its parent body, the Knights Templar, in 1188.) Jesus did not merely survive but also fathered children by Mary Magdalene, who was in fact his wife. His descendants, in France, became the ancestors of the Merovingian dynasty, which ruled most of what is now France and Germany between A.D. 447 and 750. Much of the information about the Priory of Sion (*Prieuré de Sion*) came to the three collaborators from Pierre Plantard (1920–2000), a mysterious Frenchman with a deep knowledge of esoterica, the occult, secret societies, and royal genealogies, whose aim was seemingly to restore a descendant of the Merovingians (preferably himself) to the throne of a unified Europe. The Priory of Sion had been headed by twenty-three Grand Masters, all known officially as 'John', followed by successive numbers, John XXIII being the most recent. Their number included Leonardo da Vinci, Botticelli (Sandro Filipepi), Sir Isaac Newton, Victor Hugo, Claude Debussy, and Jean Cocteau, as well as a long line of continental noblemen. Apart from Newton, three other Englishmen have headed the Priory: Robert Fludd (1595–1637), Robert Boyle, the eminent scientist (1654–91), and Charles Radclyffe (1727–46), a Jacobite nobleman in exile. What all of those on this curious list had in common was a deep interest in the occult, alchemy, secret societies, and the like.[4]

Although this rather remarkable series of claims is often considered as a single coherent narrative, it will be seen that it is actually composed of a number of very different factual claims which are quite independent of one another. To enumerate, there is a claim that, in the 1890s, an obscure Catholic priest in a village in the French Pyrenees became enormously wealthy through his discovery of secret documents in his church; that these documents disclosed that Jesus had married, survived the Crucifixion, and fathered the ancestors of the Merovingian dynasty; that these secrets were known to a mysterious secret society, the Priory of Sion, which has been headed by an often-renowned Grand Master; and that – most crucially – Jesus *did* marry, survive the Crucifixion, and beget children. None of these claims is actually dependent on any of the others; all or any may be false or true, and should be considered independently. All of these claims were the product of non-academics; with the rarest of exceptions, university theologians and historians have had no truck with anything as unorthodox and improbable as Rennes-le-Château.

It is therefore useful to consider these points one by one. There is no evidence that Sauniére's new-found wealth had anything to do with his secret discoveries. According to *The Holy Blood and the Holy Gail*, in 1891 Saunière began to carry out a restoration of his church (built in 1059 on an even earlier site) and, in the renovations of the altar, found four old parchments concealed therein, dating to 1244, 1644, and the 1780s. After consulting the local bishop Saunière brought these parchments to the Seminary St. Sulpice in Paris for examination. (He also allegedly bought reproductions of paintings by Teniers and Poussin, mentioned in the parchments.) On returning to Rennes-le-Château, Saunière behaved strangely. Among other things he defaced inscriptions on gravestones and amassed a collection of apparently worthless piles of rocks from the countryside. He also began a voluminous correspondence with persons throughout Europe and opened several bank accounts. By 1896 he was extremely wealthy, redecorating his local church with bizarre religious drawings but also improving conditions in the local village. Eventually the local bishop, suspecting that Saunière was illegally selling masses, suspended him; Saunière appealed and his suspension was overturned by the Vatican. It is also said that the priest who attended him on his deathbed refused to administer the last rites to him.[5] What Saunière actually found is still as much a matter of dispute as how he became so wealthy. In Michael Baigent's 2006 book, *The Jesus Papers*, however, the author, one of the three writers of *The Holy Blood and the Holy Grail* (published twenty-four years earlier), states that 'we now know that there were two sources of his funds'. The first was 'the Hapsburg wife of Henri de Chambord, the [Bourbon] pretender to the French throne during the nineteenth century. This money was passed over to Saunière for a specific task which he carried out.'[6] But 'having tasted wealth, Saunière then embarked upon a more venal money-making exercise: trafficking in masses – simony – a crime in the Catholic Church.'[7] In the 1980s, Baigent and his co-authors were given 'access to a wooden chest once owned by Saunière that contained the daily financial records of his business', by the French internal security organisation.[8] Saunière's career in trafficking masses extended from the late 1890s until the early 1900s, when it apparently stopped.[9]

As with almost everything in this saga, one has the feeling that not all has been revealed. After the mid-1890s, Saunière allegedly spent the equivalent of millions of dollars; plainly, neither of these sources can account for wealth on this scale. But more significantly, neither source has any apparent connection with the secret of Jesus' survival. Indeed, the linkages between Saunière and the great secret appear tenuous. As noted, the three authors of *The Holy Blood and the Holy Grail* were first informed of a possible linkage by an Anglican vicar, Rev. Dr. Douglas William Guest Bartlett, after the 1972 television broadcast on Saunière. In an unsolicited letter to them, Guest claimed that 'The clues left behind by the good curé [Saunière] have never been understood, but it is clear from the script [of the document proving that Jesus was alive in A.D. 45] that a substitution was carried out by extreme zealots on the journey to the place of execution. The document was exchanged [presumably by Saunière] for a very large sum and concealed or destroyed.'[10] A visit with Rev. Bartlett, then resident in Leafield, Oxfordshire, revealed that in 1930, when living in Oxford, he had met and become friendly with Canon Alfred Lilley (1860–1948), who, until his retirement in 1936, was Canon and Chancellor of Hereford Cathedral and an expert on medieval French, on which he was often consulted. The two men became friendlier and Lilley revealed to Bartlett an extraordinary secret. In the early 1890s he had been asked by a former pupil of his to travel to the Seminary of Saint Sulpice in Paris to advise on the translation of a 'strange document', possibly at one time in the possession of the Cathars of southern France.[11] The document had so shaken Lilley that, by the end of his life, he had lost his conviction in the truth of the Gospels.[12] Nothing more is known of the nature of this document except that, as noted, it offered 'incontrovertible evidence' that Jesus was alive in A.D. 45. Bartlett believes that it is likely to have been destroyed by the Vatican, or perhaps still held there in the most secret of Vatican secret archives.

Essentially, this strange story is the only thing, and certainly the most potentially believable assertion, to identify Saunière's secret with the survival of Jesus. Presumably, Lilley's trip to Saint Sulpice was to view the materials brought there from Rennes-le-Château by Saunière, but even that should not be taken for granted: it is not clear whether Lilley actually mentioned Saunière's name to Bartlett, or even knew it; Saunière remained totally unknown in the English-speaking world until the 1972 television programme. Even apart from the story being virtually incredible *per se*, it contains many very curious features. It is far from clear why or whether an English Protestant vicar would be brought to Paris, in the 1890s, to assist a Catholic seminary with translating from medieval French: were there no experts in medieval French in France? If the document in question was written in medieval French (presumably deriving from the Cathars), it must date from roughly 1000 years after the Crucifixion; it is difficult to see how any such document could constitute 'incontrovertible evidence' that Jesus survived. 'Incontrovertible evidence' must surely date from the first century A.D., and have been written in Latin, Greek, or Hebrew, languages which the seminary's faculty would surely have no trouble in reading. To constitute 'incontrovertible evidence', any such document must have had to pass a battery of scientific tests as to its authenticity, some of which, for example ascertaining the chemical constitution of its ink, might have been available in the 1890s, but many of which were devised only much later. If in the 1890s Canon Lilley indeed found 'incontrovertible evidence' that the Crucifixion and Resurrection – the central doctrines of Christianity – never occurred, it is also difficult to understand why he embarked on a forty-year career in the Church of England, rising to a senior position and writing many works of Christian apologetics.[13] Without knowing far more about what Lilley actually saw than the tantalising titbit made known to the three authors by Rev. Bartlett, it is impossible to do more than set out what he is quoted as saying and note its obviously very questionable features. One might also point out that our only knowledge of what Lilley saw is an anecdote related at second hand in 1972 about a conversation which took place forty-two years earlier, concerning a document read in France thirty-five years or more before that: hardly the most reliable evidence one could hope for, however honourable and intelligent these two men might have been.

Baigent suggests that what Lilley saw might have been relevant to 'a curious statement in the works of the Roman historian Suetonius', in his history of the Emperor Claudius that 'because the Jews at Rome cause continuous disturbances at the instigation of Chrestos, he expelled them from the city', events which also took place around A.D. 45.[14] Could 'Chrestos' have been 'Christ'? Perhaps, but 'Christ' is (of course) a title, 'the anointed one', or – loosely – 'Messiah', not a proper name; moreover, it is unclear if 'Chrestos', whoever he was, instigated disturbances in Rome against the population – which would plainly have met with summary executions, not expulsions – or whether the disturbances were aimed at Chrestos himself, at his followers, or occurred between warring Jewish factions.[15] This is indeed another intriguing piece of the puzzle. One wonders if what Lilley saw was a further version of this passage from Suetonius. But if this was so, it surely does not constitute 'incontrovertible evidence' for Jesus's survival in and of itself. Moreover, the Jesus universally known from the Gospels was hardly likely to have stirred up civil 'disturbances'. By 45 A.D., too, Rome was already full of Christians (possibly including St. Peter), for whom the Crucifixion and Resurrection of Jesus was central to their faith, and for whom a living, mortal Jesus, alive and in the flesh, would have been (to put it mildly) disconcerting.

This curious passage by Suetonius is also well-known to mainstream religious scholars, and has been widely discussed.[16] No firm conclusions about it can be reached, but some points are clear. Suetonius was born about A.D. 69. His *Lives of the Caesars*, where the 'Chrestos' passage occurs, was written about A.D. 120.[17] Suetonius could thus have no first-hand knowledge of Jesus (whose Crucifixion is dated to A.D. 30–33), of events in Rome in A.D. 45, or of anyone who had a direct knowledge of 'Chrestos' the 'instigator' seventy-five years before he wrote. Whence Suetonius derived his information about 'Chrestos' is unknown: according to Robert E. Van Voorst, a Christian source is unlikely, given the passage's vagueness, and an official Roman source, perhaps the imperial archives or a police report, is more likely.[18] Contrary to what Baigent implies, this passage has been widely discussed by Christian scholars, with the consensual view being that 'Chrestos' is a garbled account, by a writer evidently unfamiliar with Christianity, of the followers of the spirit of Christ rather than an individual person – 'Chrestos' was, however, also a fairly common Greek personal name (although unknown among Jews).[19] There is no evidence that a Jewish political rebellion of any kind took place in *c.*45 A.D., and the reference might well be to Christian missionaries of Jewish background attempting to convert ordinary Romans to the new religion of Christianity.[20] Others have argued that 'Chrestos' was an unknown religious agitator, but not (of course) Jesus Christ.[21] Many scholars believe that the Jews were not expelled from Rome – for which there is no real evidence – but merely limited in their right to hold public meetings.[22] The passage by Suetonius should also be taken in conjunction with another passage by Tacitus (*c.*56–120 A.D.), the great Roman historian, whose famous *Annals* was written at almost precisely the same time as *The Lives of the Caesars*, about A.D. 116. In his Chapter 44, dealing with the Roman fire of A.D. 64, during the reign of the infamous Emperor Nero, Tacitus states

> ... *Nero substituted as culprits and punished in the most unusual ways those hated for their shameful acts, whom the crowd called 'Chrestians'* (sic). *The founder of this name, Christ, had been executed in the reign of Tiberius by the procurator Pontius Pilate. Suppressed for a time, this deadly superstition erupted again not only in Judea, but also in [Rome] ...*[23]

Most scholars regard this passage as authentic, not a later, fraudulent interpolation, although Pilate was not technically the 'procurator' of Judea but its 'prefect', the title of 'procurator' not coming into official use until A.D. 41.[24] Nevertheless, if authentic, this passage, written at virtually the same time as the statement by Suetonius, shows that a leading Roman historian certainly did not think that Jesus had survived the Crucifixion. Many variants of *The Holy Blood* ignore the possibility that Jesus might have survived the Crucifixion altogether, or accept that, while he died a normal and mortal death on the Cross, his widow and progeny survived. (This is the viewpoint in Dan Brown's novel *The Da Vinci Code*.) Nevertheless, that Jesus might have survived the Crucifixion and lived for many years afterwards is also a view frequently put both in authentic folk-traditions and in recent fringe works.

The second contention made in *The Holy Blood and Holy Grail* is that Jesus was not unmarried, as he is tacitly depicted in the New Testament, but was actually married to Mary Magdalene. According to this view, Magdalene was not a prostitute or an outcast, but Jesus's loyal follower, probably identical with Mary of Bethany, and possibly (like Jesus) of royal Hebrew lineage.[25] The Marriage at Cana depicted in the Gospel of John might well be an account of Jesus's own marriage. After the Crucifixion, Jesus (probably), but certainly Mary Magdalene and their earthly child or children, fled to France, where they continued to live. A Provençal legend indeed ties Mary Magdalene and her daughter, Sara the Egyptian (St. Sarah, the 'black madonna', regarded as the patron saint of Gypsies), the subject of a well-known annual festival every 23–25 May in the Camargue.[26] Jesus might also have had an earthly son, James.[27] To many orthodox Christians, the notion that Jesus married and fathered children was even more shocking than his alleged survival of the Crucifixion, and engendered an enormous backlash when *The Holy Blood and the Holy Grail* was published. However, the possibility that Jesus was married had been suggested many times before, for instance by Hugh Schonfield in *The Passover Plot*, published in 1965. There is nothing in the New Testament which explicitly states that Jesus was unmarried. As has been pointed out many times, rabbis – as Jesus was regarded – were expected to marry and father children as part of their religious obligations. On the other hand, in first century Palestine there were ascetic Jewish sects such as the Essenes, among whom marriage was discouraged, while many of the peripatetic and evangelical early Christian leaders, including Saints Peter and Paul, were likely to have been unmarried, as was John the Baptist. No absolutely certain view of this matter is possible.

The Holy Blood and the Holy Grail does proceed from this proposition, however, to posit a further extraordinary claim, that Jesus's descendants not merely survived but became the ancestors of the Merovingian dynasty, which ruled throughout much of France and Germany from about A.D. 447 to 750, when they were replaced by the Carolingians. The Merovingians, this theory asserts, were aware of their remarkable ancestry; after their passing, the celebrated search for the Holy Grail (the cup or chalice which held the blood of Jesus when he was pierced by a Roman spear at the Crucifixion) was actually a metaphorical search for the physical 'bloodline' (*sang real*) of Jesus and his descendants. The search for this bloodline and the safeguarding of its secret was the central motivating theme among the secretive and mystical groups and orders – the Cathars, the Knights Templar; perhaps the Freemasons; and the shadowy Priory of Sion – half-public, half-unknown and underground, which have existed since the Middle Ages and which continue to exist. The central claim made by *The Holy Blood and the Holy Gráil* is that Jesus and Mary Magdalene were the ancestors of the Merovingian dynasty.[28] Although the book presents some intriguing evidence for this conclusion, there are also many objections to it. Absolutely nothing of a definitive nature is known about the Merovingian dynasty before about A.D. 417. The Merovingians claimed descent from Noah – not surprisingly, since Noah and his family were the only humans left alive after the Flood – and also from the ancient Trojans.[29] In fact, they were almost certainly a Frankish tribe who entered western Europe ahead of the Huns.[30] The founder of the dynasty, Merovech, who died in 448, was also allegedly descended from an unidentified marine creature known as a Quinotaur.[31] The first Merovingian to be baptised as a Christian was Clovis I (the best-known ruler of the dynasty) around A.D. 496. With the best will in the world, it is very difficult not to be highly sceptical of any ancestral linkage between Jesus – assuming, of course, that he did survive and father descendants, hardly a belief enjoying universal assent – and the Merovingian dynasty, who appear to have entered western Europe, as it were, from the wrong direction. In any case, the names of the ancestors of Merovech in the 400 years – sixteen generations or so – separating him from Jesus and Mary Magdalene are, of course, a complete blank. And if Jesus *did* have descendants who lived in what is now south-western France, and if these survived and engendered further descendants, the number of their progeny must have been enormous: possibly everyone, or virtually everyone, in that region and beyond must have been descended from Jesus as well.[32]

Another central assertion in *The Holy Blood and the Holy Grail* concerns the Priory of Sion (*Prieuré de Sion*), allegedly a secret society founded in the eleventh century which existed to preserve the secret of the bloodline of Jesus and Mary Magdalene. It allegedly created the Knights Templar as its military arm and, as noted, reputedly has had twenty-six Grand Masters between 1188 and 1963. There seems absolutely no doubt that the Priory is entirely fictitious, a hoax created in 1956 by Pierre Plantard and others. It is not entirely clear why such an elaborate deception should have been created – possibly a mixture of fantasy and extreme right-wing politics – but that it is pure fiction cannot be doubted.[33] The Priory of Sion never existed, and certainly not in the form given centre stage in *The Holy Blood and the Holy Grail*. The list of its alleged Grand Masters, although certainly very cleverly constructed, contains many anomalies.[34] As noted, the Priory was allegedly headed by four Englishmen. The first was Robert Fludd (1574–1637) who reputedly served as its Grand Master from 1595 until 1637. Fludd was – later – indeed a leading English occultist. When he was supposedly chosen as head of the Priory, however, he was an unknown twenty-one-year-old student at St. John's College, Oxford, which he had entered in November 1592 and from which he graduated in February 1596. At Oxford, Fludd indeed mixed in occult circles, but was also very friendly with George Abbot, a future Archbishop of Canterbury.[35] His occult interests seem to have centred on astrology. From 1598 until 1604 he travelled on the Continent, visiting France, Germany, and Spain, and was in Avignon and other places in southern France in 1601–2. Thereafter, however, he lived in London, where he was a leading Society doctor. He later wrote a work defending Rosicrucianism (a secret organisation, similar to the Freemasons, linked by some 'bloodline of Jesus' advocates with the Priory of Sion), but he denied being involved with it or even having heard of it until 1614–15.[36] As with other alleged English heads of the Priory, Fludd's career raises the question of how he could have been the Grand Master of a secret society in France when he apparently never set foot in France after he was twenty-eight. Fludd – supposedly the successor to Leonardo da Vinci, Botticelli, and Charles, Duke of Bourbon as head of the Priory of Sion – was, as noted, an unknown twenty-one-year-old college student in a foreign country when, according to Plantard, he was selected as its head. Similar questions must be asked of Sir Isaac Newton, the illustrious scientist who was supposed to have been the Priory's Grand Master from 1691 until 1727. Newton never left England, so far as is known, and never set foot in France, spending the whole of his life between 1691 and 1727 (when he died) living at Cambridge, where he was a professor, and in London, where he was given the sinecure position of Warden of the Mint, and was also a member of Parliament. Leaving aside any other objection one might make to the notion that Newton was the Priory's Grand Master, how could he have headed a secret society in France when he never set foot in France? Similarly, Robert Boyle (1629–91), allegedly Newton's successor as Grand Master between 1654 and 1691, and another illustrious scientist, did indeed travel on the Continent between 1639 and 1644, but apparently never journeyed outside Britain or Ireland thereafter. Although the Priory had a subversive view of Christianity, based in its alleged knowledge that Jesus married and fathered a child, Boyle was a devout Evangelical Protestant, who provided in his will 'for the setting up of a series of lectures for the defence of the Christian religion against atheists and others'; these, the Boyle lectures, are still delivered each year.[37] The fourth supposed English Grand Master, Charles Radclyffe (1693–1746), Earl of Derwentwater in the Jacobite peerage, led 1727–46. He lived in France for most of his adult life but was a devout Roman Catholic (two of his aunts were nuns) who was a leading French Freemason until 1738 when the Catholic Church proscribed Freemasonry, and he resigned. Radclyffe was an ardent supporter of the Jacobite cause (restoring the Catholic House of Stuart, deposed in the 'Glorious Revolution' of 1688, to the British throne). He took part in 'the 45', the ill-fated invasion of England in 1745 by 'Bonnie Prince Charlie', the Catholic Stuart Pretender, and was captured and executed.[38] It seems inconceivable that an orthodox, believing Roman Catholic would have taken part in a body such as the Priory of Sion, let alone headed it. Other alleged Grand Masters of the Priory also seem very dubious, although – superficially – their names have been added with a good deal of cleverness. Victor Hugo, the great novelist and purportedly Grand Master from 1844 until his death in 1885, was one of the most famous Frenchmen of his time. It is extremely difficult to believe that he could have become head of a mysterious secret society without the fact being known at the time, or to his many biographers.

In fact, although intelligently conceived and researched, the purported list of the Priory's Grand Masters is pure fiction. Later, acknowledging this, Plantard came up with a second list, in 1989, of sixteen alleged Grand Masters, quite different from the initial list. This second list began with Jean-

Timoléon Negri d'Albes in 1681, included Victor Hugo, Claude Debussy, the writer and film-maker Jean Cocteau (allegedly Grand Master from 1918 until 1963) and concluded with Pierre Plantard and his son Thomas.[39] One important point which should be kept in mind is that Plantard was apparently horrified by the claims in *The Holy Blood and Holy Grail*, absolutely denying that the Merovingian kings were descended from Jesus, or that the 'secret' of Rennes-le-Château concerned the survival of Jesus or his progeny.[40] Plantard was an extreme right-wing romanticist, document forger, and fantasist whose aim, it seems, was to have himself established as the 'rightful' heir of the Merovingian dynasty, and he himself restored to the throne of France – notwithstanding the fact that France already has three other former ruling dynasties with Pretenders to the French throne and has been a republic since 1870. Plantard's goals may seem highly curious and improbable, but he did not have the *chutzpah* to claim to be descended from Jesus Christ; this was the conclusion drawn by Baigent, Lincoln, and Leigh in *The Holy Blood and the Holy Grail*, not by Plantard.

The Holy Blood and the Holy Grail became world-famous. It has sold over one million copies since its publication in 1982 – possibly more than any book about the Christian religion apart from the Bible itself – and appeared in a revised edition in 1996 and a coffee-table-sized illustrated edition in 2005. Rennes-le-Château, hitherto an unknown village in the French Pyrenees (whose permanent population even in 1999 was only 111) now attracts over 100,000 tourists a year; the village now contains a range of books and souvenir shops and restaurants themed around its Church of Mary Magdalene and the secret unearthed by Baigent, Lincoln, and Leigh. Their book fomented an almost endless stream of speculative but allegedly factual accounts of the secret of Jesus' survival, marriage, and the holy bloodline whose imaginative powers often made the fabrications of Pierre Plantard seem as mundane as a bill of lading. Among them were further books by some or all three authors: *The Messianic Legacy* (1986); *The Temple and the Lodge* (1989); *The Holy Place: The Mystery of Rennes-le-Château* (1991); *Key to the Pattern: The Untold Story of Rennes-le-Château* (1997); and *The Jesus Papers: Exposing the Greatest Cover-Up in History* (2006). A long line of other investigators, generally even more wildly imaginative, joined in the fray. Richard Andrews and Paul Schellenberger, in *The Tomb of God: The Body of Jesus and the Solution to a 2000–Year-Old Mystery* (1996) claimed that Jesus is buried at Rennes-le-Château. Taking nearly 500 pages to set out this secret, which uses a medieval parchment manuscript as a map, brings in patterns discerned by pentagrams, hexagrams, and triangles, to say nothing of paintings by Poussin, they conclude that Jesus is buried at Lampos, a rock formation on the side of Mount Cardou near Rennes-le-Château, although the authors are unsure as to whether Jesus died there, or whether his body was brought there by Mary Magdalene and others after the Crucifixion, or was reburied there a millennium later by the Knights Templar. Marilyn Hopkins, Graham Simmons, and Tim Wallace-Murphy, in *Rex Deus: The True Mystery of Rennes-le-Château and the Dynasty of Jesus* (2000) regards the alleged Priory of Sion as a modern hoax, but believes that – nonetheless – the assertions made in *The Holy Blood and the Holy Grail* are true, and a shadowy dynasty and secret society (*Rex Deus*) has existed and continues to exist which was well-aware of the dynasty's descent from Jesus and Mary Magdalene. As is common, some of these authors have also written on Rosslyn Chapel, the Church near Edinburgh said to be founded by the Knights Templar, and on the Templars and Freemasons (*Rosslyn: Guardian of the Secrets of The Holy Grail* (1999); *The Templar Legacy and the Masonic Inheritance within Rosslyn Chapel* (1994)). The theme of a continuing, powerful secret society, with wide-ranging political plans aimed at unifying Europe was also taken – not unexpectedly – by Lyn Picknett and Clive Prince in *The Sion Revelation: Inside the Shadowy World of Europe's Secret Masters* (2006). Picknett – whom we will meet again in the chapter on Rudolph Hess – and Prince believe that Plantard's fraudulent list of Grand Masters was deliberately designed to put others off the scent as to the real secret society. Picknett and Prince have also written *The Templar Revelation: Secret Guardians of the True Identity of Christ* (1997) and, as a *ne plus ultra*, *The Stargate Conspiracy: Revealing the Truth Behind Extraterrestrial Contact, Military Intelligence and the Mysteries of Ancient Egypt* (1999). There is also Laurence Gardner's *Bloodline of the Holy Grail: The Hidden Lineage of Jesus Revealed* (1996) which, like *The Sion Revelation*, connects the bloodline of Jesus to the 'Fisher Kings', King Arthur, the Holy Grail, the Crusading Knights, Rosslyn, the Inquisition and Witchcraft, and even the foundation of the United States. It contains twenty-nine genealogical tables linking Jesus to many of the present and former ruling dynasties of Europe.[41] Gardner is also the author of *Genesis of the Grail Kings* (1999) and *Realm of the Ring Lords* (new edition, 2003). By the early twenty-first century, virtually every large bookshop in the United Kingdom, and probably elsewhere in the English-speaking world, had a section headed 'Mind, Body, and Spirit', where twenty or more such titles were readily available. Most of these books were deeply referenced – *The Sion Revelation* has twenty-nine pages of footnotes and a twelve-page bibliography of over 300 books and articles – and were published by very mainstream trade publishers, including Time Warner and HarperCollins, which clearly expected an enormous sale. Although well outside the accepted historiographical pathways, they are plainly not 'crackpot' works: they are well-written, even gripping, and contain none of the tell-tale signs of the amateur autodidact, such as repetition, incoherence, and inability to place historical facts in a wider context. (None of these works is by an academic historian.)

Several things might be said about the appeal of these works, and many other similar books, not mentioned here. The 'royal bloodline' from Jesus, involving secret societies and far-reaching political agendas which still purportedly exist, evidently appeals, at the deepest possible level, to the central driving force of virtually all 'amateur history', the sense that one has been clever or fortunate enough to learn a great secret, and has outsmarted the 'experts' and the 'Establishment' – in this case, the academic experts on the history of religion and legend and the orthodox religious establishment, especially the Catholic Church. The possible survival of Jesus Christ and his 'royal bloodline' is *ipso facto* the Secret of Secrets, dwarfing all others. Secondly, the popularity of these works has certainly been in inverse measure to the centrality and membership of orthodox religious belief and the established churches. These works appear to be most popular in countries such as Britain, where the Church of England, Protestant Nonconformist sects and, more recently, Catholicism, are all in apparent sharp decline. Britain, however, already has a longstanding, growing, and visible clientele for unorthodox quasi-religious beliefs such as witchcraft and neo-paganism, and in a British mythical tradition embracing King Arthur, Druidism, and other similar beliefs. In some (but not all) of these books, the author or authors seem clearly to be searching for deeper spiritual meanings and experiences evidently not available to them from the orthodox Christian churches.

Interest in this topic, however, became truly international and worldwide with the publication of Dan Brown's *The Da Vinci Code*, a fictionalised version of the discovery of this account of the progeny of Jesus and Mary Magdalene and their descendants, which was published in 2003. It has sold over fifty million copies and generated an entire spin-off industry, including a successful film. The book has been translated into forty-four languages and is arguably the best-selling novel in history. Brown (b.1964), was formerly a teacher at Phillips Exeter Academy in New Hampshire, and a successful novelist. As a work of fiction, his book is beyond the scope of this chapter, but it might be worth noting that Brown's next novel is apparently to be *The Solomon Key*, linking the Freemasons to the foundation of the United States and to the Mormon religion. Brown is apparently travelling down the road of secret, mysterious societies and secret, underground influences on history, in the manner of so many of the allegedly factual works noted in this chapter.[42] Whether these can avoid degenerating into the worst kind of malign conspiracy theories remains to be seen. The effect of *The Da Vinci Code* on mainstream academic research on the early history of Christianity, however, appears – so far – to be minimal.

Although we have presented very negative conclusions about *The Holy Blood and the Holy Grail*, it must also be noted that there *were* apparently authentic traditions that Jesus was married to Mary Magdalene, or did father children by her, whose offspring survived. Yuri Stoyanov, the author of *The Hidden Tradition in Europe* (London, 1994) found a document on Cathar believers which stated that the Cathars clandestinely taught that Jesus was married to Mary Magdalene.[43] The Bagrations, hereditary kings of Armenia and Georgia until 1801, apparently claim descent, if not from Jesus himself, then from his brother Jude.[44] According to the authors of *Rex Deus*, there are many legends about the survival of James, the son of Jesus by Mary Magdalene.[45] It also seems quite possible that there was a continuing tradition among royalist circles and royal families in Continental Europe, that they were descended from Jesus and Mary Magdalene.[46] Nevertheless, all this seems very strained and lacking in any real evidence.

It might, however, come as a surprise to many readers to learn that the notion that Jesus survived the Crucifixion is a very old one, found in many cultural traditions. A long-standing tradition indeed exists that Jesus survived the Crucifixion and went to northern India, living at Taxila, between the Punjab and Kashmir. St. Thomas allegedly met Jesus there in A.D. 49.[47] Mary, Jesus's mother, also allegedly travelled to India, and is supposedly buried at Murree, 45 miles from Taxila, near Kashmir.[48] Some Muslim scholars believe that the figure known as 'Jesus Christ' is composed of several different persons, the prophet 'Isa, mentioned in the Koran; a second man, Jehu bar Nagara; and a local cultic god born of a virgin, al-'Isa.[49] 'Isa, the Jesus of the Koran, was not crucified; this was the fate of someone else with whom his identity was confused.[50] This 'Isa was a human being, not the Son of God, but was also a divinely-inspired messenger. Worship of the cultic 'Isa in Arabia might well have predated the Jesus of the New Testament.[51] It might be noted that the Islamic conception of Jesus – which was virtually unknown in the West until recently – regards the historical Jesus in quite a different light from Christianity. These traditions would have no trouble with the notion that Jesus survived the Crucifixion or, perhaps, that he married and fathered children.

Nevertheless, the central claims made by the recent popular writers on Jesus's survival and the 'holy bloodline' are dismissed as fantasy by most mainstream Christian theologians and academic historians.[52] There are, in fact, many cogent reasons why a Rennes-le-Château scenario seems very farfetched. Everyone connected with the early Christian church – Jesus's brother and his other relatives, his disciples and initial followers, St. Paul and other early converts – all believed that Jesus was crucified and then – somehow – rose from the dead, but was certainly not still alive in an earthly sense. If Jesus had still been alive in France, India, or anywhere else, his followers would surely have known this and made some effort to meet him. If Jesus had been alive anywhere in the Roman Empire, presumably the authorities would have had him arrested and repatriated to Jerusalem for a second, successful execution. If Jesus actually fathered children, they would surely have quickly attained cultic status themselves and the existence of his descendants become well-known at the time.

In fact, arguably the most salient facts about early Christianity were the surprisingly early centrality of devotion to the figure of the resurrected Christ as the most basic feature of the new religion, and its extremely rapid spread.[53] Why this was so takes us well beyond the confines of this chapter, but it does raise a separate question which, to me, is at least as interesting as whether he survived the Crucifixion, namely what he was doing prior to the last year or two of his life in Judea. There has been a good deal of speculation on this as well. There is, for instance, also an apparently long-established tradition that he travelled to India as a youth and was influenced by Buddhism.[54] Many believe that he was a member of the Essene or Zealot sects among the Jews. I would like here to put the view that Jesus was already founding proto-Christian churches in the eastern Mediterranean, probably in what is today Greece and Turkey, possibly including Edessa in today's Turkey, whose king, Abgar V, was seemingly converted to Christianity *during Jesus's lifetime*. In the Hellenistic world, Jesus developed a universalised version of Prophetic Judaism of great power.[55] Many of Jesus's early followers were Greeks as well as Jews, as is stated in the New Testament.[56] Jesus might have returned to Palestine to see whether his new universalised version of Judaism could attract followers in his own country. It did, but in a manner that caused him to fall very foul of the authorities, and led to his death. As noted, however, there seems to have *already* been a preexisting proto-Christian community throughout the eastern Mediterranean, even before Paul's missionary activities began, one which might already have been debating the issues which set Pauline Christianity apart from the community of Jewish Christians in Palestine: the necessity for circumcision, *kashrut*, and other aspects of Jewish law. To reiterate, probably the most striking of all features of Christianity was its uncompromisingly universalistic message which promised salvation to all believers. This feature of Christianity arguably set it apart most clearly from rival religions and sects, and led to its eventual triumph throughout the Roman world.

Where the success of *The Holy Blood and the Holy Grail* and *The Da Vinci Code* are likely to lead is unclear. If they spark renewed and widespread interest in learning more of the actual facts of the life of Jesus of Nazareth and his immediate followers, free of both the straightjacket of orthodox Christian belief and the equally unhelpful straightjacket of automatic cynicism about the claims of religion, their impact might well be a positive one. Speculation, however, must as always be based in both evidence and common sense. Virtually no evidence at all exists about the life of Jesus of Nazareth outside the New Testament and other early Christian sources, although the discovery of such works in the Dead Sea Scrolls in the twentieth century has added to our meagre store of knowledge.[57] Lost in all the speculation about the 'royal bloodline', however, is Jesus's impact as a seminal religious figure, whose universalistic message of hope appears to have had no real precedent but did unquestionably make an immediate and real impression.

Chapter 7

The Mysteries of Rudolf Hess

The case of Rudolf Hess (1894–1987; his full name was Walter Richard Rudolf Hess) is probably the most unlikely and implausible to appear in this book. Hess is almost universally acknowledged to have been a mediocrity who was systematically marginalised from the centre of real power by Adolf Hitler in Nazi Germany in the latter 1930s and early 1940s. Officially the Deputy Fuhrer of the Nazi regime, and, in the 1920s, one of Hitler's closest associates, Rudolf Hess's story actually comprises one of the great mysteries of modern history. This was because, in May 1941, Hess flew, under mysterious circumstances, from Germany to Scotland to attempt to broker a peace agreement between Britain and Germany. Britain had been at war with the seemingly all-victorious German *Reich* since September 1939 and, under the indomitable leadership of Prime Minister Winston Churchill, stood alone against Hitler at the Fall of France in 1940. In May 1941, Germany was master of the European continent from southern France to the border of the Soviet Union, which at the time extended through the middle of Poland. British cities faced almost continuous nightly bombardment. Many suspected that, despite their Non-Aggression Pact, Hitler was poised to invade and conquer the Soviet Union, the centre of what he regarded as the Judeo-Bolshevik evil. Hitler did in fact attack the Soviet Union only six weeks later, on 22 June 1941. Rudolf Hess flew to

Figure 7.1 Rudolf Hess, Hitler's Deputy, in captivity. Few figures in modern times have attracted more unorthodox theories. Getty Images/Keystone

Scotland, attempting to meet with the Duke of Hamilton, in order to secure a peace agreement between Britain and Germany which would give Hitler a free hand on the Continent in exchange for a guarantee of German non-interference in Britain and the British Empire. Officially, Hess undertook this mission entirely without the knowledge or permission of Adolf Hitler and without any forewarning to the astonished British government. After landing, Hess, who said his name was 'Albert Horn', was immediately arrested, spending the duration of the Second World War in captivity. At the Nuremberg Tribunal of 1945–6 he was tried with the other Nazi defendants and controversially sentenced to life imprisonment. Hess was convicted on two counts: conspiracy to commit crimes and crimes against peace. He was, notably, acquitted on the charges of committing war crimes and crimes against humanity; he had left Germany for Britain before the genocide of the Jews and other Nazi enormities had begun in earnest. His sentence was carried out in full measure. He spent literally the rest of his life in Spandau Prison, and after 1966 was its sole occupant, before apparently committing suicide in 1987 at the age of ninety-three, the last surviving member of Hitler's original inner circle.

This sequence of events, although extraordinary, seems in most respects straightforward, yet Hess's flight and subsequent life story has given rise to a remarkable number of separate, perhaps only tangentially related, mysteries, all of which have been the subject of books and other discussions. Nearly thirty books, few or none by academic historians, have been written on aspects of the Hess case, most of which argue for a different and sometimes startlingly unorthodox interpretation of Hess's flight and subsequent events. The 'mysteries of Rudolf Hess' actually comprise no fewer than eight separate major questions which, these theorists have argued, contradict the official version of events:

1. Did Hitler in reality know about the Hess Mission in advance and give his approval to the Mission?
2. Did the British government, despite its strenuous denials, know of his flight in advance?
3. Was the Hess Mission not, in fact, a 'sting' operation by British Intelligence to embarrass the Nazis?
4. Or, alternatively, was the Hess Mission part of a conspiracy between Hess and right-wing, pro-peace forces in Britain to bring the war to an end?
5. In either case, did Hess actually bring with him a very detailed, official, and elaborate proposed peace treaty between Germany and Britain?
6. Was the man put on trial at Nuremberg not in fact Rudolf Hess, the Deputy Führer, but an impostor who then spent over forty years in prison?
7. Did the real Rudolf Hess in fact die in the plane crash in northern Scotland in August 1942 which killed the Duke of Kent and about fifteen other persons?
8. Although the official verdict on the man who died in Spandau Prison in 1987 was suicide, was he – whether the real Rudolf Hess or not – murdered, as much evidence suggests, and, if so, why?
9. As if these aren't enough, there are also a number of subordinate mysteries surrounding Hess's flight which have been posited by some writers, such as whether Reinhard Heydrich, the infamous head of the Reich Security main office, accompanied Hess part of the way in a separate plane, and whether the RAF was given orders not to attack Hess's plane over Britain.

Some of these questions, posed in all seriousness in long, well-argued books, may seem like sheer fantasy, but, most extraordinarily, the flight and subsequent life and death of Rudolf Hess have attracted unparalleled attention, probably more than that devoted to any other top Nazi except Hitler himself.

Rudolf Hess was born in – of all places – Alexandria, Egypt, the son of a German import-export merchant. He lived mainly in Egypt until he was fourteen, when he was sent to a boarding school in Germany.[1] This is probably more than a biographical curiosity, for his Egyptian background meant that Hess lived in a British Protectorate for most of his childhood, viewing the presumably positive effects of British rule at first hand. Hess was also probably the only very senior Nazi who had lived for a long period outside German-speaking central Europe. This made his own outlook on Britain very different from those of his Nazi associates. Even those who, like Hitler, respected Britain on 'racial' grounds and admired the British Empire, never actually lived under British rule. Hess joined the German army in 1914, serving with some distinction on the Western Front and later as a lieutenant in the Air Force. He was twice wounded at Verdun, a fact which plays a part in the Hess 'mystery'. In 1919 he joined the right wing *Freikorps* and attended the University of Munich, where he became friendly with Professor Karl Haushofer, the right-wing exponent of 'geopolitics', who provided much of the intellectual basis for the German drive to achieve *lebensraum* in eastern Europe and Russia. Hess was close, for the rest of the time he was in Germany, to Haushofer, Haushofer's half-Jewish wife, and their son Albrecht, who has been seen by many as providing a key linkage with Britain before Hess's flight. In 1920 Hess attended a meeting of the newly-formed National Socialist German Workers Party – the Nazis – and was immediately 'enraptured' by a ranting speech given by its leader, Adolf Hitler.[2] Hess quickly became one of Hitler's closest associates. In 1923 he was at Hitler's side in the unsuccessful Munich Beer-Hall *Putsch*, and was sentenced to seven months in Lansberg Prison. There, he wrote down from dictation much of *Mein Kampf*, Hitler's autobiography and political blueprint. It is widely believed that Hess actually wrote some of it.[3] Hess's devotion to Hitler was so fanatical that some have suspected that a sexual component existed in their relationship. As the Nazi Party grew, Hess's role and importance increased. In December 1932 Hess became Chairman of the Central Political Committee of the Party, and, in April 1933, a few months after the Nazis came to power, he was made Deputy-Führer. In June 1933 he was named Reich Minister Without Portfolio, with a wide ranging brief that included the right to nominate high Nazi officials. Such infamous Nazis as Martin Bormann and Heinrich Himmler were originally his protégés. Hess, apparently a presentable and likeable man, was genuinely popular in Nazi Germany and was presented as the 'conscience' of the regime, a leader in whom ordinary Germans could trust. His mild-mannered, somewhat eccentric demeanour and endearing, instantly recognisable appearance contrasted with the image of extremism, brutality, and sadistic mastery presented by most senior Nazis. Hess also remained active in non-party activities, winning a major airplane race around Germany in 1934.[4] Padfield also gives some examples of Hess's *poems* – astonishingly he wrote poetry – which, even in translation, are clearly better than doggerel.[5] Despite all this, and although Hess was made a member of the Secret Cabinet Council by Hitler in February 1938, he was slowly but surely losing out to other, more aggressive members of Hitler's inner circle. In August 1939 he was placed third in the Nazi hierarchy, behind Hitler and Hermann Göring, when Göring was officially named as the number two man in the regime. Hess had little of a direct leadership role in the organisation of the German military for the war or in the organisation of the S.S., the Nazi death machine headed by Himmler. While Hess's speeches were filled with fiery denunciations of 'international Jewry', as well as of Freemasons – a particular *bête noire* of his – and, above all, of Bolshevism, as the main peril to Germany, he was probably not a visceral antisemite or sadistic killer in the manner of Himmler, Heydrich, or Hitler himself. Hess is known to have been deeply depressed over *Kristallnacht* in November 1938 and 'thoroughly disapproved' of this infamous antisemitic pogrom.[6] Nevertheless, it appears that Hess became more overtly antisemitic and more extreme in his rhetoric during the later 1930s, in parallel with Hitler.[7] As noted, he left for Britain before the mass murder of the Jews began in June 1941. Nevertheless, he did not lift a finger to stop any of the Nazi regime's antisemitism or any other totalitarian or aggressive measures taken by the regime, and blindly followed Hitler wherever his policies led.

The flight of Hess to Britain in May 1941 was greeted by apparent universal amazement in Britain – and, as well, in Germany. Winston Churchill, when told in person by the Duke of Hamilton, that Hess had landed on his estate, replied 'Do you mean to say that the Deputy Führer of Germany is in our hands?', adding, soon afterwards, 'Well, Hess or no Hess, I am going to see the Marx Brothers!' – since a viewing of a film with the

American comedians had been scheduled to entertain the Prime Minister at Dytchley Hall, Oxfordshire, where Churchill was staying.[8] Hitler's response was far less relaxed (and it is safe to say that he was not watching a Marx Brothers movie). According to Professor Ian Kershaw, author of the most authoritative biography of Hitler, the Führer's first wish was that he was dead. 'It's to be hoped he's crashed into the sea,' Hitler was heard to say.[9]

> *The first Hitler knew of Hess's disappearance was late in the morning of Sunday, 11 May, when Karl-Heinz Pintsch, one of the Deputy Führer's adjutants, turned up at the Berghoff. He was carrying an envelope which Hess had given him … entrusting him to deliver it personally to Hitler. When Hitler read Hess's letter, the colour drained from his face. Albert Speer, busying himself with architectural sketches at the time, suddenly heard an 'almost animal-like scream'. Then Hitler bellowed, 'Bormann immediately! Where is Bormann?!'*[10]

Hitler immediately summoned Göring and Foreign Minister Joachim von Ribbentrop. He had Pintsch and another of Hess's adjutants arrested. Hitler and other top Nazis such as Goebbels thought that Hess had gone insane.[11] There would appear to be absolutely no evidence from any source that Hitler knew of Hess's flight in advance, let alone approved of it, as some writers have suggested, although there would also appear to be other evidence, not mentioned by Kershaw, for a different view.

The putative historical mysteries surrounding Rudolf Hess, and the non-voluminous alternative theories surrounding his flight and subsequent life and death, differ yet again from the other subjects surveyed in this book. In the case of Hess there is a standard version of events, which was generally accepted at the time and is still accepted by most historians, namely, that he was acting alone on a bizarre fool's errand, without the knowledge of either Hitler or the British; was captured and later tried, and spent more than forty years in Spandau Prison before committing suicide. This standard version has been repeatedly challenged not by one alternative account of the true nature of the Hess Mission, but by many alternative theories, each independently disputing one or another aspect of the standard account, often in contradictory fashion. The writers and historians responsible for these alternative theories have operated in isolation from one another: there are, so far as I know, no societies devoted to studying the Hess Mystery, no newsletters, and few or no websites dedicated to presenting an alternate view. In familiar fashion, however, none of the alternative theories about Hess has been produced by an academic historian. Most of these writers on Hess are British. The continuing popularity of the Hess Mystery in Britain is the result, of course, of the fame it achieved at the time, at one of the darkest moments of the Second World War, when Britain was fighting alone and appeared to many observers to be heading towards defeat. Hess has been described to me as 'The British Nazi', the one member of Hitler's inner circle with a direct linkage to Britain. While Hess is, of course, well-known to Americans, so far as I am aware no American writer has written on Hess. In Britain, however, Rudolf Hess has acted as a lightning-rod for eccentric and highly original theories.

Probably the first work to offer a wholly unorthodox and unexpected theory about Rudolf Hess was Hugh Thomas's *The Murder of Rudolf Hess*, which appeared in 1979 to very considerable international publicity. Thomas, a physician and surgeon who was born in 1935, had in the period from 1970 to 1978 been a consultant surgeon in the Royal Army Medical Corps. He had spent a good deal of time in Belfast, during the height of the 'Troubles', and had gained a vast experience of gunshot wounds. In 1972 Thomas was posted as Consultant on General Surgery to the British Military Hospital in Berlin, where he was responsible for treating, among others, Rudolf Hess, at the time a seventy-eight year old prisoner at Spandau Prison. Thomas was one of the Allied Physicians present at a detailed physical examination given to the elderly Hess in late 1972 and early 1973. Thomas had primed himself for the meeting with his historically important patient by reading about his life. In a collection edited by the psychiatrist J.R. Rees about Hess's experience in British captivity, *The Case of Rudolf Hess* (London,1947), Thomas found that Hess had been wounded twice on the Western Front, in 1916 and 1917, suffering a gunshot wound to the chest which injured his lung.[12] Having treated many similar gunshot wounds in Northern Ireland, Thomas knew that scars from these wounds never completely heal. On examining Hess, Thomas found several small scars, but no trace of any former wound. At Hess's second examination, in September 1973, Thomas asked Hess (in German) 'What happened to your war-wounds? Not even skin deep.'[13] Thomas reported that:

> *The question had a startling effect. The patient's manner changed instantly. From being in a sunny, cheerful mood, he turned chalk-white and began to*

shake. For an instant he stared at me in what appeared bewilderment or even utter disbelief. Then he looked down and avoided my eyes. After what felt like ages, he muttered 'Zu spät, zu spät' ('Too late, too late.')[14]

Hess, who began to shake so violently that Thomas thought he was having a heart attack, experienced immediate diarrhoea.[15]

From this, Thomas built up a long and seemingly impressive list of circumstantial evidence that 'Prisoner No.7' – as Hess was known in Spandau – was *not* the real Rudolf Hess. Prisoner No.7 declined to see any member of his family, including his wife or son, until December 1969, twenty-eight years after his flight to Scotland. At their first meeting, Frau Hess said, 'You have changed. Your voice is much different now to how I remember it.'[16] Thomas noted that the deepening of a man's voice in old age is a near-impossibility.[17] Hess's behaviour even in his early days in captivity in Britain showed many traits that were inconsistent with what is known about Nazi Germany's Deputy Führer. The German Hess was a vegetarian, the British prisoner a keen meat-eater. In Germany, Hess had possessed fastidious eating habits, but the prisoner ate everything like a starving man with no manners. The real Hess was an enthusiastic tennis player, but the prisoner said that he did not know the rules of the game.[18] Thomas records many other such anomalies. In captivity and at Nuremberg, Hess originally claimed to have had amnesia, which Thomas speculated was an obvious ploy to avoid answering telling questions. Thomas also argued that the plane which crash-landed in Scotland was not the one in which he had taken off from Germany.[19] The plane which had taken off did not have the fuel drop-tanks necessary for such a long flight; the plane which crash-landed in Scotland did.[20] Thomas concluded from all this that Prisoner No.7 at Spandau was an impostor, a false Hess, and that the real Hess had been shot down, on Nazi orders, before reaching Britain, probably on the orders of Hitler or the S.S.

Thomas's book became well-known and set a very high standard for other unusual and bizarre theories about Rudolf Hess. It must be said that the book is extremely well and intelligently written, and is plainly not the work of a crackpot. Indeed, the fact that it is by a respected physician and surgeon, one of the few British people ever to have contact with Hess in Spandau, must give it a good deal of veracity. Yet – needless to say – Thomas's claims are extremely difficult to accept. Other medical experts have asserted that scars from war wounds can indeed fade over time, while Hess, at Spandau, is reported to have joked about the wounds and Thomas's claims to a Protestant pastor and to his wife.[21] The claim that the plane which crashed in Scotland was not the one which took off from Germany is 'demonstrably wrong', according to Nesbit and van Acker. Thomas's claim that the Messerschmitt which took off from Germany bore the code 'NJ+C11' is impossible, since no German plane ever bore this registration.[22] Hess wrote many letters to his wife and associates in Germany such as Karl Haushofer which contain information and terminology known only to him.[23] His post-1942 handwriting was identical with that written earlier.[24] As Thomas admits, none of the other top Nazis in the dock at Nuremberg, Hess's closest colleagues, questioned that their fellow-prisoner was the real Hess. Nor did Adolf Hitler believe that the man who flew to Scotland was anyone other than Rudolf Hess. Above all, of course, there is the utter improbability of a 'Hess double' carrying on his charade after the end of the war. One might just imagine a double planted by the S.S. pretending to be Hess while the war was raging, either through loyalty to the Nazi regime or for fear of reprisals to his family, but no one not insane would continue this pointless deception after Germany surrendered on 8 May 1945, let alone for over forty more years. One can think of a dozen ways in which the false Hess could easily prove to the Allies he was an impostor, for instance through fingerprints, handwriting, or simply giving a verifiable account of his own life. Despite all this, Hugh Thomas's book was certainly effective in making the story of Rudolf Hess the subject of far-reaching speculation.[25]

Most unorthodox speculation about the Hess flight has, however, focused on whether his Mission was far less innocent than the official version credits. The mainstream, generally accepted account of Hess's flight is that it was carried out entirely on his own, without the knowledge of either Hitler or the British. Most unorthodox accounts of Hess's flight have suggested either that he was actually set up by a 'sting' operation orchestrated by British intelligence, or, alternately, that Hess had extensive previous contacts with right-wing pro-peace with Germany groups in Britain which collaborated in his flight; and that Hess actually brought with him official and comprehensive plans for an Anglo-German peace, ending the war and giving Germany a free hand in its imminent invasion of the Soviet Union. That Hess's mission was actually the product of a successful 'sting' operation by British intelligence was put in such works as Peter Padfield's excellent, unquestionably mainstream biography *Hess, The Führer's Disciple* (London, 1991; revised edition 2001); John Harris and M.J. Throw, *Hess: The British Conspiracy* (London, 1999), and Martin Allen's *The Hitler/Hess Deception: British Intelligence's Best-Kept Secret of the Second World War* (London, 2003), have made this view well-known. There is a good deal of evidence for this view, which Allen describes as a plot codenamed 'Messrs. HHHH' (for Hitler, Hess, and the two Haushofers, close friends and advisors of Hess). This plot was designed to convince Germany that important and influential leaders in Britain did want to bring about a separate peace with Germany, in order to lull Britain into attacking the Soviet Union, giving Britain, fighting alone, a Great Power ally. However, the plotters were not expecting the arrival of such a senior figure as Rudolf Hess, but of Ernst Bohle, the head of the *Auslandorganisation* (the Foreign Organisation), who would be taking with him secret plans directly from Hitler.[26] According to this view, the plotters were amazed when Hess himself arrived. This plot had the backing of Churchill, who also knew, through secret ENIGMA decrypts, that Hitler was about to attack the Soviet Union. Unfortunately, some of the evidence for this view may be based on fabricated documents placed in the Public Record Office (now the National Archives).[27] Padfield, in his biography, also provides information, from unnamed confidential sources, about the nature of a secret peace treaty which Hess was said to have brought with him, and which has since disappeared; official sources have always denied the existence of such a document. It allegedly 'comprised proposals for a peace treaty drafted in official language on Chancellery paper, together with an English translation'.[28] The proposals allegedly set out quite explicitly Hitler's plans for the invasion and conquest of Russia, and stipulated that Britain was to keep out of all continental involvement, in return for which she would retain the Empire, independence, and armed forces.[29] These proposals were carefully studied by British officials at the highest level, who had to maintain complete secrecy for fear, among other things, that any leakage of this document would greatly strengthen the 'Peace Party' in Britain.[30] While it is *possible* that Hess did bring with him such a document, it is difficult to believe that Germany's leaders could have expected that Britain would take any promise by Hitler at face value in 1942, or that it would be treated with anything but contempt. Most accounts of Hess's interrogation also insist that Hess did not state whether Hitler would invade the Soviet Union. On the other hand, there seems no doubt that, via the Haushofers, Hess was in contact with some well-placed persons in Britain, and quite possibly with British intelligence.

Another group of writers on Hess have concluded that Hess was indeed in contact with British sources, but for an entirely different purpose: he was in active contact with well-placed right-wing 'Establishment' figures, who wanted to displace Churchill, end the war, and conclude a treaty with Nazi Germany similar to the one just described. This view was put in Peter Allen's *The Crown and the Swastika: Hitler, Hess, and the Duke of Windsor* (London, 1993), which links the Hess Mission to rumoured attempts by the Duke of Windsor to regain the throne.[31] John Costello's well-researched *Ten Days That Saved the West* (London, 1991) also linked the Hess Mission to right-wing pro-Peace forces which had certainly been strong a year earlier. (The 'ten days' in the book's title were ten selected dates in May-September 1940 when Churchill came to power, France fell, and the situation looked grimmest for Britain.)

However, certainly the most dramatic exposition of this view, and probably the strangest book ever written on the Hess affair, is *Double Standards: The Rudolf Hess Cover-Up*, by Lynn Picknett, Clive Prince, and Stephen Prior, with additional research by Robert Brydon (London, 2001). Picknett and Prince are also the co-authors of *The Sion Revelation*, which is discussed in the chapter on Jesus, and also of *The Stargate Conspiracy*, which we will encounter in the chapter on the Pyramids: they are certainly nothing if not versatile! The thesis of *Double Standards* is that Rudolf Hess did indeed die during the Second World War, but in a way hitherto as unsuspected as it was dramatic: he died in the plane crash in northern Scotland in August 1942 which also killed the Duke of Kent, and (according to the official count) thirteen or fourteen crewmen.[32] *Double Standards* claims that there was one extra person on board the plane, whose presence was noted in some accounts at the time and afterwards, but who was not listed in any official report of the crash.[33] According to the authors, this extra passenger was none other than Rudolf Hess. Hess was being transported to neutral Sweden (not to Iceland, given in the official story as the plane's destination) to be handed over to the Germans as the first step in a settlement of the war between Britain and Germany. The Duke's plane, according to the authors, had actually landed on Loch More, a lake in northern Scotland near the estate of Sir Archibald Sinclair, Secretary of State for Air (later Lord Thurso). It crashed after taking off for the next leg of the trip, possibly through sabotage.[34] These moves to bring about a separate peace between Britain and Germany were masterminded by a powerful right-wing faction around the Royal Family (including the Duke of Windsor, then Governor of the Bahamas). The successful flight of Hess would then be followed by 'a "palace coup" in London in which Churchill would be dismissed from from office and replaced with Sir Samuel Hoare, the former Arch-Appeaser and Cabinet Minister who was serving, at the time, as British Ambassador to Spain. While this was happening, 'Kent and Hess [would make] a joint appearance in Stockholm to announce a peace deal.'[35] The plot failed, and Hess was killed, because it was discovered and fatally stymied by Churchill, probably working with a left-wing faction in the SOE (Special Operations Executive), headed by senior Labour minister Hugh Dalton and numbering Soviet spy Kim Philby among its members.[36]

There are many legitimate mysteries about the flight which killed the Duke of Kent and others. The plane had flown many miles off its apparent course, leading some to conclude that the crew was drunk or that the Duke of Kent was at the controls when the plane crashed.[37] The number of crash victims published at the time appears to be incorrect, although this may simply be due to confusion when the sole survivor, Andy Jack, unexpectedly turned up dazed a few days later. It is possible, even likely, that far too much about the fatal flight has been covered up, presumably because it involved Royalty in wartime. Nevertheless, as an account of the fate of Rudolf Hess, *Double Standards* seems breathtaking in its implausible inaccuracy. Where does one start? Perhaps with the most basic fact of all, that Rudolf Hess did not die in Scotland in 1942 but in Spandau Prison forty-five years later. As with the claim by Hugh Thomas that the man in Spandau Prison was an impostor, one must ask why anyone would agree to take the place of Rudolf Hess as a prisoner serving for the rest of his life. There is absolutely nothing to link Hess with the flight carrying the Duke of Kent. In the (utterly unlikely) event that he was a passenger on this flight, he would surely have been accompanied by a substantial staff of his own, including personal guards, a translator, and officials to negotiate with the Germans. Nor is there any evidence that Hitler would want him back: on hearing of Hess's flight, the furious Hitler promptly abolished the office of Deputy Leader, held by Hess.[38] Several days after Hess's flight, Hitler addressed a meeting of Nazi leaders in which he declared that Hess had betrayed him, had acted without his knowledge, and was mentally ill. Hitler 'was in tears and looked ten years older.' 'I have never seen the Führer so deeply shocked,' said Hans Frank, the Nazi dictator of central Poland, later hanged at Nuremberg.[39] There is also the nature of the alleged plot: no one, even Royalty, could possibly have secured Hess's release from Maindiff Court, near Abergavenny in Wales, where he was being held, without the knowledge and permission of Churchill and a handful of other very senior Cabinet ministers such as Deputy Prime Minister Clement Attlee, Home Secretary Herbert Morrison, and Foreign Minister Anthony Eden, all of whom were in favour of prosecuting the war against Hitler to the end. It simply could not have happened. There was no significant mainstream 'peace party' in England in August 1942, nine months after America had entered the war and after the Soviet Union had seen off any immediate threat to the conquest of Moscow by the Germans. Sir Samuel Hoare, a discredited 'Guilty Man', as the former pro-Appeasers were widely known, would not conceivably have been voted as Prime Minister in place of Churchill in mid-1942, and nor could there conceivably have been a 'palace coup', orchestrated by the Royal Family, to oust Churchill, since in the twentieth century any British Prime Minister must always enjoy the confidence of the House of Commons, not merely the approval of the Sovereign, who could simply not have foisted an outsider on an unwilling House of Commons. Hoare is widely seen, moreover, as an able diplomat in Spain, who was instrumental in keeping Franco neutral during the war. Similarly, far from being a pro-Nazi, the Duke of Kent worked closely with British intelligence during the war.[40] From any angle, *Double Standards* appears to be a gripping fantasy. It is noteworthy, too, that Rudolf Hess figures at the centre of this account: he appears to occupy centre-stage of many unusual accounts of Britain during the Second World War.

The death of Rudolf Hess has also come in for much speculation. Hess apparently committed suicide on 17 August 1987 at the age of ninety-three. There are some reasonable grounds for believing that he was murdered.[41] The reasons for his murder, if it occurred, are, however, obscure, and it seems overwhelmingly likely that he died by his own hand. In 1988 Hugh Thomas published a second book on the Spandau prisoner, *Hess: A Tale of Two Murders*, which contends that the frail Hess could not possibly have looped a wire round his neck – the method of his death – and committed suicide. According to Thomas, the marks recorded in Hess's post-mortem were consistent with throttling, probably by an intruder, and that Hess was probably killed at the instigation of the British government because he was at the point of being released from prison, when the identity deception Thomas previously alleged would become clear. But the post-mortem carried out by Professor J. M. Cameron, a highly-qualified pathologist, came to the conclusion that Hess's death was caused by asphyxia, compression of the neck, and suspension – in other words, suicide by hanging. Representatives of the Four Powers which still controlled Spandau and Hess's fate all concurred in the verdict.[42]

In reality, it seems fairly clear that all or virtually all of the 'mysteries' which have become attached to the flight and subsequent life of Rudolf Hess are fictitious speculation. Many well-reasoned books on Hess have also come to this conclusion.[43] Admittedly, there are indeed some remaining anomalies about the Hess 'Mission', which are set out in a detailed way in Padfield's biography. For instance, on 5 May 1941 Hess had a four-hour conversation with Hitler in the Reich's Chancellery in Berlin. No one knows what was said, but an aide later claimed that Hitler's last words to him were 'Hess, you are and always were thoroughly pig-headed.[44] It seems hard to believe that in four hours Hess said *nothing* to Hitler about his intended flight, which took place four or five days later. It might thus be that Hitler's astonishment and fury when he learned that Hess was in England was feigned. On the other hand, it appeared real enough to close observers at the time. As Ian Kershaw has pointed out, Hitler was on an extremely rigorous time-table with regard to preparations for the imminent invasion of Russia, which began on 22 June 1941, and which had if at all possible to be completed successfully, with the capture of Moscow and Leningrad, by the onset of the Russian winter in October or November. Hitler simply could not afford any extended negotiations on a possible peace treaty with Britain had the Hess Mission actually succeeded in bringing British agreement to talk with Germany.[45] Moreover, any negotiations would have had to be completed before the invasion got underway: if Germany succeeded, the British would presumably have had to negotiate in any case; if Germany failed to secure an immediate victory in Russia – as proved to be the case – Britain would never have negotiated. The balance of evidence is that the orthodox account of Hess's flight and subsequent life, however mundane, is the crrect one.[46]

Chapter 8

Ancient Mysteries: The Great Pyramid and the Sphinx

It is arguably the most famous structure in the world, certainly from the ancient world. Its image can be found on the reverse of the Great Seal of the United States as a symbol of permanence, and on every American one-dollar bill. It is the only one of the Seven Wonders of the World, as listed by the ancients, to survive. Universally known, the Great Pyramid still inspires not merely awe and wonder, but mystery and a deep sense of the enigmatic. Surveying strange structures from the ancient world, the scientist and anomaly-collector William R. Corliss stated that

> *Of all the enigmatic structures [from the ancient world] the Great Pyramid unquestionably possesses the largest inventory of intriguing and puzzling features. It is immensely old ... [and] displays superb craftsmanship and engineering know-how. Its completion some 4,600 years ago marked a zenith in human architectural feats that was not equalled for several millennia.*[1]

Unorthodox discussions of the mysteries of the Great Pyramid at Giza began in the nineteenth century, but have flourished and escalated during the past thirty years or so, becoming a significant cottage industry, often in a much wider context of unorthodox theories about the ancient world. Normally these theories claim that the builders of the pyramids were far more technologically advanced than they are credited with being by mainstream archaeologists; indeed, their technology might well be in advance of anything known even today. These theories sometimes claim that the pyramids at Giza, and the adjacent Sphinx, are far older than the normally-accepted dates of their construction.

While none of these unorthodox Egyptologists is an archaeologist, most are highly-educated and obviously intelligent researchers and writers, with an emphasis on those trained as engineers. Graham Hancock, the author of *Fingerprints of the Gods* and other very controversial works of unorthodox archaeology, is the former East African correspondent for *The Economist*. Robert Bauval, another prolific writer on this topic, is a construction engineer who has lived in the Middle East for much of his life. Edward F. Malkowski, author of *Before the Pharaohs: Egypt's Mysterious Prehistory* (Rochester, Vt., 2006), is a software developer; Christopher Dunn, (*The Giza Power Plant*) is an engineer in aerospace with thirty-five years of experience; Thomas G. Brophy (*The Origin Map*) is also an aerospace engineer. Robert M. Schoch (*Pyramid Quest*) is a professor at the College of General Studies at Boston University. The writers on this subject, although mainly 'amateurs' in the sense of only infrequently holding academic appointments, are among the most obviously well-qualified to write on any of the topics surveyed in this book. Agree with them or not, their publications are almost invariably well-written and cogent. Unlike some of the other subjects surveyed here, unorthodox Egyptology appears to have elicited no societies or organisations, but its ideas are publicised not only in many surprisingly widely-read books by mainstream publishers, but in magazines such as *Atlantis Rising*, edited by J. Douglas Kenyon, and *Fortean Times*, and by a number of publishers such as Bear & Co. of Rochester, Vermont, and Adventures Unlimited Press of Kempton, Illinois. [2]

The subject matter of this chapter also differs from the others in this book in that, certainly at its most extreme, it comes close to advancing theories which most would claim cross the borders from 'amateur history' to the full-blown crackpot. The notion of a technologically advanced civilization from 10,000 years ago, with its implications (at the very least) of 'ancient astronauts', will strike most readers as beyond the pale, as will anything smacking of the supernatural or the occult, apparent concomitants of unorthodox theories of ancient Egypt. In this book I rigorously eschew anything of this sort, and discuss the theories about Egypt examined here only because, however outrageous and implausible, they are rational ideas advanced by intelligent writers. There are limits, however, and, in this book, I deliberately go no further.

The standard account of the Great Pyramid at Giza, together with its two accompanying smaller pyramids and the Sphinx, is that it was built by slave or conscripted labour involving thousands of workmen, probably over a twenty-year period around 2,500 B.C. as a tomb for King Khufu, a pharaoh of the Fourth Dynasty. The Great Pyramid is, no doubt, singularly impressive and awe-inspiring, and has survived 4,500 years, but there is nothing about it which is inexplicable, let alone supernatural, or which could not be done, given sufficient resources and labour, with the technology and building techniques available at the time. Other extraordinarily impressive man-made structures can also be found in other cultures plainly not influenced by ancient Egypt, for instance in pre-Colombian Mexico, Central America, and the Andes.[3] Unorthodox theories of the pyramids have arisen simply through an underestimate of the organisational ability and the human cleverness of the ancient world. To some, this underestimation has a strong element of racism in it, or at least of Western chauvinism: no one ever claims that the Parthenon or the Roman Coliseum were built by 'ancient astronauts' or by means of advanced technology hardly glimpsed even now, the Greeks and Romans invariably being regarded as clever enough to have built these structures by their own efforts.

Nevertheless, the magnitude of (in particular) the Great Pyramid and the genuine uncanniness of so many of its features have been responsible for engendering a lengthy list of unorthodox theories and speculation by a variety of clearly intelligent persons. Three or four main claims are made by unorthodox archaeologists about the Great Pyramid: that it could simply not have been built by forced labour and brute force, but *must* have been constructed by advanced machinery and technological methods; that it is not a tomb, but an advanced 'machine' of some kind; that advanced knowledge has been deliberately 'embedded' in its structure; and that it, and the Sphinx, are actually far older than the normal dates ascribed to them, and evidence of a now-destroyed civilisation which existed millennia earlier than commonly thought.

Perhaps the most important enigma about the Great Pyramid (and most of the other gigantic structures of the ancient world) is just how it was built: how did the ancients quarry, transport, and raise into place the estimated *2.3 million* stone blocks necessary to build the Great Pyramid, the topmost of which are 400 feet above ground level? It should be noted that, while the Great Pyramid dwarfs all other ancient structures in sheer size, it did not use the largest and heaviest stone construction blocks known in the ancient world. This honour apparently goes to the three so-called Trilithtons in the walls at the Temple of Jupiter at Baalbek (in Lebanon), each of which weighs *620 tons*, compared with 'only' 200 tons for the largest stone blocks employed in the Great Pyramid, 130 tons for the stone blocks at Tiahmanaco, erected in Bolivia, and a mere 50 tons for the largest stones at Stonehenge in England.[4] Also at a quarry near Baalbek is a partially cut and dressed tone, still attached to bedrock, weighing an estimated *1100 tons*; apparently its size and weight defeated its ancient quarryers.[5] In 2001, when William R. Corliss compiled his *Ancient Structures*, which discusses this matter, only two lifting vehicles in the world were capable of lifting a stone weighing 620 tons: the tracked vehicle at Cape Canaveral which transports the *Saturn V* rocket to its launch pad, and some massive fixed cranes used in dam-building.[6] Corliss believes that between 9700 and 16,000 men would have been required to drag the 600–ton Baalbek stones three-quarters of a mile from the quarry to the building site, using rollers and a paved roadway 'provided they could have found a place to stand.'[7]

However,

> *The real problem may have occurred at the [Baalbek] Terrace itself. How does one lift and position 610 tons? Again, we can only guess: levers of metal bars, stone-paved ramps? The Baalbek problems are like those encountered by the builders of the Great Pyramid, except that the Baalbek Trilithons are thrice the weight of the largest pyramid stones. At Baalbek we* guess *that the big stones were pulled up the stone-paved ramps and then dragged and levered into position.*[8]

Although less heavy, the pyramid stones obviously demonstrate the same problems on a vastly greater scale. This is also the case with all other standing objects from ancient Egypt. According to Christopher Dunn's careful calculations, it would have taken ancient Egyptian workers fifty years to quarry the obelisk stone at Asuran, using the hand techniques of ancient Egypt, although the inscription on the base of Hatshepsut's pair of obelisks say that they were quarried and raised into place in a seven-month period.[9] With the Great Pyramid and the other Egyptian pyramids, the most obvious explanation is simply the use of brute force and tens of thousands of workers. Herodotus, the great ancient Greek historian, said that around 100,000 workers took about twenty years to build the Great Pyramid.[10] Modern estimates are that no more than 10,000 workmen could have accomplished the task in twenty years, although this is based on very optimistic models.[11] One ingenious idea, which has become well-known in recent years among those for whom the construction of the Great Pyramid seems an impossible task, is that the stones of the pyramid were not cut, dragged, and lifted into place, but were *poured* by casting a cement-like liquid limestone mix in wooden moulds on the spot! This theory was proposed in 1979 by a French chemist, Joseph Davidovits, who has assembled what Corliss described as an 'impressive list of observations supporting his claims.'[12] For instance, Davidovits notes that some of the limestone blocks have air bubbles which would not be expected in natural rock; there is a notable absence of cracked or spoiled limestone blocks at their supposed quarries; those supposed quarries were apparently not worked prior to 1659 B.C., centuries after the Great Pyramid was built; organic fibres and isolated limestone chunks are seen in some blocks, and so on.[13] Davidovits's theory was actually tested by several groups of scientific archaeologists, who found no evidence to support it.[14] Nevertheless, this still doesn't explain how the stones were cut if the quarries from which they were taken were not yet worked. Positing brute force by thousands of (presumably) slave labourers over many years, while it sounds fine (and may in the final analysis have to be accepted), simply does not tally with what we know is actually possible in the real world. As another sceptical amateur archaeologist, Will Hart, has noted:

> *The problem of how the ancients moved the heaviest loads is quite enough to crush the orthodox building theories and time lines into the dust, in my estimation. Academics are not noted for being mechanically inclined, nor are they the ones doing the sweat labor during excavations out in the field. It is extraordinarily easy to put pen to paper and make a one-hundred-ton block of stone move from the quarry to the temple wall. It is impossible to meet that challenge in the real world using manpower unaided by modern equipment.*

The fact is that the Egyptologist Mark Lehner discovered this years ago when he put together an expert team to try and raise a thirty-five-ton obelisk using ancient tools and techniques. It was filmed by 'NOVA' [an American educational television programme]. A master stonemason was brought in to quarry the granite block from the bedrock. Unfortunately, he gave up after trying every trick he knew. They called a bulldozer in, which cut it away from the bedrock and lifted it onto a waiting truck. That was really the end of the experiment, and it proved that it was not possible to quarry and lift a block one-tenth the size of the heaviest obelisk still standing in Egypt.[15]

In a later programme, Lehner – who 'never again tried to use the ancient tools to prove how the pyramids were constructed' – was forced to bring in locals 'with modern chisels, hammers, and a truck with a steel winch to hoist the blocks out of the quarry', although these blocks were less than half the size of pyramid stones.[16] Another Japanese group tried, also in Egypt, to build a sixty-foot scale model of the Great Pyramid using traditional tools and techniques.

Their first embarrassment came at the quarry when they discovered they could not cut the stones from the bedrock. They called in jackhammers. The next embarrassing situation came when they tried to ferry the blocks across the [Nile] river on a primitive barge. They could not control it and had to call for a modern one.

They ran into more grief on the opposite bank when they discovered that the sledges sank into the sand and they could not budge them. They called for a bulldozer and a truck. The coup de grâce *was delivered when they then tried to assemble the pyramid and found they could not position the stones with any accuracy, and had to request the aid of helicopters.*[17]

According to Hart,

How long did it take the ancient Egyptians to build [the Great Pyramid]? That is the wrong question. The right one is, Could the ancient Egyptians have built the Great Pyramid? The answer is: not with the tools and techniques that Egyptologists claim they used.'[18]

One of the best-known of the unorthodox archaeologists, Graham Hancock, summarised his feelings on making his way through the passageways of the

Third Pyramid, 'only' 200 feet high, at Giza:

> *Retracing our steps, we left the lower chambers and walked back up the ramp … Passing through the ragged aperture in its western walls, we found ourselves looking directly at the upper sides of the eighteen slabs which formed the ceiling of the chamber below. From this perspective their true form as a pointed gable was immediately apparent. What is less clear is how they had been brought here in the first place, let alone laid so perfectly in position. Each one must have weighed many tons, heavy enough to have made them extremely difficult to handle under any circumstances. And these were no ordinary circumstances. [T]he pyramid builders had disdained to provide an adequate working area between the slabs and the bedrock above them. By crawling into the cavity, I was able to establish that the clearance varied from approximately two feet at the southern end to just a few inches at the northern end. In such a restricted space there was no possibility that the monoliths could have been lowered into position. Logically, therefore, they must have been raised from the chamber floor, but how had that been done? …*
>
> *Not for the first time when confronted by the mysteries of the pyramids I knew that I was looking at an* impossible *engineering feat which had nevertheless been carried out to astonishingly high and precise standards. Moreover, if Egyptologists were to be believed, the construction work had supposedly been undertaken at the dawn of human civilisation by a people who had not accumulated any experience of massive construction projects.*[19]

Is the inference here accurate? Did the ancient Egyptians use building techniques unknown to us, but indicative of a level of technology which we have barely reached, if indeed we have reached it? Even level-headed scientists attuned to the realities of an actual building project have been mystified by the logistics of the Great Pyramid. One such very practical problem has been noted by William R. Corliss:

> *There is, however, an engineering problem that has received little attention in the literature:* scaffolding. *In these later days, although the sides of the Great Pyramid are severely stepped rather than smooth, due to the (hypothetical) removal of many acres of casing stones, pyramid climbers still slip and fall to their deaths. The ancient masons and laborers had to stand somewhere as they eased stone blocks into place. This must have been especially hazardous*

> *when the casing stones were installed near the top. Some of these stones weighed as much as 16–20 tons and, further, they were irregular in shape. How did the workers cling to the flat finished surfaces of the pyramid and maintain their footing in the presence of the lubricants that must have been used to ease the motion of rock against rock? … Remember that the slope of the pyramid's side is 54º – much steeper than house roofs! If scaffolding was constructed around those ancient work sites perched precariously hundreds of feet above the ground, no evidence of it survives today. Such 'practical' problems seem to be ignored by most Great Pyramid speculators.*[20]

Indeed, they are. Nevertheless, nearly all mainstream Egyptologists would reject anything about building the pyramid which borders remotely on science fiction, and are adamant in claiming that, given time and manpower, the Great Pyramid and the other great relics of ancient Egypt could and were built with relative ease (if that is the right word) – at least, with an effort achievable by ordinary humans in the ancient world, and not by supernatural means. For instance, Ian Lawton and Chris Ogilvie-Herald have written a useful counterweight to the more *outré* theories about the Pyramids, *Giza: The Truth – The People, Politics, and History Behind the World's Most Famous Archaeological Sites* (London, 2000). The authors usefully remind us – to take one example – that the Great Pyramid did not simply appear out of nowhere – as is strongly implied in many accounts of it – but was one of many pyramids built in a traceable progression beginning about eighty years before it, starting with the so-called Step Pyramid of the Pharaoh Djoser in 2630–2611 B.C. Six pyramids were built before the Great Pyramid, with the so-called Bent and Red pyramids at Dashur, built in the generation before the Great Pyramid, also being massive structures, each 105 metres (around 340 feet) high. The volume of these two pyramids together actually exceeds that of the Great Pyramid. These pyramids were built in a clear progression of increasing difficulty.[21] (Many other unorthodox theories are discussed and refuted – at least in the eyes of the authors – in this useful work.)

Another central point made by Christopher Dunn is that the Giza Pyramid, both externally and particularly internally, plainly shows evidence of advanced machining techniques wholly inconsistent with 'primitive' tools and techniques.[22] According to Dunn, 'several artefacts' in the Great Pyramid 'almost undeniably indicate [that] machine power was used by the pyramid builders.'[23] They are 'fragments of extremely hard, igneous rock', and, although scrutinised by the famous Egyptologist Sir William Flinders Petrie many years earlier, have, of course, not previously been recognised as having been cut by a mechanical lathe. This cutting of granite can simply not have been done, according to Dunn, by copper chisels, as conventional Egyptologists postulate.

> *Wanting to know more about the sawing of granite, I consulted John Barta, of the John Barta Company [an engineering firm], who informed me that the wire saws used in quarry mills today cut through granite with great rapidity. In fact, Barta told me that wire saws with silicon-carbide cut through the granite like it is butter. Out of interest I asked Barta what he thought of the copper chisel theory proposed by [conventional] Egyptologists. Suffice it to say that Barta, being from Cleveland [Ohio], and possessing an excellent sense of humor, came forth with some jocular remarks regarding the practicality of such an idea.*[24]

Dunn claims that only a 'power-driven saw' could possibly provide the control required for the precision he observed in pyramid artefact workmanship.[25] 'High-speed machine tools ... were evidently used by the pyramid builders to hollow out the inside of the granite coffers ...'[26] Petrie himself, writing in the early 1880s, was 'astounded' by the advanced workmanship he found when he examined these artefacts.[27] Dunn believes that 'ultrasonic drilling' techniques, in use only in the past few decades, must have produced the artefacts he found; they apparently could not be done in any other way.[28] Furthermore, the 'sarcophagus' in the King's Chamber (which, according to Dunn, is no such thing) is so 'perfectly flat' that it must have been carved by machine; so, too, are artefacts in the rock tunnels at the temple off Serapeum at Saggara, the site of the Step Pyramid.[29] Dunn contacted four precision granite manufacturers in the United States, asking if they could create several of these artefacts, which he described. One stated that his company 'did not have the equipment or capability' to produce these artefacts in one piece on the spot (as the Egyptians did); they could only create the main artefact, a granite box, in five parts, 'ship them to the customer, and bolt them together on site.'[30] Dunn concluded that the Egyptians *must* have possessed advanced machining techniques, possibly in advance of anything known today.

Even more extraordinary than the advanced techniques seen by some unorthodox Egyptologists in the construction of the Great Pyramid is the purpose for which it was built. Virtually all unorthodox Egyptologists reject the notion that the Great Pyramid – or any of the others at Giza – was ever built as a tomb for a pharaoh, or for anyone else. There is simply no evidence that the pyramids were ever used to hold a sarcophagus – none whatever. The belief that it was used for this purpose is an inference from the mummies actually found at the Valley of the Kings and elsewhere in Egypt. Giza and the Valley of the Kings are two entirely different sites. A total of eighty pyramids have been found in Egypt, not a single one of which has been found to hold a mummy or sarcophagus.[31] Newly-found pyramids, which were certainly not entered by grave-robbers, have never been found to contain mummies.[32] In the case of the Great Pyramid, its internal passageways are so narrow as to make grave-robbing virtually impossible.[33] For this reason and others, in 1998 Christopher Dunn, a British-born aerospace engineer resident in the United States, advanced the extraordinary theory that the Great Pyramid was actually a *power plant*, constructed at a truly advanced technological level.

Christopher Dunn's *The Giza Power Plant, Technologies of Ancient Egypt* (Santa Fe, New Mexico, 1998) is one of the central works of recent pyramid unorthodoxy. Dunn is an engineer and master craftsman who was born in Manchester, England, in 1946, where he started as a journeyman lathe turner. He emigrated to the United States in 1969 to work in the aerospace industry, and rose to be Projects Engineer in an aerospace manufacturer in Illinois, and is described as a 'master craftsman'.[34] He has spent more than thirty years manufacturing precision parts for jet engines, entailing the use of non-conventional methods such as laser processing.[35] His lengthy, hands-on career as a machinist and engineer should be kept in mind before dismissing his conclusions: in the field of engineering, Dunn knows what he is talking about, while his critics arguably do not.

Dunn says that he first became interested in the Great Pyramid in 1977 when he read Peter Tompkins' *Secrets of the Great Pyramid* (New York, 1971), and became convinced that this edifice was not a gigantic tomb for a pharaoh but 'a great machine'.[36] Dunn visited the pyramids several times and came to the conclusion that an advanced system of manufacturing existed in ancient Egypt. 'Undoubtedly, some of the artefacts [in the Great Pyramid] were produced using lathes'. [37] As previously noted, Dunn claims that the

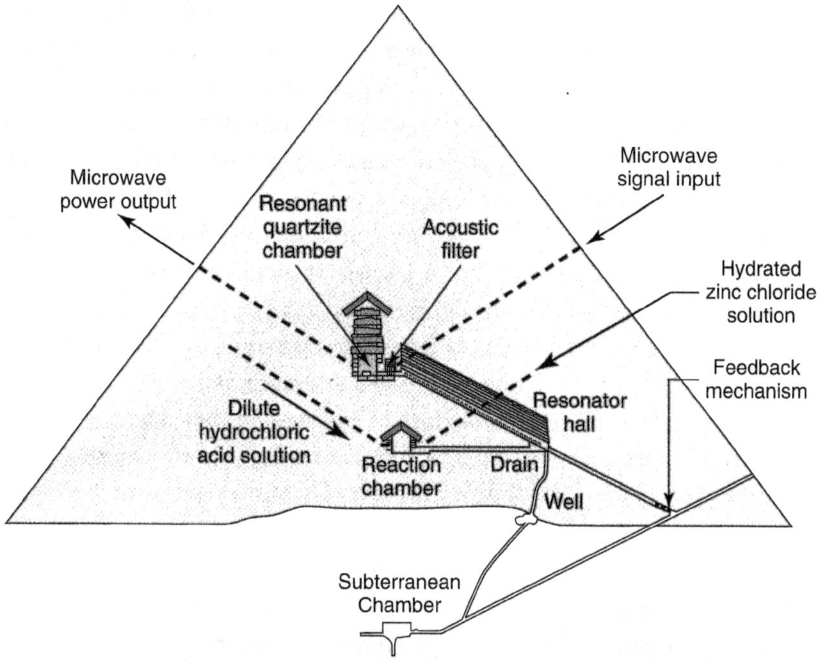

Figure 8.1 The Great Pyramid at Giza was actually a hi-tech power plant, built to produce electricity from the earth's vibrations, according to unorthodox Egyptologist Christopher Dunn. This is how it actually worked. Image from Christopher Dunn, *The Giza Power Plant* (Bear & Company Publishing, 1998), p. 220

Great Pyramid contains innumerable artefacts whose existence simply cannot be explained by the primitive technology available 4000 years ago. But he also goes beyond this to argue for something much more extraordinary, that the Great Pyramid was not a tomb at all, but a power plant. I have pointed out that both Dunn and other Egyptologists have noted that, surprisingly, there is simply no evidence that any mummy was ever entombed in the Great Pyramid; although tomb raiders might have stolen the mummy case or any nearby treasure, there are simply no surviving remnants or scraps suggesting that there was ever a tomb there at all, while the passageways in the pyramid are simply too low and narrow for the movement of a sarcophagus.[38] Indeed – and contrary to popular belief – human remains have *never* been found inside a genuine Egyptian pyramid.[39] Tomb raiders might well steal treasure, but why would they steal sarcophagi?

Dunn's explanation is that the ancient Egyptians built the Great Pyramid as a giant electric generator. Its power source were the constant vibrations of the earth's crust, drawn out by a resonator whose frequency was the same as, or a harmonic of, the earth's, producing what in engineering is called a coupled oscillator.[40] According to Dunn, the Great Pyramid is indeed in harmonic resonance with the vibrations of the earth, and acts as an acoustical horn for collecting and channelling these vibrations. The King's Chamber, the mysterious room near the centre of the Great Pyramid, is built from Asuran granite and contains 55 per cent or more of silicon-quartz crystal. It acted as a transducer, via what is known as the piezo-electric effect, to produce electricity. The Grand Gallery served as a Helmholz-type resonator (as these are technically known) to focus vibrations received throughout the pyramid. According to Dunn, the Cairo Museum holds stone artefacts which were probably the Helmholz-type resonators; they apparently have no other obvious purpose.[41] These forms of energy, both acoustical and electromagnetic, filled the King's Chamber. There they met with hydrogen gas produced from a chemical reaction in the Queen's Chamber.[42] Individual hydrogen atoms then rose to a higher state. More steps, based on high technology, were added along the way, with the hydrogen atoms amplifying and reamplifying trillions of times. This produced an extraordinary amount of electrical energy which was collected in a microwave receiver in the King's Chamber's south wall, then beamed out of the pyramid and distributed throughout Egypt. This was not done through the kind of electrical transmission we know, carried through wires, but beamed through a wireless system of the type envisioned in the early twentieth century by Nikola Tesla, the great inventor and electrical engineer who was marginalised by mainstream energy providers.[43]

To most readers, all this will surely sound as if it comes straight from the heart of Fruitcake Land, but it must be emphasised that Christopher Dunn is plainly an extremely able engineer, with decades of practical experience; I am not an engineer and nor, I suspect, are many readers of this book. It might be best to withhold ultimate judgment. Dunn's case, to a complete novice in this area, has a certain amount of plausibility, and certainly raises many questions about exactly what the Great Pyramid was built to accomplish. Nevertheless, there are self-evidently innumerable difficulties in the way of accepting even the plausibility of Dunn's theory. Apart from the general layout of the interior of the Great Pyramid, no firm evidence exists to confirm Dunn's views. No one, for instance, has ever found any sophisticated equipment, such as would indicate the existence of what we would term 'high technology', in any ancient Egyptian structure or artefact. If they ever existed, they have simply vanished. Dunn maintains that wall carvings in the cult temple of the goddess Hathor at Dendera in Upper Egypt actually depict electrical technology. This wall carving, which has been reproduced many times in Fortean works, shows three men holding transparent vessels supported on pillars and decorated with snake images; a rope of some kind connects the vessels to a statue of Atum-Ra. Dunn (and others) maintain that this depicts a Crookes tube (a cathode ray rube), a glass tube in which a partial vacuum has been created and in which an anode will allow a stream of electrodes to form a glowing image. The Crookes tube is the basis for much pre-transistor electronic tubes such as the earliest radar.[44] Needless to say, this is hard to believe and the carving surely has a more mundane explanation; there is also the fact that a carving is not an actual artefact. One fact in favour of this theory (which is also often pointed out in Fortean discussions of ancient Egypt) is that many Egyptian tombs, as well as the interior of the pyramids, show no evidence of any smoke or residue from the torches which *must* have been used to illuminate these otherwise totally dark interiors. This has led some theorists, long before Dunn, to speculate that the Egyptians must have developed some kind of electrical lighting.[45]

There is also the question of why the Egyptians generated electricity: what did they do with it? Dunn says that, when presenting his theory, he is often asked this question.[46] Dunn is vague about this, but suggests that the electricity might have been generated 'to provide power to a space ship'![47] Here, of course, Dunn goes in a direction where few would care to follow. Concerning his theory as a whole, one would perhaps be more willing to accept its plausibility if he could provide a working model of a Giza-type power plant, one employing the constant vibrations of the earth to turn hydrogen into electricity. Surely if such a generator were practical, it would potentially provide a cure for the energy crisis, global warming, and much Third World poverty, producing unlimited virtually free energy forever. The fact that no working model has ever been built must plainly count against its practicality.[48] And would the Egyptians really have used this generator merely (as it were) to power a spaceship? What 'spaceship'? Clearly, the massive amounts of electricity which the Great Pyramid allegedly generated must have been used for something; unless Dunn and others can specify what this might have been, it would be almost impossible to accept the theory, although Dunn has certainly drawn attention to many very curious features in the Great Pyramid which appear to be arguably inconsistent with its erection as a royal tomb.

Christopher Dunn, obviously a man who has the courage of his convictions, then goes on to suggest that the ancients might have fought a nuclear war, with nuclear weapons developed thousands of years ago.[49] *This* theme is examined in three books by Joseph P. Farrell: *The Giza Death Star* (Kempton, Ill, 2001); *The Giza Death Star Deployed* (Kempton, Ill, 2003); and *The Giza Death Star Destroyed: The Ancient War for Future Science* (Kempton, Ill, 2005). Farrell, an American scientist, argues that the Great Pyramid was actually a weapon of some kind, employing Tesla-like scalar impulse waves. His three-volume collection contains innumerable scientific equations and the like, which make his work difficult to assess.[50] It seems clear that the Great Pyramid retains its eternal mystery into a new millennium.

The third area where unorthodox theories of the Great Pyramid have flourished is among those who argue that the structure itself conveys advanced technological information inconsistent with its ancient date. That the pyramid was built in a way which conveys hidden but remarkable information is not a new concept. It stems from the 1850s, when Charles Pizzi Smyth, the Astronomer Royal of Scotland, published *Our Inheritance in the Great Pyramid*.[51] Smyth argued that the pyramids encoded information which could be discerned if one introduced the concept of a 'pyramid-inch' (.001 inch larger than a standard British inch), and that applying it to the passageways within the Great Pyramid gave a history of the world from its creation in 4004 B.C. to the period which would precede the Second Coming of Christ, which Smyth dated to some point between 1882 and 1911.[52] Many other similar theories, regularly finding a fundamentalist Christian account of the history of the world embedded in the dimensions of the pyramid, also appeared in the eighty years or so after 1850.

Today, those who view the Great Pyramid as an information repository of some kind are much more sophisticated. They argue that the Great Pyramid incorporated pi (π) throughout in its construction, millennia before the concept was known and that, similarly, the Golden Section (AB/AC = AC/AB, roughly 1.618, a ratio found in many natural and man-made structures) was incorporated in the pyramid many centuries before the notion was known anywhere else.[53] Some have also argued that twice the perimeter of the Great Pyramid is equal to one arc minute of longitude, meaning that the ancient Egyptians must have known, in an amazingly accurate way, the circumference of the earth. According to Smyth and others, one 'pyramid inch' is equal in length to 1/500 millionth of the earth's axis of rotation.[54] According to William Fox, in his *Pyramid Odyssey* (New York, 1978):

> *We know that someone in very deep antiquity was aware of the size and shape of the earth with great precision. The three key measurements of the earth are incorporated in the dimensions of the Great Pyramid. The perimeter of the Pyramid equals a half minute of equatorial latitude. The perimeter of the sockets equals half a minute of equatorial longitude, or 1/43,200 of the earth's circumference. The height of the Pyramid including the platform, equals 1/43,200 of the earth's polar radius ... We do not know how they measured it, but that they did so is now an article of knowledge.*[55]

There are perfectly reasonable ways in which the ancient Egyptians *might* have measured the size of the earth, for instance by observing gnomon (sundial) shadows at widely separated latitudes. The ancient Greeks did this, and estimated the size of the earth surprisingly accurately.[56] But the Egyptians built the Pyramids 2000 years before Greek civilisation reached its zenith, and their achievements are certainly uncanny. It has also been argued that the Great Pyramid is a scale model of the earth's Northern Hemisphere, with the ratio of the height of the base of the Pyramid being identical to the radius of the earth.[57] It has been argued, too, that the Great Pyramid embodies astronomical information, especially the direction of the North Star.[58] That the ancients possessed remarkable and, indeed, inexplicable astronomical knowledge is a commonplace in most unorthodox histories of the ancient, even prehistoric world. This view was probably made most familiar in Robert Temple's *The Sirius Mystery* (London, 1976), which suggested that the pre-literate Dagon peoples, living near Timbuktu in the Sahara desert, had a knowledge of the star Sirius and its invisible (without an advanced telescope) companion Sirius B, of astonishing sophistication. They also knew that the Milky Way galaxy is spiral-shaped, a fact unknown to astronomers until the 1920s. Whether this knowledge actually stems from ancient, authentic traditions, of whose nature we can only guess, or was in fact transmitted to them by twentieth-century Western anthropologists who were also astronomers, as some believe, is hotly debated.[59] More recently, Thomas G. Brophy has argued in his *The Origin Map: Discovery of a Prehistoric, Megalithic, Astrophysical Map and Sculpture of the Universe* (Lincoln, Neb., 2002), that at an Egyptian site near Aswan, Nabta Playa, a series of man-made megalithic structures are an accurate star-viewing map of the Orion constellation between 6400 B.C. and 4900 B.C. According to Brophy (a space scientist) another set of megaliths nearby most remarkably appear to be a depiction of the Milky Way galaxy – including the galactic centre, which astronomers today are unable to see – as it was in 17,700 B.C.[60] Yet another man-made object nearby – according to Brophy – depicts the Andromeda galaxy and possibly the 'Big Bang' itself.[61] . (It must be said that Brophy's book contains a series of photographs of the Nabta Playa megaliths which, to my untrained eye, appear to be nothing more than a jumble of stones.) Such theories inevitably were applied as well to the Great Pyramid, most famously by Robert Bauval and Adrian Gilbert in *The Orion Mystery* (London, 1994), which argued that the three Giza pyramids were laid out to correlate with the belt stars of the Orion constellation in *10,500 B.C.* They also argued that the so-called 'air' shafts of the Great Pyramid aligned with four major stars possessing religious significance in *c.*2500 B.C. when they were built.[62]

As will be seen, many of these very unorthodox theories about Giza claim that some or all of the renowned structures of ancient Egypt are far older than the normal dating universally accepted by academic archaeologists, and consistent with the view, held implicitly or explicitly, that a very ancient civilisation, now entirely lost or only glimpsed, had reached high levels of technological achievement millennia before the commonly-held dating. One of the best-known recent presentations of this view concerns the Sphinx, the celebrated reclining figure adjacent to the Giza pyramids. In 1979 John Anthony West published *Serpent in the Sky*, in which he argued that the Sphinx is vastly older than the 4700 years normally regarded as the period of its existence by orthodox Egyptologists, and has marked evidence, in the severe decay of its structure, of water erosion. Since northern Egypt has been arid during the past 4700 years, the Sphinx must have been built at a much earlier time than normally credited, and then experienced serious erosion by water long before ancient Egyptian history 'began'. West suggested that the Sphinx might be as old as *17–19,000* years.[63] Another well-known unorthodox Egyptologist, Robert Schoch, subsequently suggested that the weathering might have started in 10–8,000 B.C.[64] Orthodox Egyptologists have unanimously rejected this view, claiming that flash floods have occurred at Giza at regular and frequent intervals, and these account for the weathering.[65]

This theory, that the Sphinx is startlingly old, predating the normal dating of ancient Egypt by many millennia, is also consistent with an entire genre of unorthodox works on the ancient world which claim that advanced civilisations existed many tens of thousands of years ago, and perished in a catastrophe or catastrophes in the remote past. Probably the first well-known exposition of this view was made by an American professor of anthropology, Charles Hapgood, who argued, before his death in 1982, that advanced civilisations existed in America and what is now Antarctica (then, of course, not ice-covered) *100,000* years ago.[66] Such widely-distributed books as *The Atlantis Blueprint* (2001) by Rand Flem-Ath (*sic*) and Colin Wilson, Michael Baigent's *Ancient Traces* (London, 1998), and Richard Rudgley's *Lost Civilisations of the Stone Age* (London, 1998), have made this theme familiar. Still more extreme are the unorthodox archaeologists/anthropologists who argue that humans appeared on the earth, apparently reaching high levels of civilisation, *millions* of years ago. Probably the best-known exposition of this view is *Forbidden Archaeology: The Hidden History of the Human Race* (San Diego, 1993), by Michael Cremo and Richard L. Thompson, a 914–page catalogue of archaeological and anthropological anomalies ignored or disregarded by conventional academics, which is regarded as an underground classic. Beyond this I do not propose to go. I am not qualified to assess the evidence presented in any of these works, only to record that it exists, and perhaps to ask why it is not mor openly discussed or assessed.[67]

Notes

Chapter 1 Introduction: The 'Amateur Historian' and the Study of History

1 See Robert Alan Goldberg, *Enemies Within: The Culture of Conspiracy in Modern America* (New Haven, 2001) and David Southwell and Sean Twist, *Conspiracy Theories* (London, 1999). Richard Hofstadter's *The Paranoid Style of American Politics and Other Essays* (New York, 1967) is a classic work on this subject.

2 And often misunderstood by foreigners. In 2002 there occurred the well-publicised case of a group of British airplane spotters – similar to 'train spotters' – who were arrested in Greece as spies for observing a Greek military base and copying the numbers of Greek military aircraft into notebooks. They were released from serving a stiff prison sentence only after an international outcry. The Greek authorities found it impossible to understand that their interest in seeing and recording as many Greek aircraft as possible was an entirely innocent and well-known aspect of English culture entirely without a Greek equivalent.

3 In December 2006 a semi-official report on the death of Princess Diana was issued in London after a lengthy investigation headed by Lord Stevens, former head of the Metropolitan Police. In over 800 pages, it concluded that Diana and the others died accidentally, their deaths caused by the fact that their driver was drunk and speeding through a tunnel, and that there was no conspiracy of any kind.

4 See Mathias Broeckers, *Conspiracies, Conspiracy Theories, and the Secrets of 9/11* (Joshua Tree, Cal., 2006) for a sample, or try any of the innumerable internet sites.

5 See David Dunbar and Brad Regan, eds., *Debunking 9/11 Myths: Why Conspiracy Theories Can't Stand Up to the Facts* (New York, 2006), for a level-headed analysis, published by America's *Popular Mechanics* magazine.

It might be worth making the point that historical analyses of the topics treated in this book have much in common, in their use of evidence and in the element of surprise, with the classical detective stories which flourished in Britain (especially) and America between about 1900 and 1960. Indeed, reading a great many classical detective stories, where a consideration of the evidence leads to the identity of the killer, is an excellent training ground for any historian. A well-known anthology built around this theme is Robin W. Winks, ed., *The Historian as Detective: Essays on Evidence* (New York, 1970).

Chapter 2 The Assassination of President Kennedy

1 One exception to the pattern is Michael L. Kurtz, *Crime of the Century: The Kennedy Assassination from a Historian's Perspective* (Knoxville, Tennessee, 1982; revised edition 1983). Although this is a well-written and intelligent work by Professor Kurtz (of Southeastern Lousiana State University), his conclusions, that four shots were fired at Kennedy, and that the assassination was 'masterminded' by Fidel Castro 'in retaliation for the repeated attempts against his own life during the Kennedy administration', using Mafia boss Santos Trafficante (*Crime of the Century*, p.l), seem quite incredible. Only three shots were fired at Kennedy, all by Oswald, while the Mafia had been booted out of Cuba by Castro. (Kurtz believes that Castro made an agreement with Trafficante allowing him to use Cuba as a narcotics base.) Kurtz (p.ll) believes that Oswald 'was recruited as a decoy' and that there were three assassins, two firing from the Depository building and one from the 'grassy knoll'. But the Depository building was a busy warehouse; any stranger – let alone two strangers on the day Kennedy was killed – would have been noticed and reported by some of the dozens of persons employed there. No such strangers were ever noticed or reported. They would, moreover, have had to be completely familiar with the layout of the Depository building and all means of rapid escape. Professor Kurtz recently published a revised account of the assassination, *The JFK Assassination Debates: Lone Gunman Versus Conspiracy* (Lawrence, Kansas, 2006), which reiterates his position that there was a conspiracy behind the assassination. Some of Professor Kurtz's conclusions appear very dubious. For instance, he states (p.38) that 'the autopsy' conducted in Bethesda, 'concluded that Kennedy suffered four bullet wounds ... In other words, President Kennedy was shot twice from above and behind.' This cannot possibly be true because all credible witnesses heard only three shots, the first of which missed the President. He states (p.202) that 'the slaying of Lee Harvey Oswald by Jack Ruby had all the hallmarks of an organised crime hit', and that Ruby was closely connected with the Mafia. But I am unfamiliar with any gangland slaying ever carried out live on national television, in a room holding seventy policemen, where the Mafia hitman was certain to be shot dead on the spot or captured and probably executed. Kurtz also claims (p.21) that 'the Warren Commission conducted a perfunctory inquiry into the assassination'. My definition of

'perfunctory', however, is not consistent with a *Report* of ten million words following the interviewing of over 550 witnesses.

2 On Oswald's life, see Gerald Posner, *Case Closed: Lee Harvey Oswald and the Assassination of JFK* (New York, 1994), and *The Warren Commission Report: Report of the President's Commission on the Assassination of President John F Kennedy* [Volume One of the Warren Report, originally 1964] (reprinted New York, n.d. [*c.*1997], pp.375–424.

3 Posner, *op.cit.*, p.375.

4 Although some Critics believe that Ruby later invented this as a convenient motive, KRLD-TV reporter Wes Wise, who ran into Ruby (whom he knew) on the afternoon of Saturday 23 November, later recalled that Ruby then told him that 'Isn't it awful that Jackie is going to have to come back here and be a witness at a murder trial?' (*President Kennedy Has Been Shot* (Napersville, Ill., 2003), p.188).

5 See the biographical descriptions of the staff members in *The Warren Commission Report*, *op.cit.*, pp.467–481. J. Lee Rankin was the Commission's General Counsel. He had been U.S. Solicitor General in the Eisenhower administration, 1956–61, but in 1963 was in private practice in New York.

6 *Ibid.*, p.xii.

7 *Ibid.*, pp.637–668.

8 Posner, *op.cit.*, p.409, footnote.

9 *Ibid.*, p.399.

10 Thomas G. Buchanan, *Who Killed Kennedy?* (London, 1964), dust jacket.

11 Posner, *op.cit.*, p.412.

12 Buchanan, *Who Killed Kennedy?*, p.77.

13 *Ibid.*, pp.81–87.

14 *Ibid.*, pp.87–93.

15 *Ibid.*, pp.98–100.

16 *Ibid.*, p.119.

17 *Ibid.*, pp.121, 132, 136–140. Ruby was 'a "frontman" for the Chicago gang which was once run by Al Capone'. (*Ibid.*, p.137)

18 *Ibid.*, p.121.

19 *Ibid.*, p.137.

20 *Ibid.*, pp.146–154, 171.

21 *Ibid.*, p.183.

22 In 1964, German leftist Joachim Joesten also published a similar book, *Oswald: Assassin or Fall-guy?*.

23 Weisberg, *Never Again!*, pp.viii-ix.

24 Posner, *op.cit.*, p.412.

25 *Ibid.*, p.413.

26 *Ibid.*, p.414.

27 All his works were published together in one volume, *The Assassination Chronicles* (1992).

28 Two sets of medical documents exist for the period just after President Kennedy was shot: the first, briefest set by doctors treating him in Dallas, and the second, some hours later, from a fuller autopsy by doctors at Bethesda Hospital near Washington, D.C. There is general agreement that neither set of medical reports is wholly satisfactory. The fuller autopsy at Bethesda was briefer than it should have been, in large part because Kennedy's family wanted it completed as soon as possible. None of the Bethesda physicians were forensic specialists.

29 Another frequently reiterated point made by the Warren Critics is that by1978 there were over 100 'mysterious deaths' of persons involved in the case. As Posner (pp.481–498) points out with detailed evidence, there have been *no* mysterious deaths of anyone connected with the assassination. As he wryly notes, too, no Warren Critic has ever died mysteriously; most, indeed, appear to be unusually long-lived. Lifton's *Crossfire* is original in claiming that Kennedy's body was secretly removed from the plane carrying it to Washington D.C., and tampered with to make it seem as if he had been shot from the rear.

30 Jim Marrs, *Crossfire: The Plot That Killed Kennedy* (London, 1989), pp.580–582.

31 Harrison Edward Livingstone and Robert J. Groden, *High Treason: The Assassination of JFK and the Case for Conspiracy* (New York, 1998), pp.350–354.

32 Twyman, *Bloody Treason*, pp.833–835.

33 Harrison E. Livingstone, *The Radical Right and the Murder of John F. Kennedy* (Victoria, British Columbia, 2004), pp.512–513.

34 Apart from the fairly crude conspiracy theories among the Warren Critics, one occasionally finds something more sophisticated from a different milieu. Peter Dale Scott's *Deep Politics and the Death of JFK* (1993), published, bizarrely, by the University of California Press, was written by a professor of English at the University of California – Berkeley. Scott, briefly a Canadian diplomat, and (I gather) a published poet, takes it for granted that Kennedy's assassination was the result of right-wing forces within the American government, and goes on from there to an extended, almost byzantine 'account' of the 'deep politics' of decision making in modern America. The result, in my opinion, is paranoia with footnotes. It is shameful that a major university academic press would publish such a work.

35 Although Scheim does claim (p.190) that 'the common desire to eliminate the Castro regime eventually led to cooperative activity between the Mob and the CIA', and that there was (p.193), a 'possible connection to the Kennedy assassination.'

36 Anthony Summers, *The Kennedy Conspiracy* (London, 1999), p. 377; Posner, *Case Closed*, p.403.

37 *The Warren Commission Report: Report of the President's Commission on*

the Assassination of President John F Kennedy [Volume One of the Warren Report] (Washington, D.C., 1964; reprinted New York, n.d.), p.374.

38 Posner, it might be said, does not sufficiently acknowledge Moore's book, referring to it only in one footnote (p.254, footnote), and certainly not acknowledging the debt he obviously owed to it. A number of excellent television documentaries, especially those made by the History Channel, have also correctly dismissed all the conspiracy theories of the assassination.

39 Posner, p.448. Posner's account of Garrison's prosecution (pp.421–450) is particularly good.

40 *Ibid.*, p.466.

41 *Ibid.*, pp.238–240.

42 *Ibid.*, p.240.

43 These include long sections of two other books edited by Fetzer, *Assassination Science: Experts Speak Out on the Death of JFK* (Chicago, 1998), pp.207–344; and *Murder in Dealey Plaza* (Chicago, 2000), pp.325–360. The essays on Zapruder were written by a number of well-known current Warren Critics, including David W. Mantik, David Lifton, Jack White, and Noel Twyman.

44 See the commentary by Richard Stolley, Los Angeles regional editor of *Life* magazine (who actually bought the film from Zapruder) in *President Kennedy Has Been Shot*, pp.177–178.

45 If there were 'two Oswalds' from the 1950s, one must have been groomed for the job of killing President Kennedy several years before Kennedy became president. On this strange theory, see John Armstrong, *Harvey and Lee: How the CIA Framed Oswald* (2003), and his two essays on this subject (pp.91–135) in James DiEugenio and Lisa Pease, eds., *The Assassinations: Probe Magazine on JFK, MLK, RFK and Malcolm X* (Los Angeles, n.d., *c.*2003). The disputed medical evidence is convincingly examined by Posner, pp.285–315 and in Sturdivan, *JFK Myths*, pp.103–21.

46 Bonar Menninger, *Mortal Error: The Shot That Killed Kennedy* (New York and London, 1992). Menninger's book is based on the research of Howard Donahue, who has been investigating the assassination since 1967. The book (p.250) identifies the agent as George Hickey.

47 The Warren Report (*op.cit.*, p.51) states that 'Special Agent George W. Hickey, Jr., in the rear seat of the presidential followup car, picked up and cocked an automatic rifle as he heard the last shot. At this point the cars were speeding through the underpass and had left the scene of the shooting, but Hickey kept the automatic weapon ready as the car raced to the hospital.'

48 *Warren Commission Report*, p.387.

49 *Ibid.*

50 See Dan Moldea, *The Killing of Robert F. Kennedy: An Investigation of Motive, Means, and Opportunity* (New York, 1995), a meticulous and level-headed study. Another book, all too little known, which should be read is Mel Ayton, *Questions of Controversy: The Kennedy Brothers* (Sunderland, 2001),

which discusses – and calmly analyses – all the rumours about the Kennedys – their alleged affairs, relations with J. Edgar Hoover, etc. The book (pp.265–288) includes an excellent discussion of 'The JFK Assassination'.
51 See Gerald Posner, *Killing the Dream: James Earl Ray and the Assassination of Martin Luther King Jr* (New York, 1998), and Mel Ayton, *A Racial Crime: James Earl Ray and the Murder of Dr. Martin Luther King, Jr.* (Las Vegas, 2005).
52 *President Kennedy Has Been Shot*, p.23
53 *Ibid.*, p.24. This was apparently an extract from his UPI dispatch of that day.
54 *Ibid.*, p.23.
55 *Ibid.*, p.34.
56 *Reporting the Kennedy Assassination*, p.32.
57 *Ibid.*, p.30.
58 *Ibid.*, p.42.
59 *Case Closed*, p.235. The 1979 House Select Committee concluded that four shots were fired. As noted, the evidence on which this conclusion was based was fundamentally and totally flawed (*Case Closed*, pp.238–243).
60 *Case Closed*, pp.244–249, and 228–234.
61 *Ibid.*, p.241. As Posner notes (*Ibid.*), this testimony is omitted by most Warren Critics, since it is so damning.
62 *President Kennedy Has Been Killed*, p.23.
63 *Ibid.*, p.24.
64 *Case Closed*, pp.245–246.
65 *Ibid.*, pp.246–249.
66 Posner, pp.xv, 281–284.
67 Posner, pp.474–478.
68 *Case Closed*, pp.220–222.
69 *Ibid.*, p.224, footnote, and *Conspiracy One*, p.46. The paper bag contained the mail order assassination rifle, which Oswald had brought from the garage of the house in which his wife was living. Oswald had previously purchased the mail order rifle.
70 *Case Closed*, p.271.
71 *Ibid.*, p.266, footnote.
72 See *With Malice*, especially pp.235–286; *Case Closed*, pp.272–279; *Conspiracy One*, pp.59–63.
73 *Case Closed*, p.277.
74 *Case Closed*, p.280.
75 *Ibid.*, p.346.
76 *The Warren Commission Report*, p.328.
77 *Ibid.*, p.329.
78 *Case Closed*, pp.20–202
79 *Ibid.*, p.200.
80 *Warren Commission Report*, p.328. Obviously, he had no credit cards, which

were not widely available in 1963, and had no travel ticket or a passport on him.

81 *Case Closed*, pp.360–364. Assertions about Ruby's participation in the Mafia build on the fact that, as a teenager in the Chicago slums, Ruby ran errands for the Al Capone gang (presumably not insisting on a tip!). Ruby had no further contact with organised crime after being drafted into the army in World War Two, and moved to Dallas in 1947. Ruby, whose original name was Jacob Rubenstein, has apparently been confused by some writers with Harry Rubenstein, a convicted Chicago gangster. The two were not related or connected.

82 *Case Closed*, p.368, footnote; *Warren Commission Report*, pp.359–364.

83 Michael O'Brien, *John F. Kennedy: A Biography* (New York, 2005), pp.865–866.

Chapter 3 The 'Jack the Ripper' Murders

1 The historical literature on Jack the Ripper is extremely large, and one can do no more here than mention a few of the most useful and important works. Many very good narrative accounts of the Ripper crimes exist. One such recent good general account is Paul Begg, *Jack the Ripper: The Definitive History* (Harlow, 2004). (Begg is one of the very best and fairest of 'Ripperologists'.) Maxim Jakubowski and Nathan Braund, eds., *The Mammoth Book of Jack the Ripper* (London, 1999), an inexpensive paperback, contains an excellent series of general and reference accounts of the Ripper, including many essays supporting one or another suspect. Philip Sugden, *The Complete History of Jack the Ripper* (New York, 2002), is also useful. There are two Ripper encyclopedias which anyone with a serious interest should own: Paul Begg, Martin Fido, and Keith Skinner, eds., *The Jack the Ripper A–Z* (London, 1996), by three renowned Ripper experts (termed Begg *et al* in this chapter), and John J. Eddlelston, *Jack the Ripper: An Encyclopedia* (London, 2002), in some respects an even more wide-ranging work. M.J. Trow, *The Many Faces of Jack the Ripper* (Chichester, 1998), is an illustrated reference-like account. A number of works contain verbatim reprinting of contemporary newspaper accounts, letters to newspapers, and the like. These include Stewart P. Evans and Keith Skinner, *The Ultimate Jack the Ripper Sourcebook: An Illustrated Encyclopedia* (London, 2000); idem., *Jack the Ripper: Letters From Hell* (Stroud, 2001); Stephen P. Ryder, *Public Reactions to Jack the Ripper – Letters to the Editor: August-December 1888* (Madison, Wisconsin, n.d. [2006]); Stawell Heard, *Jack the Ripper in the Provinces: The English Provincial Press Reporting of the Whitechapel Murders* (Blackheath, 2005); and *How the Newspapers Covered the Jack the Ripper Murders* (essays) in *Ripper Notes*, January 2005 (No.21). Robin Odell's recent *Ripperology:*

A Study of the World's First Serial Killer and a Literary Phenomenon (Kent, Ohio, 2006), is an excellent historiographical account of the development of writing on the Ripper. Other works, generally about individual suspects, are noted throughout this chapter. I would like to thank Paul Begg for helpfully answering a number of my queries.

2 'Ripperologists' refer to the five generally-accepted victims of the Ripper as the 'canonical' five. Some researchers believe that there might have been other victims of the Ripper at either earlier or later dates. For instance, on 7 August 1888, Martha Tabram, aged 39, a hawker and prostitute of Spitalfields, was found murdered in George Yard off Whitechapel. She had been stabbed thirty-nine times. At her inquest, the coroner described her murder as 'one of the most horrible crimes' of recent times. The Tabram murder took place only three weeks before the first of the 'canonical' murders. It is generally believed that she had been stabbed by a soldier-client, and was apparently not regarded as a Ripper victim by the MacNaghten Memorandum (q.v. below), although some senior police officers at the time considered that she was. Tabram was apparently killed by a soldier's bayonet, although these wounds might have been inflicted by a penknife. (Begg *et al.*, *Jack the Ripper A–Z*, pp.444–6.) On 13 February 1891, more than two years after the apparent end of the Ripper killings, Frances Coles, aged 25, was found dead with her throat cut in Swallow Gardens in the East End. A fireman on the merchant ship *Fez* named James Thomas Sadler, a client of Coles, was arrested and tried for her murder, but acquitted. (*Ibid.*, pp.83–85 and 379–380.) The killing of Martha Tabram certainly looks suspiciously like a Ripper killing, although, as with everything in this puzzling series of horrors, there is room for doubt. An important recent contribution to this question is Stewart P. Evans and Donald Rumbelow, *Jack the Ripper: Scotland Yard Investigates* (Stroud, 2006), by two leading Ripper experts, which argues that Elizabeth Stride and Mary Kelly might have been killed by someone other than the man who murdered the other victims.

3 Maxim Jakubowski and Nathan Braund, 'Just the Facts;, in *The Mammoth Book*, pp.19–21; Begg *et al.*, pp.317–321.

4 Jakubowski and Braund, *op.cit.*, pp.21–29.

5 *Ibid.*, Begg *et al.*, *A–Z*, pp.75–78; 239–341; 464–465.

6 There were many differences between the Stride case and the others, for example in the fact that she had been assaulted and thrown to the pavement by a young drunk. (Begg *et al.*, *Ibid.*, pp.434–438; Jakubowski and Braund, *Ibid.*, pp.29–37.)

7 Jakubowski and Braund, pp.37–45; Begg *et al.*,*op.cit.*, pp.121–126.

8 Begg *et al.*, *op.cit.*, pp.197–199.

9 *Ibid.*, pp.259–261.

10 Jakubowski and Braund, *op.cit.*, pp.47–57; Begg *et al.*, pp.214–220.

11 Jakubowski and Braund, *op.cit.*, p.9.

12 Begg *et al.*, *op.cit.*, pp.21–23.
13 *Ibid.*, pp.301–302. See also M.J. Trow, *Many Faces*, pp.93–106; and Begg, *Definitive History*, pp.70–104.
14 Begg *et al.*, *op.cit.*, p.300.
15 Jakubowski and Braund, *op.cit.*, p.476.
16 *Ibid.*
17 Begg *et al.*, pp.255–256. Marie Bellow Lownes (1869–1947) was the sister of Hilaire Belloc, the famous writer. She wrote four volumes of autobiography. It is possible that she received useful correspondence on the Ripper case after her book appeared. If her correspondence survives, it ought to be read by Ripper researchers.
18 Begg *et al.*, *op.cit.*, p.269.
19 *Ibid.*, pp.14, 132, 272.
20 *Ibid.*, p.273.
21 *Ibid.* It is now known that Ostrog was in France at the time of the Ripper killings. See Evans and Rumbelow, *Jack the Ripper: Scotland Yard Investigates*, p.264, citing the research of Philip Sugden.
22 *Ibid.*, pp.273–274.
23 *Ibid.*, pp.256, 279–280,
24 *Ibid.*, p.280.
25 Begg *et al.*, *op.cit.*, pp.431–434. Stowell had first mentioned this theory to the well-known writer Colin Wilson in 1960 (*Ibid.*, p.432).
26 *Ibid.*, pp.152–153, 432–433.
27 *Ibid.*, p.409.
28 It was also given further publicity in a number of other works, for instance Melvyn Fairclough's *The Ripper and the Royals* (1991) and Kevin O'Donnell, *The Jack the Ripper Whitechapel Murders* (1997).
29 Eddleston, *op.cit.*, p.247.
30 Begg *et al.*, pp.224–226; Jakubowski and Braund, pp.460–463; Eddleston, *op.cit.*, pp.202–204; Trow, pp.134–137.
31 Begg *et al.*, pp.8–13.
32 Begg *et al.*, p.12.
33 Begg *et al.*, pp.225–226; 247. Eddleston, *op.cit.*, p.140.
34 Begg *et al.*, pp.343–345; 246–247. LeQueux claimed that the Russian document implicating Pedachenko had been dictated by Rasputin (Eddleston, *op.cit.*, p.272).
35 Begg *et al.*, pp.457–458; Eddleston, *op.cit.*, pp.240–242; Trow, pp.127–130; Jabukowski and Braund, *op.cit.*, pp.465–467.
36 Begg *et al.*, p.455.
37 Begg *et al.*, p.251. The Littlechild letter came to light through the efforts of researcher Stewart Evans, a former police officer, in 1993.
38 *Ibid.*, p.456.
39 Begg *et al.*, pp.35–36; Eddleston, *op.cit.*, pp.197–199; Trow, *op.cit.*,

pp.134–135. Bruce Paley, 'The Facts Speak for Themselves', in Jakubowski and Braund, *op.cit.*, pp.228–258.

40 Begg *et al.*, p.36.
41 Begg *et al.*, pp.439–441.
42 *Ibid.*, pp.441–443.
43 Begg *et al.*, pp.228–229.
44 *Ibid.*, pp.81–82. See also Martin Fido, 'David Cohen and the Polish Jew Theory', in Jakubowski and Braund, *op.cit.*, pp.164–186.
45 Begg *et al., op.cit.*, p.82.
46 *Ibid.*
47 *Ibid.*
48 Montagu personally posted a reward of £100 for any information about the Ripper (Begg *et al.*, p.303). Montagu presumably received hundreds of letters about the Ripper (as did other local M.P.s and elected officials). If these survive, they ought certainly to be examined by researchers.
49 Begg *et al., op.cit.*, pp.16–17, 152–153; Eddleston, *op.cit.*, pp.195–196, 223–224; Trow, *op.cit.*, pp.152–153; Colin Wilson, 'A Lifetime in Ripperology', in Jakubowski and Braund, *op.cit.*, pp.417–432, and Begg, *Jack the Ripper*, pp.356–366. See also Kevin O'Donnell, *The Jack the Ripper Whitechapel Murders* (London, 1997).
50 Begg *et al., op.cit.*
51 Eddleston, *op.cit.*, p.240. He was first named as a possible suspect by Richard Patterson, in a privately printed work published in Australia in 1999, *Paradox* (*Ibid.*, p.251). How he could have leapt into eighth place on the 'Casebook' list is a mystery.
52 Begg *et al., op.cit.*, pp.109–114. Druitt was a leading cricketer at Winchester a few years after MacNaghten was at Eton, and it is perhaps surprising that MacNaghten had apparently never heard of him, describing him incorrectly as a 'doctor of about 41 years of age' (he was actually twenty-nine and not a doctor). MacNaghten claimed to have spoken to Druitt's family about him, making these errors more curious, even suspicious.
53 *Ibid.*, p.109.
54 *Ibid.*, p.112. McCormick made this suggestion, based on the evidence of an unidentified 'London doctor' in the 1986 edition of his *The Identity of Jack the Ripper*. Begg *et al., op.cit.*, suggest that this book should be used with 'extreme caution'. (*Ibid.*, p.265.)
55 Eddleston, *op.cit.*, p.110. MacNaghten stated in his 'Memorandum' that 'it was alleged that he was sexually insane'.
56 *Ibid.*, p.110.
57 *Ibid.*, p.111; Jakubowski and Braund, *op.cit.*, p.4.
58 Eddlelston, *op.cit.*, A good recent exposition of the case for Druitt is Andrew J. Spallek, 'Montague John Druitt: Still Our Best Suspect', *Ripper Notes*, Issue 23 (July 2005), pp.4–21.

59 Begg *et al.*, *op.cit.*, pp.408–410.
60 *Ibid.*, pp.410–411.
61 *Ibid.*, pp.375–376.
62 See the useful discussion of this on the 'Casebook' website.
63 Begg *et al.*, *op.cit.*, pp.428, 430. See also Jakubowski and Braund, *op.cit.*, pp.445–450; Eddleston, *op.cit.*, pp.238–239. In October 1888, Stephenson wrote a letter to the City of London police suggesting that the word 'Juwes' in the Goulston Street Graffito [graffiti] was actually the French word 'Juives', and that the Ripper was a Frenchman. (Jakubowski and Braund, *op.cit.*, pp.447–448.)
64 *Ibid.*
65 Begg *et al.*, *op.cit.*, pp.207–208.
66 Her allegedly unfair conviction became a *cause célébre* in America, remembered many years later. When she died in 1941, her death was reported on the front page of the *New York Times.* On her life see Anne E. Graham and Carol Emmas, *The Last Victim: The Extraordinary Life of Florence Maybrick, the wife of Jack the Ripper* (1999) (Anne E. Graham owned the Ripper 'Diary'), and Bernard Ryan, *The Poisoned Life of Mrs. Maybrick* (1977).
67 Begg *et al.*, *op.cit.*, pp.289–295; Eddleston, *op.cit.*, pp.225–230.
68 Shirley Harrison, ed., *The Diary of Jack the Ripper* (1993) contains the complete contents of the 'Diary'. Paul H. Feldman, *Jack the Ripper. The Final Chapter* (1997), contains a lengthy account of the Diary by a researcher who believed it to be authentic. Seth Linder, Caroline Morris, and Keith Skinner, *Ripper Diary: The Inside Story* (2003) contains an even-handed account of the 'Diary', without arriving at any firm conclusion. See also Shirley Harrison, 'The Diary of Jack the Ripper', in Jakubowski and Braund, *op.cit.*, pp.204–227.
69 A video cassette exists of Barrett's talk on the 'diary' at the Cloak and Dagger Club in 1998. Barrett made a number of claims about forging the 'Diary' which are not regarded as reliable.
70 Another theory, explored by Feldman (*op.cit.*) is that William Graham was the son of Florence Maybrick and a shipowner named Henry Flinn.
71 This is consistent with the fact that the Ripper did not have sexual relations with any of his victims. Maybrick was fifty in 1888, it should be noted.
72 Feldman, *Final Chapter*, pp.106–108. Christie's book on Florence Maybrick was *Etched in Arsenic.*
73 Michael Maybrick has an entry in the *Oxford Dictionary of National Biography.* He wrote the song 'The Holy Boy', which has often been recorded.
74 Feldman, *Final Chapter*, p.294. The 'Stage' is apparently a reference to the Liverpool docks.
75 Shirley Harrison's more recent book, *Jack the Ripper: The American Connection* (London, 2003), outlines the view that Maybrick was responsible for a series of brutal murders of black women in Austin, Texas, in 1884–85

Maybrick was known to have been in Virginia in 1884, but his whereabouts during most of the 1884–85 period are unknown.

76 Drysdale gave evidence about this on oath at Mrs. Maybrick's trial. See also Feldman, *Final Chapter* p.80, and Ryan, *Poisoned Life*, p.29.

77 The letter is reprinted in Ryan, *Ibid.*, p.58.

78 One question which has sometimes been raised by 'Diary' opponents in connection with Mrs. Maybrick is why she did not expose her husband as Jack the Ripper at her trial (for instance, see Odell, *Ripperology*, p.187). The reason for this is simple: Mrs. Maybrick pleaded *innocent* at her trial. If she had pleaded guilty and confessed to killing her husband, she would have automatically been sentenced to death. No judge, jury, or Home Secretary was likely to have accepted in mitigation the utterly incredible claim that her husband was Jack the Ripper. She did not have the 'Diary' (which she had presumably never seen), and she would obviously have been asked why, if she knew that her husband was Jack the Ripper, she didn't go to the police. An assertion that her husband was Jack the Ripper would have sent her straight to the gallows.

79 Feldman, *Final Chapter*, p.189.

80 See Rob Sindall, *Street Violence in the Nineteenth Century: Media Panic or Real Danger* (Leicester, 1990).

81 See Begg *et al.*, *op.cit.*, pp.294–295; Linder *et al.*, *Ripper Diary*, pp.40–43.

82 Begg *et al.*, *op.cit.*

83 Marriott, *op.cit.*, pp.295–302.

Chapter 4 The Shakespeare Authorship Question

1 The three leading books on the Authorship Question are: R.C. Churchill, *Shakespeare and His Betters* (London, 1958); H.N. Gibson, *The Shakespeare Claimants* (London, 1962; reprinted 1971); and John Michell, *Who Wrote Shakespeare?* (London, 1996). The development of the 'anti-Stratfordian' position (i.e., that someone else, apart from William Shakespeare of Stratford, wrote the works bearing his name) is discussed in detail, but in a highly negative way, in S. Schoenbaum, *Shakespeare's Lives* (New Edition, Oxford, 1991), pp.385–454. See also my brief overview of the subject, 'Who Was Shakespeare?', *History Today*, August 2001. All of the main 'candidates' as Author have generated a literature in their favour by partisans, with, in recent decades, the Oxfordian output dwarfing all others. Among the works supporting the claims of Edward De Vere, seventeenth Earl of Oxford as the author are: Charlton Ogburn, *The Mystery of William Shakespeare* (London, 1988), a 779–page paperback described as an *abridged* edition of a work originally published in 1984; Joseph Sobran, *Alias Shakespeare* (New York, 1997); Richard F. Whalen, *Shakespeare: Who Was He?* (Westport, Conn.,

1994); and the recent lengthy and sophisticated work by Mark Anderson, *'Shakespeare' By Another Name* (New York, 2005). One of the best Oxfordian works of recent years is a collection of essays by more than twenty advocates of the De Vere thesis, Richard Malin, ed., *Great Oxford: Essays on the Life and Work of Edward De Vere, 17th Earl of Oxford, 1550–1604* (Tunbridge Wells, 2004), with a Foreword by Sir Derek Jacobi. While Baconism has been in decline in recent years, some highly intelligent Baconian works continue to appear, such as N.B. Cockburn, *The Bacon Shakespeare Question: The Baconian Theory Made Sane* (Surrey, 1998), and Peter Dawkins, *The Shakespeare Enigma* (London, 2004). The Shakespeare Oxford Society of Washington D.C. produces an excellent annual journal, about 200 pages long, with extremely impressive articles, *The Oxfordian.* Possibly the best account of the deficiencies of the orthodox account of Shakespeare's life, without naming or suggesting a specific alternative Author, is Diana Price, *Shakespeare's Unorthodox Biography: New Evidence of an Authorship Problem* (Westport, Conn., 2001). Another general account of the deficiencies of the normal view is Bertram Fields, *Players: The Mysterious Identity of William Shakespeare* (New York, 2005). Few books specifically *defend* the orthodox viewpoint, but see Scott McCrea, *The Case for Shakespeare: The End of the Authorship Question* (Westport, Conn., 2005), and the valuable website of David Kathman and Terry Ross, *The Shakespeare Authorship Page* (www.shakespeareauthorship.com). The book I co-authored, Brenda James and William D. Rubinstein, *The Truth Will Out* (London, 2005), discusses the Authorship Question and makes the case, which we believe to be convincing, for Sir Henry Neville as the real author.

2 Shakespeare was baptised, married, and buried as a conforming Anglican, and both of his daughters married Anglicans, one a Puritan, Dr. John Hall. Nevertheless, in recent decades an extensive genre of biography has appeared claiming that Shakespeare was a secret Catholic, for example Ian Wilson, *Shakespeare: The Evidence* (London, 1993); Richard Wilson, *Secret Shakespeare: Studies in Theatre, Religion and Resistance* (Manchester, 2004); Stephen Greenblatt, *Will in the World: How Shakespeare Became Shakespeare* (London, 2004); and Clare Asquith, *Shadowplay* (New York, 2005). Asquith's book claims (p.28) that Shakespeare might have secretly attended Oxford University and then attended the English College in Rome, for English Catholics. There is, needless to say, not one iota of evidence to support this supposition. The traditional account of how Shakespeare came to London claims that he poached deer illegally, fled to London, held horses at the stage door, and then attached himself to a theatre company. The new view is that he spent two years in two wealthy Catholic households in *Lancashire* (a county with Shakespeare had no known connections) as a kind of tutor-entertainer, and then attached himself to Lord Strange's acting company and came to London. The only evidence for this suggestion comes

from the 1581 will of Alexander Houghton of Lea, Lancashire, which left a small legacy to a 'William Shakeshaft (*sic*) now dwelling with me.' A virtual industry has arisen on the basis of the far-fetched proposition that this was William Shakespeare. See E.A.J. Honigman, *Shakespeare: The 'Lost Years'* (Manchester, 1985).

3 Schoenbaum, *Shakespeare's Lives*, pp.99–110.

4 Chambers, *William Shakespeare*, II, pp.147–254. Aubrey (who is regarded as notoriously unreliable) apparently derived much of his information from an interview with William Beeston, the son of an actor in Shakespeare's Company in 1598, eighty-three years earlier, and from Sir William Davenant, who claimed, without evidence, to be Shakespeare's illegitimate son (*Ibid.*, pp.252, 254).

5 Cited in *ibid.*, p.264.

6 *Ibid.*, p.265.

7 *Ibid.*, p.169; F.E. Halliday, *Shakespeare Companion*, p.195.

8 Halliday, *Companion*, p.299.

9 Schoenbaum, *Shakespeare's Lives*, pp.99–272.

10 Michell, *Who Wrote Shakespeare?*, p.103.

11 *Ibid.*, pp.103–104. Schoenbaum, *op.cit.*, pp.397–399. There is some doubt about the authenticity of Cowell's paper.

12 Schoenbaum, *Shakespeare's Lives*, pp.395–404.

13 *Ibid.*, p.405.

14 I refer to him throughout as 'De Vere' rather than as 'Oxford' to avoid confusion with the town or university.

15 Schoenbaum, *Shakespeare's Lives*, pp.430–440; Michell, *Who Wrote Shakespeare*, pp.61–189.

16 *Ibid.*, p.164; Schoenbaum, *op.cit.*, pp.440–444.

17 Michell, *Ibid.*, pp.164–165 and Schoenbaum, *op.cit.*, pp.431–432, reprint Looney's list.

18 See, for instance, William Farina, *De Vere As Shakespeare: An Oxfordian Reading of the Canon* (Jefferson, N.C., 2006), p.195.

19 *Ibid.*, pp.189–194.

20 Churchill, *Shakespeare and His Betters*, p.225.

21 This is the solution apparently preferred by John Michell, *Who Wrote Shakespeare?*, pp.259–261.

22 Halliday, *Companion*, p.140; Schoenbaum, *op.cit.*, pp.354–362.

23 Today, the most frequently encountered example of an *outré* opinion about an historical event is probably 'Holocaust denial', the notion that the Jewish Holocaust of the Second World War was a 'hoax'. No academic historian could ever take the exposition of 'Holocaust denial' as anything other than malign propaganda and none ever has. Its exponents would be asked to provide evidence for their viewpoint. Since none exists, while there is overwhelming factual evidence, accepted by all historians of the period

without exception, that the genocide of the Jews actually occurred, anyone making such a claim would be dismissed as an antisemitic crackpot, with, of course, all such claims emanating from the extreme right or, more recently, Islamist sources. Asserting that someone besides William Shakespeare wrote his works is frequently compared by orthodox Stratfordians to 'Holocaust denial', as well as to 'Creationism' in evolution and to a denial that HIV infections cause AIDS. All of these are subjects on which vast libraries of evidence exist; the *point* is that no or virtually no evidence on Shakespeare's supposed life *as an author* exists, despite centuries of ceaseless research.

24 The attitude of my colleagues in the History Department of The University of Wales, Aberystwyth, towards my co-authorship of *The Truth Will Out*, was very much as here described: they were intrigued and bemused but certainly not hostile to me.

25 Alan H. Nelson, *Monstrous Adversity: The Life of Edward De Vere, 17th Earl of Oxford* (Liverpool, 2003), back cover.

26 Alan H. Nelson, 'Stratford Si! Essex No! (An Open-and-Shut Case)', talk delivered *c.*2004 at the University of Tennessee Law School debate on the Shakespeare Authorship Question. I am grateful to Professor Nelson for letting me read this paper, most of which consists of a trenchant attack on De Vere as a plausible 'Shakespeare' and an extremely unconvincing defence of Shakespeare of Stratford as the actual author. Nelson qualifies the above statement by saying 'But having tenure means never having to say you're sorry, while retirement means a release from all constraints, so it may seem surprising that anti-Stratfordians within the profession remain vanishingly small ...' But Nelson fails to address the question of how many current, former, or tenured English Literature academics have actually carried out objective historical research on the Authorship Question. My estimate would be a figure very close to zero.

27 Michell, *op.cit.*, pp.167–168.

28 For instance, Mark Anderson's 598–page Oxfordian biography, *'Shakespeare' By Another Name*, mentions Tyrrell twice – once (p.xiv), in two lines, in a long list of more than one hundred persons who figured in De Vere's life, and once (p.37) in part of a single paragraph. Tyrrell is not mentioned at all in many Oxfordian biographies, for instance Joseph Sobran's *Alias Shakespeare*. In fact, there are much closer historical parallels to the Hamlet plot in both the Essex rebellion and the story of Mary, Queen of Scots than in the life of De Vere, both of which would have been more apparent to knowledgeable playgoers when *Hamlet* first appeared in 1602–03. See the extremely interesting study by Lilian Winstanley, *Hamlet and the Scottish Succession* (Cambridge, 1921).

29 Probably the most convenient discussion of this is 'Appendix A: Edward De Vere's Geneva Bible and Shake-speake (*sic*)' in Mark Anderson, *'Shakespeare' By Another Name*, pp.381–392. Dr. Stritmatter's dissertation (at the

University of Massachusetts) was probably the first ever awarded to an explicitly anti-Stratfordian work. Dr. Stritmatter is now an assistant professor of English at Coppin State College in Baltimore, Maryland. See also Scott McCrea, *The Case for Shakespeare*, pp.177–179. Stritmatter's 2001 doctoral dissertation, *The Marginalia of Edward De Vere's Geneva Bible* (Oxenford Press, Northampton, Mass.) is available from Oxfordian sources.

30 McCrea, *op.cit.*, p.177.

31 Stanley Wells and Gary Taylor, *William Shakespeare: A Textual Companion* (Oxford, 1997), pp.89–109.

32 Farina, *op.cit.*, p.49.

33 See, for instance, Hank Whittemore, *The Monument* (2005), which argues that *all* of the Sonnets were addressed by De Vere to Southampton when he was imprisoned in the Tower in 1601–03.

34 The exception being that Southampton was willing to pay £5000 to avoid marrying De Vere's daughter. But there is no evidence of any kind that they ever met over this matter, let alone discussed it.

35 Michell, *op.cit.*, p.125.

36 *Ibid.*, pp.154–156.

37 *Ibid.*, p.56.

38 *Ibid.*, p.131. Chambers, *William Shakespeare*, II, pp.196–198.

39 Except in December 1594, when *A Comedy of Errors* was performed at Gray's Inn, Bacon *probably* writing the accompanying masques. See N.C. Cockburn, *The Bacon Shakespeare Question* (Surrey, 1998), p.106.

40 *Ibid.*, pp.292–294.

41 Although Bacon was friendly with the dedicatees of the *First Folio*, Lords Pembroke and Montgomery. (*Ibid.*, pp.277–279.)

42 *Ibid.*, p.629.

43 See Cockburn's fine book and Peter Dawkins, *The Shakespeare Enigma* (London, 2004).

44 Michell, *op.cit.*, p.237.

45 *Ibid.*, p.197–204.

46 *Ibid.*, pp.190–212.

47 Chambers, *op.cit.*, II, p.214.

48 Diana Price, *Shakespeare's Unorthodox Biography* (Westport, Conn., 2001), p.63

49 *Ibid.*

50 James Shapiro, 'Shakespeare's Genius in the Theatre …' (London), *The Guardian*, March 25, 2006.

51 *Ibid.*

52 Colin Burrow, 'Introduction: *Venus and Adonis*', to *William Shakespeare: The Complete Sonnets and Poems* (Oxford, 2002), pp.8–9.

53 Michell, *Who Wrote Shakespeare?*, p.131 (cited incorrectly in its index as at p.181). When Neville's mother died in 1573, his father remarried Bacon's

much older half-sister. It does not appear that they were blood relatives. Neville (as Shakespeare) and Bacon were associated in the famous production of *The Comedy of Errors* at Gray's Inn in 1594 but there is no real evidence that they were 'close associates'.

54 That *Hamlet* is in part 'about' the Essex rebellion is a view that has been put forward before by Stratfordian scholars, most notably in Lilian Winstanley's fine and neglected book, *Hamlet and the Scottish Succession*, *op.cit.*

Chapter 5 Richard the Third and the Princes in the Tower

1 Bertram Fields, *Royal Blood: King Richard III and the Mystery of the Princes* (originally 1998; Stroud, 2006), p.1; Paul Murray Kendall, *Richard the Third* (originally 1955, new edition, New York, 2002), p.465. Although this subject is always known as the mystery of 'Richard III and the princes in the Tower', the elder of the two 'princes' was in fact a king, or deposed king, Edward V.

2 Rosemary Horrox, *Richard III: A Study in Service* (Cambridge, 1989), p.viii.

3 'Josephine Tey' was the pseudonym of Elizabeth Mackintosh (1896–1952), who also wrote plays using the name Gordon Daviot. She was born in Inverness and was (implausibly) a physical education teacher, chiefly in Tunbridge Wells. Her first detective novel featuring Inspector Alan Grant, *The Man in the Queue*, appeared in 1929. She died of liver cancer aged fifty-five, a year after *The Daughter of Time* appeared. Gillian Avery, 'Elizabeth Mackintosh (1896–1952)', *Oxford Dictionary of National Biography.*

4 The two best recent biographies of Richard III are probably A.J. Pollard, *Richard III and the Princes in the Tower* (Stroud, 1991) and Charles Ross, *Richard III* (London, 1981). Other good biographies include Kendall, *Rop. cit.*; Michael Hicks, *Richard III* (Stroud, 2003); Rosemary Horrox, *Richard III: A Study in Service* (Cambridge, 1989); Desmond Seward, *Richard III: England's Black Legend* (London, 1997); and P.W. Hammond and Anne F. Sutton, *Richard III: The Road to Bosworth Field* (London, 1985). The older (1906) biography by Sir Clements R. Markham, *Richard III: His Life and Character*, was among the first to present a positive view of his life. Other works specifically concerned with the princes in the Tower will be noted in a later footnote.

5 If – as I believe– Sir Henry Neville (*c.*1562–1615) was the actual author of Shakespeare's works, it is easy to see why he painted Richard III as a demonic figure. By confiscating the vast Neville holdings in the north of England, Richard began the process by which the family declined from 'kingmakers' to ordinary nobility and minor gentry. Shakespeare also believed that Richard murdered Anne Neville, Richard's queen. Another influence on Neville's attitude might well have been his mentor at Oxford, Sir Henry Savile,

who, in 1596, was the first to print part of the manuscript of the *Croyland Chronicle*, a contemporary source covering Richard's misdeeds. See Jeremy Potter, *Good King Richard? An Account of Richard III and His Reputation, 1483–1983* (London, 1983), p.68. Of course this date (1596) was the first appearance of Shakespeare's play, but Neville had been in close contact with Savile for the previous eighteen years.

6 Pollard, *op.cit.*, p.69.
7 *Ibid.*, pp.90–92; Ross, *op.cit.*, pp.63–95.
8 Pollard, pp.212–213 citing Desmond Seward.
9 *Ibid.*, pp.144–177; Ross, *op.cit.*, pp.170–209; Horrox, *passim*, esp. pp.178–225.
10 Jeremy Potter, *Good King Richard?*, pp.68–77.
11 *Ibid.*, pp.78–86.
12 Pollard, *op.cit.*, p.7; Alison Weir, *The Princes in the Tower* (London, 1993), p.3.
13 Potter, *op.cit.*, pp.99–121.
14 *Ibid.*, pp.161–164.
15 *Ibid.*, pp.175–183; Fields, *op.cit.*, pp.125–130.
16 Apart from the biographies of Richard III noted above, many other books specifically deal with the fate of the princes. These include two particularly useful works: Alison Weir's fine *The Princes in the Tower* (London, 1992) and Bertram Fields's book cited above; as well as Elizabeth Jenkins, *The Princes in the Tower* (London, 1978), and Audrey Williamson's *The Mystery of the Princes* (Stroud, 1981). None of these authors, it should be noted, are academics: Fields is an American lawyer, the others are professional novelists and biographers. Virtually every biography of Richard III, including those by academics, contains long discussions of the fate of the princes.
17 Taken from Pollard, *op.cit.*, pp.115–139, etc.
18 *Ibid.*, p.120.
19 *Ibid.*
20 Fields, *op.cit.*, pp.200–229; Pollard, *op.cit.*, pp.130–132.
21 Pollard, *op.cit.*, p.132.
22 Weir, *op.cit.*, pp.249–258.
23 Fields, *op.cit.*, p.291.
24 *Ibid.*, pp.231–233.
25 Pollard, *op.cit.*, pp.125–126.
26 Polydore Vergil, described as Henry VII's official historian, stated in *English History* (published 1534) that there was a general belief that 'the sons of Edward IV were still alive, having been conveyed secretly away ... [to] some distant region.' (Fields, *op.cit.*, p.234.)
27 'Mission Statement' of the Richard III Society (www.richardiii.net).
28 'The Society – Origins', *Ibid.*
29 *Ibid.*

30 'Activities of the Richard III Society', *Ibid.*
31 *Ibid.*
32 I am most grateful to Sara J. Gremson of Radcliffe, Lancashire, for sending me some back issues. A particularly interesting and useful article it published was Helen Maurer's 'Whodunit: The Suspects in the Case', in *Ricardian Register* XVII (1983), which discusses all the possible candidates. It is available on the society's website 'Online Library of Primary Texts and Secondary Sources Sponsored by the Richard III Society, American Branch'.
33 'Achievements', Richard III Society, *op.cit.*

Chapter 6 Did Jesus Marry and Survive the Crucifixion?

1 In this chapter, I use the lower case 'he' and 'him' etc. in referring to Jesus, although most believing Christians would prefer capital letters. I have not done this to be either offensive or provocative, but simply because this is a secular discussion of an historical topic.
2 Michael Baigent, Richard Leigh, and Henry Lincoln, *The Holy Blood and the Holy Grail* (London, 1996 edition), pp.xvi-xix.
3 Michael Baigent, *The Jesus Papers: Exposing the Greatest Cover-Up in History* (London, 2006), p.7.
4 See *Holy Blood and Holy Grail*, esp. pp.111–294; Lynn Picknett and Clive Prince, *The Sion Revelation* (London, 2006), esp. pp.470–472. A useful account of this affair is Marilyn Hopkins, Graham Simmans, and Tim Wallace-Murphy, *Rex Deus: The True Mystery of Rennes-le-Château and the Dynasty of Jesus* (Shaftesbury, Dorset, 2000), esp. pp.1–28.
5 *Holy Blood and Holy Grail*, pp.24–37.
6 Michael Baigent, *The Jesus Papers*, p.297, Chapter Two, n.1. Baigent does not state what that 'task' might have been, or why a Hapsburg princess would have paid a substantial sum to an obscure village priest.
7 *Ibid.*
8 *Ibid.*
9 *Ibid.*
10 *Ibid.*, p.7.
11 *Ibid.*, pp.9–10.
12 *Ibid.*, p.10
13 According to his entry in *Who Was Who, 1941–1950*, Canon Lilley was born in County Armagh, Northern Ireland, and attended the Royal School. Armagh, and Trinity College, Dublin (not Oxford), where he won several medals. He became a curate in County Derry in 1889, but was a vicar in London from 1891–1912, when he became Canon of Hereford Cathedral. He is listed as having written thirteen books including *The Soul of St. Paul* (1909); *Prayer in Christian Theology* (1924); *Sacraments: Their Meaning for Christian Worship*

(1928), and others of like ilk. Lilley was, however, a Modernist (one who accepted the truth of modern science, saw no contradiction between science and religion, and favoured naturalistic explanations for Biblical miracles), who wrote several influential works on Modernism; according to *The Jesus Papers* (pp.11–17), St. Sulpice was a centre of Catholic Modernism before it was banned by the Vatican, although this might well have had very different implications in Catholic seminaries than within the already far more liberal Anglican church.

14 Baigent, *Jesus Papers*, p.16, citing Suetonius, *The Twelve Caesars* (Harmondsworth, 1979), p.202.

15 Baigent, *ibid.*, p.17.

16 An excellent recent discussion may be found in Robert E. Van Voorst, *Jesus Outside the New Testament: An Introduction to the Ancient Evidence* (Grand Rapids, Mich., and Cambridge, 2000), pp.29–39. This very useful and accessible scholarly study, which examines both the certain and supposed non-Biblical references to Jesus from the Roman period, provides a useful counterweight to the many unorthodox theories about Jesus which have flourished in recent years.

17 *Ibid.*, p.30

18 *Ibid.*, p.38.

19 *Ibid.*, p.33.

20 *Ibid.*, p.37.

21 *Ibid.*, p.32.

22 *Ibid.*, p.31, n.32.

23 *Ibid.*, pp.41–42.

24 *Ibid.*, p.48.

25 *Holy Blood and Holy Grail*, pp.346–362.

26 Marilyn Hopkins *et al.*, *Rex Deus: The True Mystery of Rennes-le-Château and the Dynasty of Jesus* (Shaftesbury, Dorset, 2000), p.80

27 *Ibid.*, pp.83–84.

28 *Holy Blood and Holy Grail*, pp.245–294.

29 *Ibid.*, p.249.

30 *Ibid.*, pp.250–251.

31 *Ibid.*, p.246.

32 Paradoxically, the Merovingian kingdom did *not* rule over south-western France or the area around Rennes-le-Château (see the map in *Holy Blood and Holy Grail*, p.258). In fact, the boundary of their realm ended about 250 miles away from Rennes, which was part of the kingdom of Aquitaine.

33 This was made clear on a 1998 BBC documentary *Timewatch* programme, *The History of a Mystery*. See also the illuminating 'Priory of Sion' on Wikipedia; *Rex Deus*, pp.31–40; Lynn Picknett and Clive Prince, *The Sion Revelation* (London, 2006), etc.

34 This list is given and discussed in nearly all accounts of the alleged marriage

and survival of Jesus, e.g. *The Holy Blood and the Holy Grail*, pp.441–466. The first three Grand Masters were Jean de Gisors (1188–1220), Marie de Saint-Clair (1220–1266), who was possibly de Gisors' wife, and Guillaume de Gisors (1266–1307).

35 Ian Maclean, 'Robert Fludd (*c.*1574–1637)', *Oxford Dictionary of National Biography*.

36 *Ibid.*

37 Michael Hunter, 'Robert Boyle (1627–1691)', *Oxford Dictionary of National Biography*.

38 Leo Gosch, 'Charles Radclyffe (1693–1746)',*Oxford Dictionary of National Biography*. Needless to say, absolutely no real evidence exists that any of these men were Grand Masters of the Priory of Sion – which never existed.

39 *Sion Revelation*, p.472.

40 'Pierre Plantard, *Wikipedia*.

41 Gardner is described on the back cover of the paperback edition of the book in these terms: 'Distinguished as the Chevalier Labhràn de St. Germain, he is Presidential Attaché to the European Council of Princes, a constitutional advisory body established in 1946. He is also a Knight Templar of St. Anthony and the appointed Jacobite Historiographer Royal.'

42 Many 'instant' guides to *The Da Vinci Code* have appeared in conjunction with the book and movie. Generally, these are surprisingly useful and helpful. They include René Chandelle, *Beyond the Da Vinci Code: The Book That Solves the Mystery* (London, 2005), Simon Cox, *Cracking the Da Vinci Code: The Unauthorized Guide to the Facts Behind the Fiction* (London, 2004); Michael and Veronica Haag, *The Rough Guide to the Da Vinci Code* (London, 2004), and the lengthy collection of essays edited by Dan Burstein, *Secrets of the Code: The Unauthorized Guide to the Mysteries Behind the Da Vinci Code* (New York, 2006). Oxford University Press – no less – also quickly published a useful and sensible discussion of Brown's book by Bart D. Ehrman, professor of religious studies at the University of North Carolina – Chapel Hill, *Truth and Fiction in the Da Vinci Code: A Historian Reveals What We Really Know About Jesus, Mary Magdalene, and Constantine* (Oxford, 2004).

43 Cited in 'Postscript, 1996', in the 1996 edition of *The Holy Blood and the Holy Grail*, pp.479–471. On Mary Magdalene and her treatment in Christian writing see Dan Burstein and Arne J. De Keijzer, eds., *Secrets of Mary Magdalene: The Untold Story of History's Most Misunderstood Woman* (London, 2006); and Susan Haskins, *Mary Magdalene: The Essential History* (London, 1993). Mary Magdalene has been adopted in recent years as a feminist icon. Previously, however, – in Catholic teaching at least – many of the admirable female attributes (compassion, forgiveness, etc.) were seen as held by the Virgin Mary, Jesus's mother.

44 *Ibid.*, pp.471–473.

45 *Rex Deus*, pp.83–86.

46 See, e.g. *The Holy Blood and the Holy Grail* (1996 ed.), p.486.
47 Fida Hassnain, *A Search for the Historical Jesus* (Bath, U.K., 1994), p.154.
48 *Ibid.*, p.158–159.
49 Kamal Salbi, *Who Was Jesus?: Conspiracy in Jerusalem* (London, 1998; reprinted 2002); Rugaiyyah Waris Maqsood, *The Mysteries of Jesus* (Oxford, 2000), pp.142–150.
50 Maqsood, *Ibid.*, p.147.
51 *Ibid.*, p.149.
52 There are some exceptions. The Catholic theologian Margaret Starbird, author of *The Woman With the Alabaster Jar* (1993), believes that Jesus was married and fathered children. So, too, does the very controversial Sydney University theologian (now retired) Barbara Thiering, who believes that Jesus was married twice, divorced, and fathered four children! (See her *Jesus the Man: New Interpretations from the Dead Sea Scrolls* (1992) and *Jesus of the Apocalypse: The Life of Jesus After the Crucifixion* (1995).)
53 Two excellent recent objective and deeply researched accounts of early Christianity, well worth reading, not least of all as contrasts to the books discussed in this chapter, are Larry W. Hurtado, *Lord Jesus Christ: Devotion to Jesus in Earliest Christianity* (Grand Rapids, Mich., and Cambridge, 2003), and Margaret M. Mitchell and Frances M. Young, eds., *The Cambridge History of Christianity, Volume I – Origins to Constantine* (Cambridge, 2006). These works were – one assumes – written by believing Christians, but employing all of the canons of objective scholarship. The notion that Jesus did not really exist, as has been argued in a range of recent works, strikes me as highly implausible, since the main facts of his life are spelled out in the New Testament in remarkable detail.
54 Hassnain, *A Search for the Historical Jesus*, pp.53–75.
55 That many of the very early Christians were 'Hellenists' is apparently a well-developed theme in modern New Testament scholarship. See Hurtado, *Lord Jesus Christ*, pp.208–214.
56 There is a debate as to whether these were Greeks or Greek-speaking Jews. (*Ibid.*)
57 The imaginative and interesting works of the late Carsten Thiede, whose aim was to show that very early evidence about Jesus, tending to add weight to the orthodox account of his life, does exist, ought to be noted. These include his *Jesus: Life or Legend?* (Oxord,1990); *The Jesus Papyrus* (London, 1996); and *the Quest for the True Cross* (London, 2000); the latter two works co-authored with Matthew D'Ancona. Thiede's works have also given rise to a great deal of speculation among orthodox theologians. Beyond the scope of this chapter are the many works on the Shroud of Turin, and the enormous controversy this supposed relic of the Crucifixion has generated. One of many recent works about the Shroud, which links it to bodies such as the Templars, is *The Divine Deception: The Church, The Shroud and the Creation of a Holy Fraud*

by Keith Laidler (London, 2000). Although carbon dating has *apparently* revealed the Turin Shroud to be a medieval artefact, the last word on its origins certainly remains to be said. Some peripheral but useful 'unorthodox' essays on this whole topic may be found in J. Douglas Kenyon, ed., *Forbidden Religion: Suppressed Heresies of the West* (Rochester, Ct., 2006).

Chapter 7 The Mysteries of Rudolf Hess

1 Peter Padfield, *Hess: The Führer's Disciple* (London, 1991; revised edition 2001), pp2–4.
2 Padfield, p.15.
3 *Ibid.*, p.24.
4 Padfield, pp.71–84.
5 *Ibid.*, pp.8, 30.
6 *Ibid.*, p.101, citing the diary of Ulrich von Hassell.
7 Peter Longerich, 'Hitler's Deputy: The Role of Rudolf Hess in the Nazi Regime', in David Stafford, ed., *Flight From Reality: Rudolf Hess and His Mission to Scotland* (London, 1002), pp.104–120.
8 *Ibid.*, p.217.
9 Ian Kershaw, *Hitler – 1936–45: Nemesis* (London, 2000), p.369.
10 *Ibid.*
11 *Ibid.*, pp.372–374.
12 Hugh Thomas, *Murder of Rudolf Hess*, p.14.
13 *Ibid.*, p.24.
14 *Ibid.*
15 *Ibid.*, pp.172–173.
16 *Ibid.*, p.172, citing Eugene Bird, *The Loneliest Man in the World* (London, 1974), pp.180–181.
17 *Ibid.*
18 Thomas, *op.cit.*, pp.118–119.
19 *Ibid.*, pp.36–52.
20 *Ibid.*, p.196.
21 Roy Conyers Nesbit and George Van Acker, *The Flight of Rudolf Hess: Myths and Reality* (Stroud, 1999), pp.138–139. This valuable book offers many doses of common sense to the various unorthodox theories about Hess. I am most grateful to Mr. Nesbit for our conversation and further information. It should be noted that Hugh Thomas's medical experience would largely have come from observing victims of high-powered modern weapons in Northern Ireland soon after they were wounded, not from treating First World War veterans over fifty-five years later.
22 *Ibid.*, p.137.
23 Padfield, *op.cit.*, pp.286–287.

24 Nesbit and Conyers, *op.cit.*, p.138.
25 Thomas, *op.cit.* (p.89) readily admitted that he did not know the real identity of the 'Hess Double'.
26 See, e.g., Allen, *op.cit.*, pp.228–230.
27 Information provided to me by Roy Nesbit, to whom I am most grateful, based on a report (5 July 2006) in the (London) *Daily Telegraph* newspaper.
28 Padfield, *op.cit.*, p.369.
29 *Ibid.*, p.370.
30 *Ibid.*
31 Allen, *op.cit.*, argues (p.238) that Hess was killed soon after his landing in London, citing *The Secret War of Charles Frazer-Smith* (London, 1981), by Charles Frazer-Smith, a tailor who was asked by MI5 in May1941 to make an exact copy of the captured Rudolf Hess's uniform in four hours, while Hess lay drugged in the Tower of London. MI1 then found a Hess look-alike among German POWs, and subjected him to prolonged brainwashing to pose as the real Hess. (Hess, however, was forty-seven in 1941. Most German POWs – of whom there were surely very few in May 1941 – were much younger.)
32 *Double Standards*, pp.406–409. There was one survivor, tail gunner Andy Jack. Jack was sworn to secrecy and gave only one interview about the flight, to a Scottish newspaper in 1961. He died in 1978. (*Ibid.*, pp.392–393.)
33 *Ibid.*, pp.406–409.
34 *Ibid.*, pp.410–421.
35 *Ibid.*, p.434. It should be noted that Picknett, Prince, Prior, and Brydon, are inveterate Royal-haters who *also* produced a muckraking account of the British Royal Family, *War of the Windsors: A Century of Unconstitutional Monarchy* (Edinburgh, 2002).
36 *Ibid.*, pp.116, 417–421.
37 *Ibid.*, pp.394–395.
38 Kershaw, *op.cit.*, p.372.
39 *Ibid.*, p.373.
40 Martin Allen, *The Hitler/Hess Deception* (London, 2003), pp.182–184.
41 Padfield, *op.cit.*, pp.338–345.
42 Nesbit and Van Acker, *The Flight of Rudolf Hess*, p.140.
43 For instance, James Douglas-Hamilton, *Motive for a Mission: The Story Behind Hess's Flight to Britain* (London, 1971). The author is the son of the Duke of Hamilton with whom Hess was trying to make contact. See also Stafford, ed., *Flight from Reality*, and Wolf Rüdiger Hess, *My Father Rudolf Hess* (London, 1976).
44 Cited in Padfield, *op.cit.*, p.186.
45 Kershaw, *op.cit.*, p.377.
46 Nesbit and Van Acker also (*op.cit.*,pp.110–142) effectively refute other claims made about Hess, e.g. that Hess was escorted for part of his flight by Reinhard Heydrich.

Chapter 8 Ancient Mysteries: The Great Pyramid and the Sphinx

1 William R. Corliss, *Ancient Structures: Remarkable Pyramids, Forts, Towers, Stone Chambers, Cities, Complexes: A Catalogue of Archaeological Anomalies.* (Glen Arm, Ma., 2001), p.170.

2 Some of the key books written by the unorthodox Egyptologists will be discussed throughout this chapter. Others include J. Douglas Kenyon, ed., *Forbidden History: Prehistoric Extraterrestrial Intervention, and the Suppressed Origin of Civilizations* (Rochester, Vt., 2005); Preston Peet, ed., *Underground! The Disinformation Guide to Ancient Civilizations, Astonishing Archaeology and Hidden History* (New York, 2005); Robert M. Schoch with Robert Aquinas McNally, *Voices of the Rocks: A Scientific Look at Catastrophes and Ancient Civilizations* (New York, 1999); and *idem.*, *Pyramid Quest: Secrets of the Great Pyramid and the Dawn of Civilization* (London, 2005). The last is a particularly interesting account of this question.

3 Although there is a long-standing school of thought that the Egyptians, through ancient factors and travellers, did influence these cultures.

4 Corliss, *op.cit.*, pp.70–71. William R. Corliss is the compiler of the 'Sourcebook Project' catalogues of anomalous events. The works of a sceptical scientist, Corliss's 'Sourcebook Project' newsletter and published *Catalogue of Anomalies* are unquestionably the most interesting and well-researched 'Fortean' publications currently available, and should be read by anyone with an interest in this area. ('Fortean' is the commonly accepted term for 'unexplained events' and their study, named for Charles Fort (1874–1932), the American cataloguer of such occurrences.)

5 Corliss, *Ancient Structures*, p.71.

6 *Ibid.*, p.71.

7 *Ibid.*, p.72.

8 *Ibid.*, p.72. A look at a photograph of the Baalbek Temple (*ibid.*, p.70) will show how difficult it must have been to do this precisely.

9 Christopher Dunn, 'The Obelisk Quarry Mystery', in J. Douglas Kenyon, ed., *Forbidden History*, p.262.

10 Cited in Corliss, *op.cit.*, p.179.

11 Corliss, *ibid.*, pp.178–179.

12 *Ibid.*, p.182. The theory of poured pyramid stone concrete was revived in 2006 by Professor Michael Barsoum of Drexel University, Philadelphia, who found 'concrete glue' in stone samples from the Great Pyramid ('Ancient Concrete Rises Again' (London), *New Scientist*, 9 December 2006, p.6.)

13 *Ibid.*, pp.182–183.

14 Cited in *ibid.*, p.183.

15 Will Hart, 'Archaeology and the Law of Gravity', in Kenyon, ed., *op.cit.*, p.211.

16 *Ibid.*, pp.211–212.
17 *Ibid.*, p.212.
18 *Ibid.*
19 Graham Hancock, *Fingerprints of the Gods: The Quest Continues* (London, 1996), pp.327–328. This work is probably the all-time best-seller in the field of unorthodox archaeology, having sold over a million copies.
20 Corliss, *op.cit.*, pp.177–178. These labourers would have been working in the (presumably) blazing Egyptian sun, and also needed constant supplies of water to stay alive. How was this water brought to them?
21 Lawton and Ogilvie-Herald, *Giza: op.cit.*, pp.78–79.
22 Christopher Dunn, 'Advanced Machining in Ancient Egypt', *The Giza Power Plant: Technologies of Ancient Egypt* (Sante Fe, N.M., 1998), pp.67–91. Dunn originally gave his theories in an article in *Analog Magazine* in August 1984.
23 *Ibid.*, p.72.
24 *Ibid.*, p.76.
25 *Ibid.*, p.78.
26 *Ibid/*. pp.79–80.
27 *Ibid.*, p.84.
28 *Ibid.*, p.87.
29 *Ibid.*, pp.94–97
30 *Ibid.*, pp.98–99.
31 Dunn, *Giza Power Plant*, p.11
32 *Ibid.*, p.13.
33 Edward F. Malkowski, *Before the Pharaohs: Egypt's Mysterious Prehistory* (Rochester, Vermont, 2006), pp.115–120.
34 'About the Author', in *The Giza Power Plant*, p.281.
35 Malkowski, *op.cit.*, p.75.
36 *Ibid.*
37 *Ibid.*, citing Christopher Dunn, 'Advanced Machining in Ancient Egypt', *Analog Magazine*, August 1984
38 Malkowski, *op.cit.,* p.118.
39 *Ibid.*
40 *Ibid.*, p.120; Dunn, *Giza Power Plant*, pp.125–150.
41 *Ibid.*, pp.160–171; Malkowski, *op.cit.*, p.124.
42 Dunn, *Giza Power Plant*, pp.179–204; Schoch and McNally, *Pyramid*, p.50.
43 *Ibid.*, pp.50–51. Tesla (1856–1943) was born in what is now Croatia and emigrated to the United States in 1884. He was unquestionably one of the very greatest inventors of his time, and was apparently robbed blind by Thomas A. Edison, who employed him. At the end of his life Tesla was said to be experimenting with anti-gravity devices, teleportation, and time-travel. (See Marc J. Seifer, *Wizard: The Life and Times of Nicola Tesla – Biography of Genius* (Syracuse, N.J., 1996). In recent years Tesla has emerged as

one of the leading cult figures among those who believe that the ancients employed forms of energy unknown even now. Adventurers Unlimited Press of Kempton, Illinois, which publishes many books on this subject, also produces works such as *The Tesla Papers* and *The Fantastic Inventions of Nikola Tesla.*

44 Dunn, *Giza Power Plant*, pp.231–234. See also David Hatcher Childress, *Technology of the Gods: The Incredible Sciences of the Ancients* (Kempton, Illinois, 2000), pp.124–126. The Fortean researcher Ivan T. Sanderson also investigated the Dendera image, coming to the same conclusion

45 'Frightfully Ancient Electrics', in Ivan T. Sanderson, *Investigating the Unexplained* (Englewood Cliffs, N.J., 1972), pp.179–196. Sanderson posited the theory many years before Dunn that the Egyptians invented electric lights. It is also well-known that the Parthians apparently developed a primitive battery used for electroplating around 250 B.C. (*Ibid.*). Examples of this are (or were) on exhibit at the Baghdad Museum. It might be relevant to note a story which appeared on BBC News On-line (15 November 2006), 'Physics Promises Wireless Power', by Jonathan Fildes, which reports that 'U.S. researchers have outlined a relatively simple system that could deliver power to devices such as laptop computers ... wirelessly.' "The answer the team came up with was 'resonance', a phenomenon that causes an object to vibrate when energy of a certain frequency is applied ... Instead of using acoustic vibrations, the team's system exploits the resonance of electromagnetic waves." The system they described, however, 'would be able to transfer energy over three to five meters', but no further. There was no mention of the Great Pyramid.

46 Dunn, *Giza Power Plant*, p.233.

47 *Ibid.*, p.237.

48 Dunn apparently does not indicate how much energy would have been produced in the 'Giza power plant'. Surely, however, its output would be colossal.

49 Dunn, *Giza Power Plant*, pp.219–25.

50 Farrell is also the author of *Reich of the Black Sun* (2006), which argues that both the Nazis and the Japanese set off atomic bombs in 1944–45, before the first American atomic bomb! He employs a wealth of intriguing evidence, making it impossible to dismiss.

51 A slightly earlier work of the same kind, John Taylor's *The Great Pyramid: Why Was It Built?* (1860) also saw the pyramid as encoding advanced knowledge in its measurements. Taylor believed that the pyramids were erected on the direct instruction of God. (Schoch and McNally, *op.cit.*, pp.83–84.)

52 Corliss, *op.cit.*, p.205, citing Martin Gardiner, *Fads and Fallacies in the Name of Science* (New York, 1957), p.177.

53 Corliss, *op.cit.*, pp.201–203.

54 Dunn, *Power Plant*, p.132.
55 William Fix, *Pyramid Odyssey* (New York, 1978), p.232. cited in *ibid.*, pp.133–134.
56 *Ibid.*, p.203.
57 Corliss, pp.203–204.
58 *Ibid.*, p.205.
59 See, e.g. Francis Hitching, *The World Atlas of Mysteries* (London,1978), pp.108–111,
60 See the discussion of Brophy's work in Malkowski, *op.cit.*, pp.83–95.
61 *Ibid.*, pp.94–95.
62 See the critique of this view in Lawton and Ogilvie-Herald, *op.cit.*, pp.334–359. The 'ancient Sphinx' theory is set out at length in Graham Hancock and Robert Bauval, *The Marriage of the Sphinx: A Quest for the Hidden Legacy of Mankind* (New York, 1996). Many other well-known works of unorthodox anthropology can only be mentioned here in passing. They included Robert Bauval and Graham Hancock, *Keeper of Genesis: A Quest for the Hidden Legacy of Mankind* (London, 1997), by two of the best-known writers in this field, and *The Stargate Conspiracy: Revealing the Truth Behind Extraterrestrial Contact, Military Intelligence and the Mysteries of Ancient Egypt* (London, 2000), by the ever-present Lynn Picknett and Clive Prince. Rather surprisingly, Picknett and Prince reject most of the claims of the 'New Egyptologists', claiming that a vast contemporary conspiracy is behind these claims.
63 West, *op.cit.*, pp.228–229.
64 Cited in Lawton and Ogilvie-Herald, *op.cit.*, p.297. The initial suggestion that the erosion of the Sphinx was caused by water apparently came from Rene Schwaller de Lubicz (1887–1961), regarded as the father of unorthodox Egyptology. Schwaller de Lubicz, an exponent of esoteric philosophy, who lived in Egypt from 1938 to 1952, believed that profound knowledge was deliberately concealed in many ancient Egyptian structures and is there to be decoded. He outlined this in his work, *The Temple of Man*. Schwaller de Lubicz may be seen as the link between unorthodox Christian fundamentalist views of knowledge concealed in the pyramids and modern non-religious views. He is regarded as beyond the pale by many because of his pro-Nazi views. See Joseph Ray, 'R.A. Schwaller de Lubicz's Magnum Opus: Keys to Understanding the Wisdom of the Ancients Have Been Preserved', in Kenyon, ed., *op.cit.*, pp.191–110 and Malkowski, *op.cit.*, pp.219–238.
65 Lawton and Ogilvie-Herald, *op.cit.*, pp.297–320. The geological issues are quite complex. The face on the Sphinx certainly appears to be that of an Old Kingdom king.
66 Rand Flem-Ath and Colin Wilson, *The Atlantis Blueprint* (London, 2001), pp.1–30.

67 Nor do I propose to discuss the theories of 'ancient astronauts', made familiar by Eric von Daniken, in his many works. For a devastating critique of von Daniken's theories, see Hitching, *op.cit.*, pp.144–149. On anomalous small artefacts apparently much older than they 'should' be, or found in the 'wrong' place, probably the best objective account is another work by William R. Corliss, *Archaeological Anomalies: Small Artefacts – Bone, Stone, Metal Artefacts, Footprints, High Technology* (Glen Arm, Md., 2003).

Index

CPSIA information can be obtained
at www.ICGtesting.com
Printed in the USA
BVHW031054301021
620267BV00003B/30

9 781911 454441